Improvement Science in the Field

Cases of Practitioners Leading Change in Schools

Edited by
Edwin Nii Bonney
Sarah A. Capello
Maxwell M. Yurkofsky

ROWMAN & LITTLEFIELD
Lanham • Boulder • New York • London

Acquisitions Editor: Nathan Davidson
Acquisitions Assistant: Hollis Peterson
Sales and Marketing Inquiries: textbooks@rowman.com

Published by Rowman & Littlefield
An imprint of The Rowman & Littlefield Publishing Group, Inc.
4501 Forbes Boulevard, Suite 200, Lanham, Maryland 20706
www.rowman.com

86-90 Paul Street, London EC2A 4NE

Copyright © 2024 by The Rowman & Littlefield Publishing Group, Inc.

All rights reserved. No part of this book may be reproduced in any form or by any electronic or mechanical means, including information storage and retrieval systems, without written permission from the publisher, except by a reviewer who may quote passages in a review.

British Library Cataloguing in Publication Information Available

Library of Congress Cataloging-in-Publication Data

Names: Bonney, Edwin Nii, editor. | Capello, Sarah A., editor. | Yurkofsky, Maxwell, editor.
Title: Improvement science in the field : cases of practitioners leading change in schools / edited by Edwin Nii Bonney, Sarah A. Capello, Maxwell Yurkofsky.
Description: Lanham, Maryland : Rowman & Littlefield, [2024] | Includes bibliographical references and index.
Identifiers: LCCN 2023044638 | ISBN 9781538180167 (cloth) | ISBN 9781538180174 (paperback) | ISBN 9781538180181 (ebook)
Subjects: LCSH: School improvement programs—United States. | Educational evaluation—United States. | Educational change—United States.
Classification: LCC LB2822.82 .I484 2024 | DDC 372.12/207—dc23/eng/20240116
LC record available at https://lccn.loc.gov/2023044638

We dedicate this book to all improvers working to create equitable educational systems for all children from diverse backgrounds and experiences like our Teddy, Bella, Abigail, Samuel, Isabel, and Evelyn.

Contents

Foreword *Brandi Hinnant-Crawford, PhD*	vii
Acknowledgments	xi
Introduction: The Practitioner Voice in Improvement Science *Edwin Nii Bonney, Sarah A. Capello, and Maxwell M. Yurkofsky*	xiii
PART I: CASES ON LEADING CHANGE	**1**
Chapter 1: Leading Change in Racial Disparities in Discipline *Courtney Browning, EdD*	7
Chapter 2: Leading Change in Enrollment of Black and Brown Students in Gifted Programs *Kelly A. Huff, EdD, and Tracy Kwock, EdD*	35
Chapter 3: Leading Change in Teacher Stress and Mental Health *Jessica Cromer, EdD*	63
Chapter 4: Leading Change in the Overrepresentation of Students of Color in Special Education *Shanice Harrington, EdD*	79
Chapter 5: Leading Change in Onboarding and Support of Novice Teachers *Elisabeth Harman, EdD*	109
Chapter 6: Leading Change to Improve Academic Outcomes for Traditionally Marginalized Students *Jamie Soltis, EdD*	131
Chapter 7: Editors' Commentary *Edwin Nii Bonney, Sarah A. Capello, and Maxwell M. Yurkofsky*	165

PART II: CASE STUDIES FOR PRACTICE AND DISCUSSION   169
Megan Crew; Michelle Greene, EdD; Megan Hawley; Amy Johnson, EdD; Andrew Nester, EdD; Felicia Preston, EdD; and Kim Rygas

Case 1: EL Family Engagement and Sense of Belonging   173

Case 2: Discipline and In-School Suspensions   177

Case 3: Transitioning from Middle School to High School   183

Case 4: Reading Achievement   187

Case 5: Teacher Burnout   193

Afterword   199
Wendy Durham, EdD; Sandy Strayer, EdD; Elizabeth Motley, EdD; and Matthew Woods, EdD

References   203

Index   217

About the Contributors   219

Foreword

Brandi Hinnant-Crawford, PhD

> The eyewitness to these things has presented an accurate report. He saw it himself and is telling the truth so that you, also, will believe.
>
> —John 19:35 (The Message)

TESTIFY!

In my faith tradition we often talk about the power of testimonies. Testimonies are not a brag, but they are a recounting of someone's experience. Those who have overcome are encouraged to share their testimony. But the testimony is not for the overcomer. It is for those who have not yet experienced the hardship, or it is for those who are currently experiencing it and need some encouragement and proof that they too can overcome and prevail in a particular situation. A testimony is a testament. A story. A case. It tells the listener or reader what happened. There is a setting, a plot, a conflict, and a resolution. In the ones that follow, there is context, a problem of practice, an improvement strategy employed by the protagonist, and growth and learning.

Testimonies can grow our self-efficacy. In social cognitive theory, Albert Bandura (1999) talks about the building of self-efficacy. Self-efficacy is an individual's belief in their capability to do something; self-efficacy is domain-specific. Individuals may believe they are good teachers or good leaders and struggle to believe they have the capability to dismantle oppressive structures that plague our educational system (read more about teacher self-efficacy in chapter 5). Ellen Usher and Frank Pajares (2008) discuss the sources of self-efficacy and how it is cultivated. They identify four primary sources, the first of which is mastery experience. When someone does something successfully, they are more likely to believe they can do it again in the future. Another source of self-efficacy is verbal persuasion. My book, *Improvement Science in Education: A Primer*, is a text that seeks to use verbal persuasion to convince the reader of their ability to apply improvements to a variety of problems and practices. Another source of self-efficacy is physiological and emotional states—when one's own body gives them feedback about whether or not they can do something (i.e., anxiety). The fourth source of self-efficacy is vicarious experience.

Unlike most how-to texts on improvement science, the experienced educators in this text offer something different altogether—vicarious experience. Instead of persuading the reader, the first six chapters provide powerful testimonies of improvement work. Through eyewitness, first-person accounts, practitioners describe their experience employing improvement methodologies. Vicarious experience comes from observing others who are similar to oneself. Usher and Pajares (2008) explain, "Vicarious information gained from others perceived to be similar in ability yields the most influential comparative information, but the experiences of those perceived as having similar attributes (e.g., age, gender, ethnicity) are often powerful sources of self-efficacy information" (p. 753). In the authors' testimonies, the readers of this text can observe—dare I say, witness—practitioners like themselves engage in improvement work to address a variety of educational dilemmas.

The authors of the chapters that follow are honest in their accounts. They share their positionality, experiences of resistance, and hiccups along the way. In these chapters that address underrepresentation of minoritized individuals in gifted education, overrepresentation in special education, disproportionality in discipline, disparate achievement, teacher retention, and teacher well-being—the experience of the authors provides clear evidence that improvement work can be employed to engineer a more just society. Each chapter is clear about who is involved and who is impacted, the two "whos" all improvers must keep in mind to improve for equity. Yes, the authors provide specifics on the types of measures used and the length of cycles—but their details of team composition (and turnover), empathy interviews, and changing plans are what makes the cases more than cases—testimonies.

In addition to self-efficacy beliefs, Shewhart introduced the concept of degree of belief (Deming, 1942; Langley et al., 2009). While self-efficacy deals with beliefs about oneself, degree of belief deals with beliefs about a possible intervention. Degree of belief is how much faith one has in their theory of improvement, and it is based on two things: whether or not the intervention has been successful before and how similar one's context is to the context where it worked. If the reader is wondering whether or not this "improvement stuff" has merit, if it can be used to intervene in the face of some of education's most pressing problems, I believe this text may increase the reader's degree of belief. It provides one of the keys to the degree of belief, evidence! The authors write about implementing changes during a time of unstable leadership and a shifting policy landscape. Does that context seem similar? Browning (chapter 1) recounts how pursuing Culturally Responsive Teaching in the current political climate felt dangerous. Furthermore, even when authors did not meet their aim, such as was the case with Huff and Kwock (chapter 2), they were still able to move "the equity needle."

Beliefs are important. Beliefs about one's own capabilities, beliefs about the utility of improvement methodologies, and beliefs about the people and communities we serve matter. Yolanda Sealy-Ruiz (2022) explains that educators' "beliefs about students and their community dictate how much or little they will invest in them" (p. 24). When it comes to improvement, while effective the methods are not magic, the people are. As the reader bears witness to the testimonies of the authors, I hope it's evident that there is a recurring theme of educators who believe in themselves, their students, and the possibility of equitable education. As we seek to improve, we must realize the educational system we have inherited has never served all children well. So, it is incumbent on us to imagine a system we have never seen before and then pursue that imagined system—relentlessly—continuously. Designing, developing, testing, and spreading interventions that lead to equitable opportunities to learn for all students is the responsibility of all educators. But our pursuit is contingent upon our beliefs.

The authors in this text testify and in doing so, they provide evidence. The purpose of this book is for the reader to see themselves in these educators. Recently, Brandon Bennett (a guru in improvement and a colleague I admire) and I were having a conversation about proof points in improvement work and how people question the effectiveness of it because the scholarly literature is not overflowing with examples of where improvement works. We talked about the dilemma of the practitioners who engage in improvement work versus the scholars who consume literature about improvement work. Often, practitioners do not have the luxury of time to write articles or chapters showcasing the good work they have done. So, the field owes a debt of gratitude to Edwin Nii Bonney, Sarah A. Capello, and Maxwell M. Yurkofsky for collecting the testimonies of educators engaging in this work. In the pages that follow the reader will find evidence, proof points, and encouragement.

As you read,

May these testimonies increase your degree of belief [faith] in the power of improvement.
May the vicarious experiences increase your self-efficacy in being an improver.
May you engage in improvement for equity and go on to testify to future improvers.

Acknowledgments

We are grateful to Mark Kerr at Rowman & Littlefield for enthusiastically believing in this project and to Sarah Rinehart for working tirelessly with us to prepare this book. Nathan Davidson, Hollis Peterson, and Jenna Dutton at Rowman & Littlefield, thank you for helping us through the production process. Thank you to Vida, Nate, and Amelia for holding down the fort and making space for us to complete this book. To the many anonymous people who reviewed our original proposal and provided feedback: Your comments and questions made this book so much better than we could have imagined. We especially want to acknowledge the practitioners who accepted our invitation to review the first draft of chapters: Drs. Jessica McClung, Ken Nicely, Gregg Robinson, Amy Griffin, Ana Cingel, Alan Seibert, Jason Wimbush, Tamra Vaughan, April Small, Turonne Hunt, and Basil Marin. We are grateful to our students—Catherine Anderson, Trumaine Becoat-Wade, Jennifer Bolling, Esther Colley, Amy Hall, Debbie Harris, Erica Hazelwood, Andrea Herndon, Jason Matlock, Jessica Morris, Susan Mullins, John Otey, Steven Rayford, Melissa Roark, Derrick Sessor, Amy Varian, and Lisa Gehring—who also provided reviews of and feedback on the cases in part 2 of this book. Your insights, questions, and comments about improvement science in practice helped contributing authors strengthen their work, the case studies they created, and how they told the stories about their improvement journey. Last but not least, we would also like to acknowledge Dr. Brad Bizzell for his mentorship and support for the transformational leaders who are featured in this book.

Introduction

The Practitioner Voice in Improvement Science

Edwin Nii Bonney, Sarah A. Capello,
and Maxwell M. Yurkofsky

The field of education is particularly susceptible to reforms and initiatives that purport to solve problems and improve outcomes with scant evidence of their effectiveness. Every few years, policymakers and district leaders mandate new initiatives that are to be taken up on a large scale, provide a day or two of professional development to kick off the initiative, and send practitioners on their way to implement the various components according to their role. However, educational initiatives to solve complex problems of practice frequently fail because they are: implemented as quick-fix solutions on a large scale without a full understanding of how (or if) the initiative will actually work; developed or decided on by a single educational leader or small group of leaders without input or buy-in from those affected by the problem; not implemented with fidelity or followed through on; lacking assessment on the effectiveness and outcomes of the initiative; or lacking acknowledgment of the systematic forces contributing to the problem. Subsequently, the failure of each initiative results in policymakers and leaders looking for the next proposed solution to the same persistent problems.

In response to the problem of educational leaders and policymakers jumping from reform to reform in search of quick-fix solutions, Bryk and coauthors (2015) proposed using improvement science as a method or tool for educational practitioners to: (1) investigate how a problem is manifested in their local context and see the system-wide factors contributing to the problem; (2) collaboratively develop a theory of improvement with those impacted by the problem; (3) design and implement tests of change on a small scale along with measures that will allow the improvers to evaluate whether change is occurring and if that change is an improvement; and (4) decide whether to spread, tweak, or discard the change idea. This process helps leaders more fully understand the problem from a variety of perspectives, refrain from relying on quick-fix, band-aid solutions that fail to solve the problem, try out ideas on a small scale to identify and remediate potential sticking points before they are implemented on a large scale, and discern if the change idea is effective in addressing the problem.

Since Bryk and colleagues (2015) published their groundbreaking book on how educational stakeholders can take up improvement science as an approach to systematically and collaboratively addressing problems in education, there have been at least 10 books on improvement science, with more coming out each year. Scholars have authored books laying out a step-by-step approach to using improvement science in education (Crow et al., 2019; Hinnant-Crawford, 2020); books on how to teach improvement science to practitioners (Spaulding et al., 2021), books on using improvement science for a dissertation in practice (Perry et al., 2020), and books on how to evaluate continuous improvement efforts (Christie et al., 2017; Rohanna, 2021). Many of these texts have been largely conceptual, theoretical, and pedagogical. Bryk (2021) also presents large-scale efforts that benefit from lots of funding which many practitioners, unfortunately, do not have access to. A recent volume edited by Gomez and colleagues (2023) also highlighted partnerships between school districts and universities conducting continuous improvement. Although these books are useful for instructing higher education administrators, graduate practitioners and students, and educational leaders in the theoretical, conceptual, and pedagogical facets of improvement science (Bryk, 2021; Perry et al., 2020, Peurach et al., 2022), they omit the voice of the practitioner and fail to capture the ways practitioners are actively taking up improvement science to lead change in their school settings (Bonney et al., forthcoming).

Furthermore, the books that have centered on the practitioner's voice (e.g., Peterson & Carlile, 2021) provide few details describing the entire arc of the improvement cycle including their challenges, questions, reflections, and successes in using improvement science in their settings. Although these books provide some practitioner perspectives, they are eclipsed by the perspectives and voices of academics, researchers, and higher education faculty such that we do not fully know how practitioners are making sense of and using improvement science as a tool for educational change. This knowledge is critical not only for academics who study school improvement efforts and faculty who teach improvement science to graduate students but also for educational leaders who are looking to learn from their peers in similar school settings or who are facing similar challenges. Nonetheless, the available works have been essential in advancing improvement science as a signature pedagogy for higher education institutions, particularly graduate programs in educational leadership and re-envisioned EdD programs (CPED, 2022), and as an approach for improving schools. However, to support and spread the theoretical and conceptual underpinnings of improvement science in education (Lewis, 2015), it is crucial to hear more from practitioners themselves at this time and how they are employing and grappling with improvement science as a tool for solving problems of practice in their local contexts.

WHY THIS BOOK?

The three of us were hired as new EdD faculty at Radford University. This Carnegie Project on the Education Doctorate (CPED) member institution had just enrolled its second cohort six months prior. We were tasked with creating a program that centered on improvement science in core coursework, program assessments, and the dissertation in practice (DiP). We had both formal and informal conversations with students about their learning. We wanted to know where students needed more support in their learning and application of improvement science. We interviewed program coordinators and faculty in other CPED-affiliated programs (Yurkofsky et al., 2023) about their work to center improvement science in their program. Based on our learning, we then shifted from a traditional research methods sequence in our program to a practitioner inquiry sequence that blended both quantitative and qualitative inquiry tools and supported students in their DiP work (Capello et al., 2023). We still had questions and more questions as we kept learning more from different key actors, and then we noticed that the voice of scholars, researchers, and higher education faculty dominated most things we read about improvement science, how it should be used, and how it was used. We decided to learn about how practitioners made sense of improvement science including the affordances and tensions they experienced (Bonney et al., forthcoming), but more so we wanted them to speak and tell us how they view and use improvement science as a tool for transformation in education. We also sought their perspectives and insights into how improvement science is taken up in the field during habituated practices in education of temporary band-aids, quick fixes, and rapidly implemented interventions.

This book was written for us, for you, for various key actors and partners in education such as educational practitioners in K–12 schools, students enrolled in graduate degree programs in education, and faculty in higher education institutions involved in preparing current and future educational leaders as a resource for learning and teaching. The book is also for interest and advocacy groups, school boards, and professional learning communities (PLCs) in education that are interested in critically examining problems of practice and collaboratively working together toward finding evidence-based solutions that will improve their schools and communities.

ORGANIZATION OF THE BOOK

The book is divided into two parts. Part 1 presents real problems of practice authored by practitioners leading continuous improvement efforts. In chapter 1, Dr. Courtney Browning, a principal of a rural elementary school, shares how she and her team investigated the racial disparities in discipline, and how that affected the school climate including the negative perceptions students had about the school. Their inquiry into racial disparities in discipline highlighted a much more pressing and broader problem related to the school culture. In chapter 2, Drs. Kelly Huff and Tracy Kwock describe their journey of inquiring into why students of color were not applying to a regional gifted program where Kelly works as a regional director. Their improvement team, which included faculty, staff, and students, after rounds of perspective seeking, discovered that transportation was not the main issue as initially thought. In chapter 3, Dr. Jessica Cromer, a district leader, focuses on teacher wellness in the immediate aftermath of the COVID-19 pandemic. In addition to teachers in her division feeling overwhelmed, burnt out, and overworked, they were also experiencing secondary trauma from their students' lived experiences. Jessica and her team, in collaboration with a community mental health organization, led interventions on self-awareness and secondary trauma, supportive peer support sessions, and the development of a personal mindfulness practice. In chapter 4, Dr. Shanice Harrington describes her work aimed at reducing the overrepresentation of students of color in special education. Her intervention is starting to address the lack of culturally competent teachers, a culturally relevant curriculum, and a need for professional development on equity for practitioners. In chapter 5, Dr. Elisabeth Harman and her team wanted to make sure the school district had qualified special education teachers who felt competent even as novice teachers to implement high leverage practices (HLP). The applicant pool for special education teachers in the division was limited and so, to ensure that hired novice teachers were competent, the change idea involved job-embedded and supported professional learning experiences. In chapter 6, Dr. Jamie Soltis, an assistant superintendent, worked with his team to learn why the opportunity gap for students of color and white students continued to widen. Empathy interviews with students and parents in addition to class observations highlighted the need for culturally relevant teaching (CRT) that will help students see themselves in their learning. Two Plan-Do-Study-Act cycles with two groups of teachers were conducted to provide individualized and targeted support and CRT training to teachers.

While the first section of the book presents cases of practitioners who have gone through a full cycle of improvement, part 2 of the book follows a tradition of case-based teaching where authors only provide part of their journey of improvement to invite readers to practice, discuss, brainstorm, and reflect on how *they* would address the problem of practice presented. Therefore, the second part of the book also presents multiple *practice* cases, authored by practitioners that are based on real problems of practice. The case narratives provide details about a problem of practice including relevant contextual information, secondary data, and data from empathy interviews. Readers, students, and groups will be invited to explore and discuss the next steps to addressing the problem using the tools of improvement science. We included these practice case studies for discussion because, as faculty who teach and introduce improvement science to practitioners, there were few teaching tools we found that could engage students authentically. These hypothetical cases serve to start the conversation and also practice with students, practitioners, and professional learning communities what improvement science looks like and should look like. We found in our own teaching and learning that practitioners wanted examples and more examples of improvement science studies and opportunities to analyze sample cases to determine what the process can look like. We present cases describing a problem in a K–12 educational setting based on real experiences of practitioners and educational leaders. The cases were creatively developed by practitioners—Megan Crew, Dr. Michelle Greene, Megan Hawley, Dr. Amy Johnson, Dr. Andrew Nester, Dr. Felicia Preston, and Kim Rygas—to capture the various complexities of problems of practice they have observed, experienced, or are experiencing in education. Each case ends either with what a practitioner and their team found during their inquiry or what they planned to do next after learning about the problem. Readers are invited to analyze the case, examine how the inquiry was conducted, discuss what they would have examined further, and speculate how they would proceed using improvement science processes and tools. The case studies tackle problems of practice such as an English language learner's sense of belonging, teacher demoralization, reading achievement, middle to high school transitions, and discipline and in-school suspensions.

This book presents the practitioner's voice, their uptake of improvement science, their challenges, and how they use the tools of improvement science to lead to educational change. In this book we share multiple examples of how practitioners are using improvement science to lead and create educational change. If you have tried to solve problems in your school community without seeing much change, this book with the stories of leaders and their teams creating and leading change will show you not just the *what* of improvement science but especially the *how*. We invite you to bring your questions and your curiosities about improvement as you begin to read these chapters. For our fellow scholars of improvement science, we invite you to consider the successes and especially the challenges practitioners experience in using improvement science in their organizations to inform how we theorize and expand what improvement science should look like in the field.

Part I

CASES ON LEADING CHANGE

In each chapter in this section, a practitioner presents a case describing their setting and a problem of practice they observed or experienced that created inequities in their schools. The chapter tells the story of how the educational leader formed a team to inquire into the problem including the various forms of inquiry processes and tools of improvement science they used to learn more about how the broader system contributed to the problem facing stakeholders in their setting. Each leader also describes how they and their team worked to understand what change ideas might work well to address the problem. The conclusions of the chapters describe the intervention—the Plan-Do-Study-Act (PDSA) cycle—that the team designed and implemented. These narratives pay particular attention to the lessons learned, challenges, and successes that the scholar-practitioner and their team experienced at each stage of the improvement science process from problem inquiry to intervention implementation and subsequent iterations. Each chapter is interwoven with tools and resources for inquiry and implementation that the practitioner and their team used in addressing their specific problem of practice (e.g., fishbone diagram, driver diagrams). The chapters conclude with lessons learned for leadership, improvement science, or social justice in addition to discussion questions to guide readers in analyzing and discussing the case. The abstracts of each chapter are listed here.

CHAPTER 1: LEADING CHANGE IN RACIAL DISPARITIES IN DISCIPLINE

In this case study, the primary investigator, a principal in a rural elementary school that has struggled to gain accreditation since being restructured in 2021, outlines the work of her research team in investigating and impacting the problem of racial disparity in discipline resulting in students being excluded from the classroom and the negative impact on student perceptions of school culture. By investigating the initial problem of racial disparity in discipline and high office-level referral rates while carefully considering the school and community context, the team's understanding and resulting change theory evolved. The team collectively realized that what began as an issue connected to office-level discipline was rooted in a broader, more pressing school culture problem. The core team, consisting of teachers with varying backgrounds and experiences, a school counselor, school administrators, a school social worker, and a behavior interventionist sought to gather pieces of the puzzle through parent interviews, a school division leadership focus group, and a parent focus group by using the tools of improvement science. After researching and identifying possible change theories, the team sought to consider the level of impact and readiness for each change theory to ensure it was rooted in the school's context. During this time, the team developed a change theory tailored to the school context and carried out PDSA cycles. Despite the feeling of moving slowly, the team remained steadfast and committed to fully understanding the problem and context to develop a change theory and refine existing practices and ultimately found unexpected results and more opportunities to continue applying the tools of improvement science to drive meaningful change.

CHAPTER 2: LEADING CHANGE IN ENROLLMENT OF BLACK AND BROWN STUDENTS IN GIFTED PROGRAMS

Racial and ethnic disproportionality in gifted education is a persistent inequity, especially in Virginia's Academic-Year Governor's School (AYGS) program. Why are students of color not applying to this regional gifted program? This chapter shows why and how a brand-new Equity Team at Mountain Vista Governor's School (MVGS) came together to use improvement science married with implementation science to increase the number of Black and Latinx applicants in less than a year to directly address the program's historically and predominantly white applicant and enrollment pool. The chapter focuses on the use of improvement science to explore, identify, and install a set of tailored communication systems and recruitment practices (including site visits, application kick-offs, and an expanded online presence) to address specific misconceptions and information barriers experienced by potential Black and Latinx applicants. By providing a successful example, the change idea will convey the importance of elevating the voice, perspective, and role of stakeholders closest to the problem to ensure an effective and sustainable solution. This chapter also highlights the researchers' attempt to not only spread the change within the organization but also to other AYGSs and programs examining challenges with disproportionality through a series of asynchronous process modules. These modules take participants through the same processes utilized by the MVGS Equity Team to identify their own potential solutions. The modules highlight the work of MVGS not as a blueprint, but rather as a guide or roadmap, to help participants better understand the processes and tools to seek their own equitable outcomes based on their own organization's needs.

CHAPTER 3: LEADING CHANGE IN TEACHER STRESS AND MENTAL HEALTH

This case focuses on supporting educators' mental health and resiliency as they work with youth who have experienced childhood trauma. This secondary trauma can have physical, mental, emotional, and spiritual impacts on those in a helping profession such as education. Previous research on this topic has centered on the fields of social workers, healthcare workers, and first responders. Given the rise in the number of students experiencing trauma, educators in a rural PK–7 elementary school planned interventions to combat the impact of secondary trauma on the teaching staff. A research team consisting of central office administrators, a building principal, and a school psychologist used ongoing data from staff and assistance from community mental health organizations to guide interventions that targeted teacher wellness. The interventions were concentrated in the areas of teacher training on self-awareness and secondary trauma, supportive peer support sessions, and the development of a personal mindfulness practice. The work encountered several challenges due to a change in leadership at the school, a high rate of staff turnover, and the general impact of the COVID-19 pandemic on the field of education. The team found a decrease in the levels of secondary traumatic stress among staff throughout the project and plans to spread this change into the future school year.

CHAPTER 4: LEADING CHANGE IN THE OVERREPRESENTATION OF STUDENTS OF COLOR IN SPECIAL EDUCATION

In education, disproportionality, often used interchangeably with overrepresentation, is defined as, "the high probability of being placed in special education, based on membership in a historically marginalized group" (Oswald et al., 1999). Research findings have identified root causes of disproportionality as a lack of culturally competent teachers, a curriculum that is not culturally relevant, or a need for professional development on equity. This chapter provides an analysis of the implementation and outcomes associated with one school's improvement process that was aimed at reducing the overrepresentation of students of color in special education. The intermediate goal was to address disproportionality and implicit bias and improve capacity to implement culturally relevant practices through professional development. Pre- and post-test data were collected in the form of survey responses and an efficacy scale related to evidence-based culturally relevant practices. Qualitative data were collected in journal reflections and a focus group and analyzed to develop themes. Quantitative data were analyzed using a one-sample t-test to determine if there was a statistical significance. The results demonstrated statistical and marginal significance in teachers' self-efficacy to implement culturally relevant practices, and themes of awareness related to disproportionality and implicit bias. The results of implementation revealed that the professional development was effective at addressing the intermediate goal of awareness. While this chapter focused on teachers being self-reflective to improve their efficacy, future cycles would be needed to determine if improved efficacy translates to proportional representation of students of color in special education.

CHAPTER 5: LEADING CHANGE IN ONBOARDING AND SUPPORT OF NOVICE TEACHERS

The purpose of this study was to determine if novice special education teachers self-reported improved efficacy of knowledge and skill after being provided quality, engaging learning opportunities that were relevant, job-embedded, and grounded in the high-leverage practices (HLP) in special education framework. Due to the growing need for quality and qualified special educators, but a limited applicant pool, it is critical to ensure that hired staff, often with minimal to zero experience, are provided with high-quality, job-embedded, and supported professional learning experiences. The research team, which consisted of seven division-level special education administrative staff, believed that providing professional learning in multiple modalities (i.e., in-person, asynchronous online, mentoring) over an extended period and grounded in a framework would provide a better first-year experience for our novice teachers than in previous years. The team believed that novice teachers who have professional learning opportunities that improve their knowledge, skills, and self-efficacy in their ability to perform the duties of their role are more likely to be successful and remain in the field. Data collected through the course of this study with pre- and post-intervention surveys revealed that, when comparing individual responses pre- and post-intervention, growth was demonstrated in all categories surveyed. It can be surmised that the targeted aim of the study was met because data indicate improved working knowledge of and ability to implement the HLP and reported increases in self-efficacy related to targeted skills by all participants. Teacher retention will be determined over time. Results from this study may be applied to other disciplines as an effective approach to onboarding novice teachers.

CHAPTER 6: LEADING CHANGE TO IMPROVE ACADEMIC OUTCOMES FOR TRADITIONALLY MARGINALIZED STUDENTS

This chapter highlights the importance of addressing the racial disparities in reading outcomes between Black and white students. It is the moral responsibility of all educators to determine the factors contributing to these disparities and to implement strategies to eliminate them. An assistant superintendent and his research team used improvement science to address the reading racial disparity at their community's only middle school. They analyzed data, used improvement science tools, and developed a working theory of improvement using a driver diagram. The team found that culturally relevant pedagogy (CRP) was necessary to close the reading racial disparity. They developed and provided an ongoing professional development program to increase teacher self-efficacy in understanding and implementing CRP. The team collected data on the effectiveness of the professional development on the CRP program through driver surveys, process surveys, class observations, and discussions with teachers and modified the program based on the data collected during and after the PDSA cycles. The data indicated that providing teachers with ongoing personalized professional development in CRP increased their self-efficacy, and they were more likely to implement CRP in their classrooms. The team plans to expand their change idea throughout their school division in the coming school year.

Chapter 1

Leading Change in Racial Disparities in Discipline

Courtney Browning, EdD

THE CONTEXT

Slateville Elementary School opened its doors in Slateville County after the school board consolidated and restructured the four existing small community primary and elementary schools. The goal of the school division was to increase opportunities for all preschool through fifth grade students, more fully leverage resources, and improve academic opportunities. Through this restructuring, a central preschool, a primary school, which serves kindergarten through second grade, and an elementary school, serving third through fifth grade were opened. A former middle and elementary school were renovated as buildings for the new primary and elementary schools. The primary and elementary are situated on a shared campus and were designed with open learning spaces, green features, and cutting-edge technology. The design of the building and selection of furniture was intended to promote movement and health. The building was also intended to foster collaboration and inquiry. Breakout spaces were created outside of classrooms and at the end of hallways with soft seating areas throughout, teacher collaboration rooms for each grade level, and informative signs hung on the walls throughout the building to teach students about the mechanics of the facility, different habitats in Virginia, and environmental science. The campus was designed as a potential hub for place-based learning.

    The shared primary and elementary complex was intended to be not only a place of educational excellence for students but also a resource for the community. Slateville is a geographically large, yet sparsely populated county populated with an average of 29 citizens per square mile (U.S. Census Bureau, n.d.). The county has limited community resources and a small tax revenue base. There are only 253 employers in the county and a median income of $49,841, as compared to the state's overall median of $80,615. The demographics of the county mirror those of the elementary school, where 64% of the Slateville county population is white and 33% are African American. Slateville Elementary School has a high poverty rate with 82% of its students considered economically disadvantaged (School Division, 2023).

    Before the consolidation, Slateville had a primary school serving about 150 students in preschool through fourth grade, a primary school serving about 350 students preschool through third grade, a primary school serving about 160 preschool through fifth grade students, and an elementary school serving about 220 fourth and fifth grade students (School Division, 2020). The decision to consolidate and restructure the schools came after many years of discussion, debate, and disagreement within the community. There was disagreement about whether merging schools would best serve all students and not negatively impact the small local communities the schools served. However, there was a great need to renovate three of the four schools and resources were extremely limited. At the time of the newly reconfigured schools, all the smaller community schools were fully accredited and exceeded state accreditation guidelines (School Division, 2020).

During its first year, Slateville Elementary School faced numerous struggles. The full weight of the recession was hitting the state when the new preschool, primary school, and Slateville Elementary School opened. During the restructuring, several teaching, administration, and support positions were cut across the division; this caused an increase in class sizes and reduced the number of administrators, instructional support teachers, and staff. Additionally, the primary school and Slateville Elementary School opened while still under construction and with an unanticipated increase in student enrollment, causing the primary and elementary schools to open above capacity. Rooms that had been slated to be learning and science labs were turned into general education classrooms to house the additional students at the schools' inauguration.

Throughout the year, Slateville Elementary School experienced the growing pains of merging schools, higher class sizes, and the establishment of new systems. In the spring, end-of-year state testing revealed Slateville Elementary School had fallen far below state accreditation guidelines in reading and math as compared to previous accreditation results for each school before the consolidation. The impact of restructuring and opening of the new schools was compounded by the newly increased rigor of state curriculum standards and changes to the assessment format being felt across the state, with the statewide percentage of fully accredited schools falling from 90% to 77% in the year of the change (Reporter, 2013). Being a new school, Slateville Elementary was unable to rely on a three-year average to help offset the impact of the increased rigor on the end-of-year state assessments in reading. In contrast, other schools that were previously successful were able to average the past three years together for accreditation purposes. However, despite each of the small schools having pass rates over the past three years that were well above the state requirement, Slateville was only able to use the pass rate from the year of the change. As a result, the school was identified for comprehensive school improvement due to being in the bottom 5% of all Title 1 schools in the state, based on state testing (State Department of Education, 2020). Had Slateville been able to average the prior two years of performance by the small community schools that were merged into Slateville, it would not have been identified for comprehensive school improvement.

In the first seven years of opening, Slateville was part of three different federal models of school improvement. The school worked with external coaches and state Office of School Improvement staff, conducted two needs assessments, wrote three different school improvement grants, and wrote two school improvement plans.

Nonetheless, Slateville failed to reach full accreditation. Although initial gains were made in math and science with Slateville meeting state accreditation guidelines in those subjects within the first three years, Slateville began to experience a downward trend in math and science. In 2016–2017 and 2017–2018, Slateville was denied accreditation. By 2019–2020, Slateville met accreditation with conditions. According to the State Department of Education (2020), Level 1 signifies that a school or division "meets or exceeds state standards or has made sufficient improvement in that area." Level 2 denotes that the school or division is "near state standards or has made sufficient improvement" in that area. Level 3 signifies that a school or division is "below state standards" and has not made sufficient growth in that area.

In the 2019–2020 school year, Slateville Elementary School was a level 2 in English, Science, and Achievement Gap groups in Math and a level 3 for Achievement Gaps in English as outlined in Figure 1.1 (State Department of Education, 2020). Level 1 means that a school is performing at or above the state standard for the indicator. Level 2 means that a school is performing near the state standard for the indicator or improving while Level 3 means that a school is performing below the state standard for the indicator.

Figure 1.1. 2019–2020 School Quality Indicators Table

In addition to the poor academic achievement, Slateville experienced high teacher turnover, a change of administration at the division and school level, and limited parent involvement. Furthermore, Slateville had high rates of office-level discipline and out-of-school suspensions (State Department of Education, 2020).

THE PROBLEM

In February 2020, I rounded the corner of finishing my 17th year in education and serving Slateville public schools and my fourth year as an assistant principal at Slateville Elementary School. I began to explore a problem of practice that was affecting the school and something I was invested in helping to solve. The problem of practice I selected would drive the research study my school-based research team and I developed over the next three years. My research team and I would employ the tools of improvement science to study the problem in-depth, consult existing research, and develop an intervention that would be tested and refined as we conducted two Plan-Do-Study-Act (PDSA) cycles. As a former reading specialist and instructional coach, my passion was instruction. Slateville clearly had a problem at the Tier 1 reading instructional level. This meant that the overall initial reading instruction or curriculum provided to all students needed to be improved, in contrast to needing an intervention for a smaller population of students. While there was a problem with Tier 1 instruction for all student populations, it also resulted in a significant opportunity gap among African American students in reading and math. However, as the assistant principal, one of the greatest areas of focus for my daily work was school discipline. I was often faced with multiple significant behavior incidents while simultaneously struggling to understand the lack of academic improvement, despite creative efforts among our teachers, staff, and administrators.

At the time, Slateville had an extremely high rate of in-school suspensions (ISS) and out-of-school suspensions (OSS). I began my study of the problem by examining the types of referrals, locations of referrals, and, overall, number of referrals. I found that from 2016–2020, Slateville issued the highest number of referrals for defiance, disrespect, and minor altercations. This matched my anecdotal observations as the assistant principal. As I dug deeper, I decided to look at the quantity, locations, reasons for referrals, and disciplinary measures given to students when comparing the rate among African American students and their white peers. The racial breakdown at Slateville has remained consistent since opening its doors with African American students making up approximately 36% of the population and white students making up about 52%. However, ISS and OSS rates were almost the opposite of the demographic makeup with just over 67% of all ISS and about 64% of OSS in 2019 being given to African American students in the 2019–2020 school year despite African American students only making up 36% of the population. Additionally, there was a historical trend of disproportionate ISS and OSS rates among African American students as compared to their white peers as noted in Figures 1.2 and 1.3. Furthermore, a comparison of office and bus referral rates revealed that the disparate rate in which African American students were referred was consistent across multiple settings as demonstrated in Table 1.1. Rates were similar on the bus and in the school. In both cases, rates continued to be disproportionate as compared to the demographic makeup of the school population. The overall racial disparity in discipline was comparable to the high-level disparity in achievement gap groups among African American students and their white peers as noted in Table 1.2.

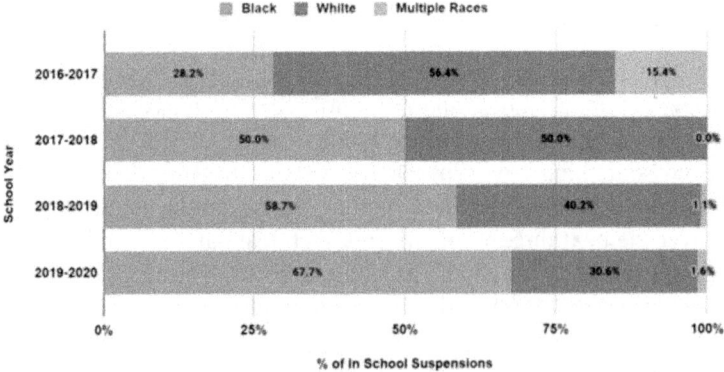

Figure 1.2. Percent of In-School Suspensions by Race

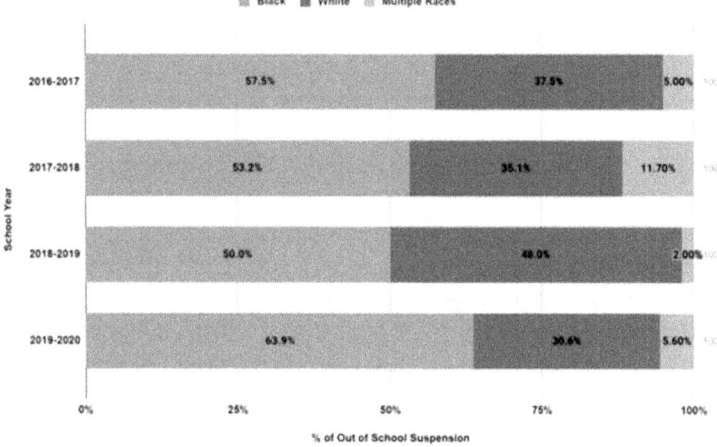

Figure 1.3. Percent of Out-of-School Suspensions by Race

Table 1.1. Setting of Referrals by Race 2019–2020

Race	Bus	School	Total
	Rate of Referral	Rate of Referral	Rate of Referral
African American	65%	67%	66%
White	27%	29%	28%

Table 1.2. 2018–2019 Opportunity Gap Data

Academic Achievement 2018–2019

Subject	% Passing			% Not Showing Proficiency or Growth	
	African American	White	Difference	African American	White
English	38%	62%	24%	44%	25%
Math	48%	71%	23%	36%	18%

At first examination, the problem appeared rooted in the disparate rate of behavior incidents. As I dove into the first round of disciplinary data and initial study of research, I realized that at my school and in my context, this was a historical, multifaceted problem that could no longer be avoided. As research indicates, OSS negatively impact student engagement and academic achievement (Blake et al., 2020; Gastic, 2017; Rocque, 2010; Skiba et al., 2002; Skiba et al., 2019), attendance (Losen, 2015), and retention (Blake et al., 2020; Heilbrun et al., 2017). Given the breadth of research suggesting a correlation between OSS and negative outcomes for students (Girvan et al., 2017; Skiba et al., 2002, Skiba et al., 2019), the corresponding correlation between suspensions and achievement among racial groups observed at Slatesville Elementary School provided serious cause for concern along with direction for potential improvement.

This disproportionate rate of office referrals, ISS, and short-term suspensions that African American students were experiencing at Slateville was not unique to the school. Racial disparity in discipline and short-term suspensions has increased across the nation since the 1970s (Skiba et al., 2019). While the overall rate of suspensions has grown over time for all populations in the educational setting, the rates have increased more dramatically and more quickly for African American and Latino students than for white students (Gastic, 2017). Blake et al. (2020) found that according to the US Department of Education, "African American male and female students received 25% and 14% of OSS, respectively, but each accounted for 8% of total enrollment" (p. 131). Suspension rates of African American students are two to three times higher than those of white students (Skiba et al., 2002; Skiba et al., 2019). Research also indicates that the problem of racial disparity in discipline is impacted at both the teacher (Skiba et al., 2002; Skiba et al., 2019) and administrative levels (Gastic, 2017; Skiba et al., 2019) as can be seen in the disparity Slateville Elementary was experiencing in the rate of initial office referrals written and of instances of ISS and OSS between African American and white students.

The disparity continued to deepen when I examined the types of referrals students received. As noted in Table 1.3, African American students received disparate rates of referrals for incidents deemed disrespectful, defiant, disruptive, and a fight/minor altercation.

Table 1.3. Historical Referral Rates by Race Based on Sanction Code

School Year	2016–2017		2017–2018		2018–2019		2019–2020 (through January)	
Race	Black	White	Black	White	Black	White	Black	White
Disrespect	35%	60%	65%	18%	60%	40%	61%	33%
Defiance	43%	51%	57%	32%	47%	51%	59%	41%
Disruption	50%	36%	57%	33%	65%	35%	56%	44%
Fight/Minor Altercation	57%	36%	40%	60%	56%	36%	73%	17%

For each type of referral, the ratio remained disproportionate in comparison to the population makeup of the school. Through my research, I learned that the disparate rates of referrals for defiance, disrespect, disruptions, and fights or minor altercations extended beyond the elementary school. This disparity is present across the nation (Gastic, 2017; Girvan et al., 2017; Monroe, 2005; Harvard Civil Rights Project, 2000; Skiba et al., 2002; Skiba et al., 2019). Research indicates that African American students are more likely to be disciplined for fighting than white students (Gastic, 2017; Losen, 2015). Furthermore, research has also found African American students largely experience higher rates of racial disparity in office referrals and exclusionary discipline for subjective offenses such as defiance, disrespect, and disruption (Girvan et al., 2017; Harvard Civil Rights Project, 2000; Skiba et al., 2019), as was the case at my elementary school. In addition to disproportionately receiving office referrals, African American students are more likely to receive more severe consequences for comparable misbehavior than white students (Blake et al., 2020; Gastic, 2017; Skiba et al., 2002; Skiba et al., 2019). It has been proposed that the disparate rates of office referrals among African American students as compared to their white peers are a result of higher rates of misbehavior occurring among African American students as compared to their white peers; however, a wealth of research has shown that the disparate number of office referrals for African American students as compared to their white peers is not the result of higher instances of actual misbehavior (Fenning & Jenkins, 2018; Girvan et al., 2017; Rocque, 2010; Skiba et al., 2002; Skiba et al., 2019).

To further my study of the problem in my context, I conducted empathy interviews with 11 teachers from Slateville. I posed a combination of three questions to participants, such as:

- Paint me a picture of what you think about when you hear that a high number of students exhibit verbal and physical aggression at Slateville.
- What do you wonder about the disproportionate number of referrals for African American and white students for verbal and physical aggression?
- What advice would you give a fellow teacher about working on the schoolwide problem of verbal and physical aggression?
- Suppose you could have three wishes to make the rate of disproportionality between African American and white students the best it could be. What would they be, and why?

Participation in the empathy interviews was completely voluntary.

Of the 11 participants, all were women. Six were core classroom teachers, one was a librarian, one was a school counselor, one was a school social worker, one was a director in the central office, and three were parents. Two of the parents were also teachers. Responses varied, but there were common trends among them. Responses fell into the themes: factors related to outside of school, factors of school organization and process, factors related to teacher impact, and factors related to community actions. Many of the responses connected to building relationships among students, creating a safe and consistent place for students, teaching students how to communicate with one another, fostering stronger communication with parents, building parent and community partnerships, and supporting social-emotional learning.

After administering empathy interviews, I facilitated a faculty meeting in which all teachers and staff examined referral data, discussed "hot spots" and types of behaviors they were seeing, and created a goal for how to reduce negative behavior. Groups worked in grade-level and cross-grade-level teams to share ideas and collaborate. During this analysis, it was determined that there was an escalation from third through fifth grade in the types of behaviors. Third grade teachers reported that they were struggling most with horseplay. Fourth grade teachers struggled with defiance and fights. Fifth grade teachers identified behaviors related to disrespect, defiance, fighting, and safety issues as most pressing. Encore teachers (art, music, library, and PE) teachers experienced high levels of defiance and disrespect in their classes. The group noted that the behaviors in third grade began as horseplay, with students roughhousing, play fighting, or playing football or basketball with some light contact such as pushing or ball checking. However, the behaviors shifted into physical escalations such as pushing, hitting, and fighting out of anger as students moved into fourth and fifth grade. These findings gave a sense of what types of behaviors teachers felt were occurring most often and where.

Next, I began a close examination of our discipline and school culture policies and procedures. The school discipline policy was critically evaluated to identify strengths and weaknesses. Additionally, I considered components of the policy that may be impacting the discrepancy in overall office referral rates, instances and rates of ISS, and instances and rates of OSS between African American and white students. The policy was also reviewed to determine what types of behaviors led to ISS and OSS. In 2018–2019, the school adopted a written discipline policy outlining schoolwide discipline steps, types of behaviors warranting an immediate office referral and the associated consequences, types of behaviors requiring corrective actions on the part of the teacher to prevent future occurrences or escalations of the behavior, and the consequences for the types of behaviors requiring corrective measures if an office referral is issued. Lastly, the policy outlined what types of referrals result in ISS and OSS sanctions. It was revised in the summer of 2019. In the revision, an ISS room was established that employed a support paraprofessional to monitor students in ISS.

While the discipline policy established consistency and clear expectations that had the potential to become strengths, a review uncovered strong similarities to a zero-tolerance approach. According to Monroe (2005), while zero-tolerance policies were created to promote safety in the light of school violence, such policies may be aggravating the problem and increasing racial disparity overall, in part, because educators extend the application of the policies and fail to make distinctions between severe and minor infractions. The Harvard Civil Rights Project (2000) found discipline policies that were "overly inelastic and uncompromising did not meet the developmental needs of school-aged children. They inhibit a student's ability to develop enduring trusting relationships with critical adults and can negatively impact a student's perception of fairness and justice around them" (p. 22). The increased office referrals at Slateville for minor behavioral infractions, as research suggested, can have the opposite effect than intended. Rather than deterring future misbehavior, office referrals can become predictive of more significant future escalations of defiance (Amemiya et al., 2020; Girvin et al., 2016). Additionally, office referrals for subjective behaviors such as defiance, disrespect, and disruption, as is the case at Slateville, correlate to increased racial disparity in school discipline (Gastic, 2017; Girvan et al., 2016).

This early study of research began opening my eyes to the fact that my initial assumption was that the problem was a result of disparate incidents, rather than a systemic problem. As I learned more, I began to realize my assumptions and implicit bias were built into my statement of the problem of practice. I assumed that the root of the problem was student behaviors, and I realized that this was an example of my own implicit bias. This awakening became a critical aspect of the work of my research team and me.

In February 2020, before the pandemic and all that followed, I started to fully lean into the problem that I had uncovered and found so troubling. I also began to awaken to the realization that this issue was strongly connected to, if not at the root of, many other problems my school was facing. While it seemed insurmountable, I started to have hope for change. However, I had no idea how relevant, pressing, and critical my problem of practice would become.

THE TEAM

After my initial research and study of the problem, I formed the research team. My team began with seven members and was supported by two subcommittees whose members were not part of the research team. Initially, my research team included five white and two African American team members. However, the members and the demographic makeup of the team changed throughout the study, as members were unable to continue participating due to reasons outside the study. Both initial members who were unable to continue on the team were African American due to reasons outside of the school and the research study. The two team members who had to leave the research team were replaced with white team members due to the limited diversity among Slateville Elementary School staff. My final team included a grade level teacher, an art teacher, a social worker, a school counselor, a behavior interventionist, another school administrator, and myself. The selection of members was based on creating a team with varying backgrounds, experiences, expertise, and perspectives. I sought members of the team who had demonstrated a desire to be agents of change, reflectiveness, leadership, and creative problem-solving. As a result, I invited members who had previously demonstrated these qualities. The team members had shown leadership by acting as grade level leads or the chair of a school-based committee. The research team members had previously demonstrated an openness to collaborate, analyze problems, and be reflective during school leadership team meetings, grade level data meetings, or faculty meetings.

In addition to my research team, I created two focus groups that helped at different times throughout the study. My division leadership subcommittee included three representatives, two who were white and one who was African American. The division leadership subcommittee team met to consider contributing factors and assess the readiness and capacity of the school system concerning the problem of practice. The family stakeholder subcommittee included three parents; two were African American and one was white. Initially, I met with each member of the family stakeholder subcommittee individually because there was hesitation from members to meet as a group to discuss racial disparity in discipline. Later in the study, the family stakeholder subcommittee met as a group to review findings from the study of the problem and to develop our change idea.

PROBLEM INQUIRY AND ANALYSIS

To start our inquiry into the problem, I shared my initial data with my core research team. Based on our initial discussions, I realized I needed to adjust the structure of how we approached our fishbone diagramming. A fishbone diagram is created by considering potential contributing factors related to a problem. From each main contributing factor, additional subfactors are identified therein. This can be done through an open group discussion. However, talking about race, racial disparity, and the underlying causes was not something any of us had previously done together as a group. Initial discussions of the problem, study, and data were cautious and somewhat limited. As a white woman who was their supervisor, I was also timid about how to engage them in these types of open, honest, and difficult conversations. As a result, I adapted the fishbone diagram process to build time for individual thought and reflection before sharing ideas. I also structured our process to strategies that would ensure full participation while creating a feeling of safety among participants. To ensure reflection and wide discussion, participants spent time independently recording possible contributing factors on sticky notes. Each contributing factor they came up with was written on a sticky note. I allotted five minutes for this and asked that no one share ideas before the time was up. As a group, we established basic rules for sharing that included: there are no wrong answers and Vegas rules (what is said in the research team stays with the research team). Although we may disagree, we will be honest and respectful of one another, and we should share all ideas. With these parameters in place, we came together to share each idea, one at a time, and discussed any connections, similarities, or additional thoughts this prompted. As we discussed the ideas, we identified additional possible contributing factors and added them to the chart as well. We also began to share our feelings and open up with one another. Our group continued in this fashion, literally creating our fishbone diagram on chart paper until all sticky notes were shared as noted in Figure 1.4. Once we finished, we looked

Figure 1.4. Fishbone Diagram

for broad trends, considered the frequency of responses, which were visible by the number of sticky notes for each offshoot, and made connections across factors. This process seemed to bring us together and helped us feel more comfortable talking about our problem of practice as a team.

After developing our initial fishbone diagram, we engaged in system mapping. We used an open discussion forum and then spent time considering any connections between responses from both tools.

Due to COVID restrictions, our fishbone diagram and system mapping were conducted virtually with the school district subcommittee. I decided to use an open discussion format with this subcommittee, as they appeared more comfortable discussing the topic as a group. We then did the fishbone diagram and system mapping individually with the family participants before combining their answers into one table.

Once all initial causal analyses were complete, the research team and I reviewed the fishbone diagram tables and system maps to consider similarities, differences, and frequency of responses. We noted overlap and differences in Table 1.4. All three groups noted that cultural differences between students and staff were a critical factor. The staff is primarily composed of white female teachers. The student population includes more diversity in race and gender. All three groups also felt that the school culture and discipline policies were contributing to the problem. The groups agreed that teachers needed more training in restorative justice. The teams also felt that there were inconsistencies across the school and that the policy needed to build in steps to improve the behavior rather than rely so heavily on punishments. Additionally, all three groups noted the home environment as being impactful in the racial disparity in discipline. Under this category, all three groups felt that the impact of acute childhood trauma experiences outside of school, the high levels of poverty families of Slateville experience, and the limited outside resources to support families all contributed to the problem of practice. The research team and division groups also felt that the lack of social-emotional learning and support at the school were also critical to the problem. The division and parent groups more often noted teacher response to students, lack of professional development, and the impact of teachers' and staff's implicit bias, stereotypes, and presumptions being an important contributing factor.

As we compared the findings from all three groups against our research, we began to recognize that the problem went beyond the referrals themselves. At that time, we recognized we were missing critical pieces of data that we had not considered: the student and parent perceptions of school climate and existing policies and practices. Much of our research spoke to the school climate, culture, and policies, however, we had not examined these pieces.

As a result, we examined school climate data that had been collected as part of Slateville's annual Comprehensive Needs Assessment. Students and parents were given the University of Oregon's Office of Special Education Programs (OSEP) Technical Assistance Center on Positive Behavioral Interventions and Supports School Climate Survey. The findings were startling. There were three areas in which there was a wide discrepancy, 10 or more percentage points, between African American and white or all student groups' positive perceptions about school. African American students expressed far less positive feelings about liking school, feeling safe at school, and the

Table 1.4. Comparison of Responses from Fishbone Diagrams

Research Team		
Majority of staff are white women; we have five black teachers and two male teachers; this does not match the makeup of our student population	Inconsistency on how corrective measures are applied; No school-wide common expectations	High rates of trauma among students (ACE score-addiction, neglect, parent incarcerated, drug use), handling emotions (neurological impact of trauma)
Mismatch in teacher/student messages and interpretations of messages and actions (communication barriers from differences)	Corrective actions in some cases became steps to check off quickly to get to referral while other teachers did more to prevent and correct behavior	Modeling at home (learned reactions and behaviors)
Life experiences are different (many teachers have not grown up in similar situations as our students) many teachers from outside of the county	Evidenced in cases where students are successful in one setting and not another, inconsistent use of teacher timeouts (length of time, frequency, contact with parents, follow-up), becomes long undocumented exclusion in some cases or for specific students	Limitations of foster care in county causing students to remain in these environments, limitations of DSS and outside agencies
Preconceptions from teachers can stem from these cultural and life experience differences	Different management styles from room to room and as a result environment	Limited local counseling and community resources (Crossroads of Farmville serves the county, 30–50 minutes away from many families), limited funding compared to close regions like Region 10
	Policy does not connect to follow-up with teaching the behaviors, offering counseling support or positive supports after the behavior referral	Discipline approaches (authoritative versus authoritarian) typical to SES
	Discipline policy focuses on punishment	Language Gaps/Patterns typical to SES
	Restorative justice is not built into policy	Lack of socially mitigated involvement (sports, play dates, etc.) outside of school, very rural, limited opportunities for socialization outside of school
	No training on restorative justice has taken place	Parent work hours and commutes result in not seeing parents as often
		High percent in single-parent, grandparent, or foster setting

Division Team	Cultural differences between students and teachers, families and teachers Teachers assume the reason for a response but it may be that it is a mismatch (e.g., using ma'am and sir, making eye contact) Reponses from students are often rooted in their family dynamics, experiences in community, and cultural expectations, and teacher's interpretations of this are rooted in theirs Limited diversity among staff (composition of staff backgrounds and demographics does not mirror that of students (includes life experiences, race, socioeconomic status, and backgrounds) Teachers have not had training in culturally responsive teaching and behavior management practices	Lack of cohesive school culture that is responsive to cultural differences and community Discipline policy does not have consistent corrective and preventative actions across all rooms/settings Policy has punishment but not a lot of preventative, relies on ISS and OSS instead of alternate or restorative practices (has become a fast track for punishment rather than deterrent or correction of behaviors) Norms within classes are different from one grade to the next, one teacher to the next Discipline policy leaves room for subjectivity regarding what aggression is and is not, does not have a way of ensuring consistency in writing	Trauma outside of school Limited resources and poverty in the home Students act out behaviors they see in the home Cultural differences and expectations at home differ from school (e.g., use of sir or ma'am, eye contact, not responding verbally)
Parent Group	Mismatch between students and staff demographics and cultural backgrounds: Majority of staff are white, female Need to have conversations among staff about cultural differences, stereotypes, implicit bias, and white privilege (begin tough conversations to unpack problem)	Need to develop steps for teachers to take before just disciplining Need to consider what may be causing the behavior before just punishing Need to remediate the behaviors, treat them like something a student needs to learn rather than just punishing The school needs to incorporate restorative justice practices Teachers need training in how to approach students and to be reflective about messages sent in tone, actions, and reaction	Act out behaviors modeled out home (yelling, aggression, physical violence, anger, mistrust) Trauma outside of school Many students have a parent or family member who is or has been incarcerated Many children, in particular African American males, do not have a strong male role model at home Limited resources and supports in the home cause pressures and impacts family (poverty, drug abuse, lack of employment) High rates of poverty in the community High rates of single-parent households and of kids living with grandparents or guardians

behavior of their peers as compared to white or all students. Parent responses mirrored this despite being taken separately from their children.

This was a pivotal moment for the team. Each member was shocked and saddened to realize that the school experience student survey responses indicated that African American students expressed less positive feelings about liking school, feeling safe, and the behavior of their peers as compared to their white peers. This finding was not something that could be explained by disparate rates of actual misbehavior. This was not something that any of us could avoid feeling in part responsible for contributing to, regardless of our intentions. Yet while this realization for the team hurt each one of us deeply, it also motivated us to dig deeper to develop our change idea and create a path toward equity. This finding helped us to fully own our problem of practice and come together to improve it.

The team recognized that our change idea needed to focus on a Tier 1 level to improve African American students' perceptions of school given that student perceptions about school impacted their achievement, behavior, and engagement (Gastic, 2017; Okonofua et al., 2016; Skiba et al., 2002; Skiba et al., 2019).

CHANGE IDEAS AND INTERVENTIONS

With this new conclusion at the forefront, the team went back to our consolidated fishbone diagram data to conduct an assessment of our locus of control on the causal factors that were most frequently noted. We did this to frame what factors may be solidly within our locus of control, may be within our locus of control, and what was not within our locus of control. My team and I recognized that those factors that were outside of our locus of control, while important of which to be aware, were not things that we could or should root our change idea. We needed to ground our change idea in something that was within our potential to alter significantly if we were truly going to create sustainable change.

Next, the research team reviewed the research about change ideas, approaches, and strategies that could be used to improve school culture overall and reduce racial disparity in discipline as compared to the main contributing factors that we identified as impacting Slateville Elementary. From there, our team created and modified a driver diagram. We began reviewing the contributing factors solidly or partially in our control and considering how these could become primary and secondary drivers. Once we developed our list of primary and secondary drivers, the team began an open brainstorming session to list possible change ideas individually and then compiled our ideas as a group. As we shared our change ideas, we connected them to the driver to which they related. This, again, was done using sticky notes with one answer on each note to help the team gauge the frequency of our responses, foster more reflective responses, and avoid groupthink. The approach also helped us not get "stuck" in one or two change ideas because it required us to keep the problem of practice and our inquiry into it at the forefront. Improvement science tools can be very effective; however, if a shift in our disposition to tackling problems is not made, their effectiveness is lost as we fall into the common pattern of committing to a change idea without fully understanding the problem. By forcing ourselves to focus continually on understanding our school's context concerning our problem of practice, rather than quickly jumping to a solution, my research team and I had to stay in the unknown or gray zone where there are many possible solutions but no definite answer. In this zone, it doesn't always feel like forward progress or accomplishment are being made. Most often, our instinct is to avoid rather than embrace that feeling.

After completing our driver diagram, we consulted the research again on practices, strategies, and factors that had the potential to positively impact school culture and racial disparity in discipline. We reconsidered our list of change ideas and whether:

1. Each change idea was something we were already doing with fidelity.
2. Each change idea was something we were doing with limited fidelity.
3. Each change idea was something we were not doing at all.
4. The change idea was something we may not be doing now but based on future division or state initiatives, we would likely be doing it in the future.

Once again, we used the approach of each participant rating every change idea on their own before coming together to create a final rating. This created discussion and careful consideration about each change idea. Once we made our ranked list, we discussed the leading change ideas, considered our school context, and how many primary or secondary drivers to which each top change idea related. One trend that the team noted was that the school was already in the process of many initiatives to foster relationships, social-emotional learning, and student support. Many of the initiatives began in the spring of 2020 or during the 2020–2021 school year. However, for the majority of the initiatives, the implementation was limited due to the pandemic, which resulted in school closure and full remote learning for the first two and a half quarters of the 2020–2021 school year, and the limitations created by social distancing and health/safety mitigation measures. During this discussion, the team weighed the ease of implementation versus the potential for positive impact for each change idea and which change ideas overlapped multiple drivers.

Initially, we considered trying to improve some of the current social-emotional learning and support programs Slateville was currently undertaking. We saw from our research that programs such as these can help to foster a school culture that values mutual respect and collaboration among students and teachers while equipping students with the tools they need to resolve conflicts (Harvard Civil Rights Project, 2000). However, we recognized that the direct impact on student behavior and social-emotional learning was not as solidly in our locus of control. There are several additional factors, including poverty and the early childhood trauma that a high number of Slateville Elementary students experience, which can contribute to their behavior and social-emotional regulation. As a result, the team felt that changing student behaviors and building self-regulation and coping skills were less within our locus of control and, therefore, not a suitable change idea for our study at this time.

The team also considered our existing discipline policies and practices. We had found that over time Slateville's discipline policy took on attributes of a zero-tolerance policy. Research from the National Summit on Zero Tolerance (2000) noted that an important aspect of reducing racial disparity in discipline is to shift discipline policies and practices from being a rigid means of "control" to "a way to help a child solve a problem, develop inner controls and learn better ways of expressing feelings" (p. 23). Additionally, Schiff (2018) pointed out that "zero tolerance and other exclusionary discipline policy," like those used at Slateville, "have resulted in unprecedented numbers of mostly minority youth entering what is now being called 'the school-to-prison pipeline'" (p. 143). While changing the policies was solidly in our locus of control, we recognized that simply changing policies didn't ensure change.

Through our research, we began to recognize that supporting teachers with professional learning opportunities in appropriate classroom management and conflict resolution may be critical to reducing racial disparity in discipline and is a critical component to reducing racial disparity (Harvard Civil Rights Project, 2000). We noted that there was power in supporting teachers and staff in approaching discipline and classroom management with an empathetic mindset (Okonofua et al., 2016). Okonofua and coauthors (2016) found that in school environments that rely largely on punitive measures to correct and prevent misbehavior, students' levels of respect for their teachers and their internal motivation to behave in school were diminished; whereas, in schools that promoted teachers taking an empathetic mindset when addressing discipline, suspensions rates were halved within one year. We realized that a critical element to taking an empathetic mindset toward students is building relationships and making connections with students. It also meant getting to know, understand, and honor the diversity of our students. As we considered our driver diagram with this idea, we recognized that this was also a fundamental aspect of culturally responsive teaching.

The team also discussed the use of restorative justice, as it had also been found to reduce the use of overall exclusionary discipline and positively impact racial disparity in discipline (Schiff, 2018). We recognized there was an increasing body of research that indicated that restorative justice practices could help to reduce racial disparity in discipline and reduce the "school-to-prison pipeline" by helping schools shift away from reliance on exclusionary discipline practices, instead fostering a school culture that promotes "inclusiveness, respect, trust, honor and engagement" (Schiff, 2018, p. 134). However, Schiff's research helped the team recognize that, at this point, for our context, centering our change idea on restorative justice would be futile if we did not first build in reflective examinations of implicit bias, systemic racism, and cultural views beyond simply implementing a program or new practice (Schiff, 2018). Additionally, Girvan et al. (2017) contend that while changes to discipline policies and behavior management practices may reduce the problem, they will not eliminate it. The team recognized that jumping directly to building in restorative justice practices, revamping the discipline policy, building in more time for student social-emotional support, or supporting teachers with professional learning opportunities to improve classroom management and implement restorative justice practices may fall short. There is a greater need to first support teachers and staff in improving the equitable practices in their classrooms and throughout the school by increasing their cultural competency, engaging them in reflective considerations of implicit bias and their own cultural views, helping them learn how to build learning partnerships and deeper student relationships, and equipping them with the ability to operationalize culturally responsive teaching and classroom management practices.

Before committing to our change idea, the team took time to consider teacher readiness and perceptions of school culture. Slateville Elementary gave teachers and staff the same school climate survey given to students and parents. Thirty teachers and staff responded. The team reviewed this secondary data. Teachers and staff reported higher rates of positive feelings of safety at school than African American students. Teachers and students had similar levels of concern about student behaviors and their impact on learning. Additionally, teachers and staff also showed concern over how students treat one another with 20.7% of teachers and staff perceiving that students do not treat one another with respect and 13.8% of teachers and staff feeling that students base their treatment of one another on academic ability. This area of concern among teachers and staff was similar to that of the concern among African American students. When asked about how their peers behave in class, only 43% of African American students expressed positive perceptions. While there were some similarities among student and teacher responses, there was a noted difference. Only 6.9% of teachers and staff who completed the survey, 90% of whom identified as white, felt that students' treatment of one another is impacted by race, ethnicity, or culture. Furthermore, 90% of teachers and staff felt all students were treated with respect by adults and that race, ethnicity or culture did not impact student treatment by adults. The high rates of agreement from staff that the treatment of students is not impacted by race, ethnicity, or culture conflicts, to some degree, with the disparity in perceptions of feeling safe and liking school among African American students as compared to their white peers as noted in Table 1.5.

Table 1.5. Student Perceptions of School Climate

Question	All Students		African American Students		White Students	
	Always/ Often	Sometimes/ Never	Always/ Often	Sometimes/ Never	Always/ Often	Sometimes/ Never
I like school.	54%	46%	42%	58%	63%	37%
I feel safe at school.	76%	24%	70%	30%	80%	20%
Students in my class behave so that teachers can teach.	52%	48%	43%	57%	54%	46%

The team felt that this data spoke to the teachers' and staff's readiness and potential level of buy-in for an intervention to improve racial disparity in discipline. Overall, staff had high levels of positive perceptions of school climate. Yet, this did not match the African American student and parent school climate perception data. This mismatch in perceptions between teachers and students was a critical aspect of the development of our change idea.

The team hypothesized that the change idea to have the greatest impact and highest ease of implementation was an ongoing culturally responsive teaching professional learning opportunity. This professional learning series would be rooted in supporting participants as they examined their own implicit bias, considered existing systemic racism, examined how this impacted their students of color, investigated how to build meaningful learning partnerships with students, and explored how to implement instructional and classroom management practices that would foster more equitable and engaging learning environments. The explicit goal of our change idea would be to increase African American students' positive perceptions about the school climate while eliminating racial disparity in office-level discipline at Slateville Elementary School.

At the time of this work, our school division, like many others, was struggling to reopen the school in person and rebuild relationships within our community. Additionally, the topics of social-emotional learning, equity, and culturally responsive teaching became charged with people having highly opposing views of one another. Across the nation, school board meetings were becoming very heated with people from both sides of these topics expressing their views and questioning schools' handling of these topics.

When we first brainstormed the change idea list, my research team initially considered the change idea of doing a culturally responsive teaching professional development series. However, the team quickly agreed this would likely become a problem for everyone because of the larger political discourse. As they expressed this view, I couldn't help but agree. It felt dangerous, and our program would likely be shut down before it ever started. However, after we fully considered the problem of practice through improvement science paired with our research, we all agreed that we should create a professional development series for our teachers and staff, based on our local community and school context on culturally responsive teaching. That day, as we stared at our driver diagram, we recognized that the right path for us; the thing we planned to avoid a few months earlier was going to be our change idea. As we all committed to this path, I remember holding back from my team how scared I was of this prospect. I knew that because of the local and state political landscape, we were not taking the path of least resistance; instead, we were potentially diving right into the middle of a heated and divisive topic in education across the state and within our community. However, I also knew the research was pointing us in the right direction and that my research team and I were doing what was needed for the kids, teachers, and community of Slateville.

CYCLES OF IMPROVEMENT

My research team and I developed our theory of improvement and tailored it to our context. We proposed that effective, ongoing professional development in culturally responsive teaching that included a reflective focus on implicit bias, its impact on students, and how to foster equity through culturally responsive instructional and classroom management practices would improve the school and classroom climate for African American students while reducing the racial disparity in discipline between African American and white students. We decided to create our professional development series based on the work of Zarretta Hammond's (2015) *Culturally Responsive Teaching and the Brain*. We found the Ready for Rigor Framework gave us a concrete basis from which to build and the accompanying book study resource was a very helpful guide. Ideally, we agreed that having an expert in the field do the professional development would have been best. However, we did not have access to such an expert; we recognized that by building our own professional learning cohort based on the Ready for Rigor Framework in our school context for our own people, we were more likely to develop something sustainable. Our study was guided by three measurable goals:

1. Through the development of a deep understanding of and regular implementation of culturally responsive teaching and classroom management practices by research participants, African American students will increase their positive perceptions about school so that in two years, 85% or more African American students will express positive feelings about liking school, feeling safe, feeling that students behave in class and that students treat one another well by marking strongly agree or agree on the annual school climate survey adapted from the University of Oregon's OSEP Technical Assistance Center on Positive Behavioral Interventions and Supports School Climate Survey.
2. Through an ongoing professional learning series, teacher participants will increase their self-efficacy of their ability to implement culturally responsive instructional and classroom management practices as measured by the Culturally Responsive Teaching Self-Efficacy Scale (CRTSE) survey measure.
3. Through ongoing professional learning, teachers will increase their use of culturally responsive practices in the classroom as measured by a Culturally Responsive Walkthrough form adapted from the Ready for Rigor CRT Walkthrough Observation Guide.

We used multiple measures. For the primary outcome measures, we selected the University of Oregon's OSEP Technical Assistance Center on Positive Behavioral Interventions and Supports School Climate Survey. This survey is given consistently across the Slateville school division each year. It includes teacher and staff, student, and parent components that indicate perceptions of school culture among each population. School office referral and discipline data would be reviewed, but not considered an outcome measure, due to concerns over reliability and the potential impact of confounding variables outside the control of the research team. We included two driver measures. The CRTSE was given to all participants as a pre- and post-survey. We recognized that participants' perceptions of their ability to implement culturally responsive teaching practices in their classrooms are a powerful data set that can inform researchers about factors that may impact participants' ability and level of motivation to implement culturally responsive teaching practices in their classrooms (Cruz et al., 2020). Participants were also asked to submit two self-reflection journals. Participants responded to six questions, asking about their perceptions of how much students liked school and felt safe at school, perceptions of students' behavior impacting learning, and whether they observed any difference in the perceptions of African American students as compared to white students.

We realized that we had to ask participants about their perceptions, rather than survey students, in part, due to the increasingly tense political climate across the state relating to topics such as equity, social-emotional learning, and culturally responsive teaching. These issues became the focus of heated debate and confusion with critical race theory. We also felt that we would not be able to seek direct input from students because this would create hurdles related to the institutional review board process. As a result, we excluded any direct interviewing, surveying, or working with students on the part of the research team.

For our process measures, we included post-professional development surveys based on Hammond's (2015) Ready for Rigor Framework, which required participants to use a Likert scale to rate their knowledge of and ability to implement each aspect of the framework. The Likert scale was used because the data being collected were nonparametric, and Likert scales are responsive, reliable, and valid. Additionally, Likert scales are often easier for both the respondent and researcher to use and understand (Chung et al., 2018; Hassan & Bengt, 2005). Additionally, we included two walkthroughs using an adapted culturally responsive teaching and the brain walkthrough tool. Lastly, we included two additional questions in the self-reflection journal. These two questions related to how (if at all) the learning series was impacting participants' classrooms and what (if any) takeaways related to culturally responsive teaching participants had.

Our balancing measures were built into the post-professional development surveys and self-reflection journals. Balancing measures were intended to determine what (if any) unexpected or unintended effects were happening. The first question asked participants about the amount of additional time outside of the professional learning sessions participating in the study required of them. Participation in the study was not supposed to result in a high time demand upon participants beyond the time spent in the professional learning sessions. The second question was open-ended. It asked if there was anything else they wanted to share about their engagement in the study, the professional development, or implementing culturally responsive practices in their classrooms.

As a team, we decided to start small and implement two PDSA cycles each with four participants. We decided to use convenience sampling. We opened participation in the study to all Slateville Elementary teachers and staff and ensured participants knew participation was fully optional. In the first cohort, we had four participants. All were white females. In the second cohort we had five participants because one of the initial cohort participants was unable to fully finish the series. In this cohort, all participants were female. Three were white, one was Black, and the fifth was multiracial. Each participant in both cohorts had varying educational and teaching experiences and backgrounds.

Each PDSA cycle was intended to be four weeks from start to finish. However, due to scheduling constraints and illness, both PDSA cycles extended beyond four weeks. However, the number of professional development sessions offered remained as planned.

In both PDSA cycles, we created a website that housed school, division, and state data regarding discipline and academic achievement, a synthesis of relevant research, current legislation and teacher evaluation standards, and relevant background information about the school and community. In the first session of each PDSA cycle, participants in both cohorts engaged in pairs to research the problem using the website the research team created to study the problem in multiple contexts which included: school-based data, division data, and state and national trends. The website gave participants access to relevant research in a manner in which it was more easily accessible. After reviewing the website, participants took part in a fishbone diagram activity and assessment of the system. We used these two tools of improvement science to help foster a stronger sense of connection and personalization to the problem of practice because a critical component of culturally responsive teaching grounded in Hammond's Ready for Rigor Framework is an examination of our own implicit bias and the development of awareness. After the initial sessions, we began our study of Hammond's work but incorporated empathy-style interview questions to promote deeper discussion and reflection. At the end of each session, participants were asked to set an intention about something they would do in the next few days and to have students participate in a formative "temp check" in which teachers asked students in a format comfortable for their class how much they liked school and how safe they felt at school. At each follow-up session, we revisited how it went with the intention they set and encouraged participants to share anything they noticed from the formative "temp checks." Topics for follow-up sessions were based on their post-professional development (PD) survey responses.

The biggest challenges I experienced as I facilitated the PD cohorts were scheduling and finding ways to hold the sessions during the school day to avoid requiring participants to stay after school. During this time, some participants were out unexpectedly with illnesses. Additionally, Slateville, like many schools in the state, was experiencing shortages of substitutes. When this happened, those who were going to provide coverage for teachers to participate were unable to do so. Another challenge was to accommodate all the content to the degree and depth it needed. Discussions often ran longer than anticipated, and we were not able to cover the full content planned for each session. While this was a challenge, it was also a reflection of how engaged participants were.

Another challenge was that, while we were implementing this study, the political landscape became very heated. When the PDSA cycles began, I stopped meeting with my research team and did not involve them in carrying out the professional learning series because I was concerned about pushback or fallout due to the content of the series. Though our state was slated to require all teachers to take part in culturally responsive teaching professional learning in the next year, with the recent change of state leadership, terms such as "equity" were labeled potentially "divisive." With the change of state leadership, the direction of education and efforts to foster equity and inclusivity felt as though they were on unstable ground. It felt like anything related to race and equity was potentially something that the governor had just deemed divisive concepts. In addition, our division was going through heated debates during school board meetings and critical scrutiny from community groups concerning these topics as well. As the lead researcher and the direct supervisor for all staff on the research team, I did not feel comfortable including them as facilitators of the professional learning series. While we had permission from our interim superintendent to proceed, I did not want to involve the members of my team in any controversy. As a result, I facilitated the professional learning series by myself, which was another challenge. I had just become the principal of the building that fall. As principal, my schedule and time became more limited and unpredictable. However, we ultimately made it work.

FINDINGS

The outcome measure for this project was a school climate survey completed by students annually in the fall. The outcome measures are long-term measures and trends cannot be established within one year. However, the team reviewed survey data to consider what, if any, changes in student perceptions about school had taken place over one year. A comparison of 2022 Fall school climate data to Fall 2021 as noted in Table 1.6 shows a small increased positive perception of liking school and feeling safe at school among African American students.

Table 1.6. Two-Year Comparison of African American Students' Positive Perceptions of School Climate

Question	Fall 2022	Fall 2021
	Always/Often	Always/Often
I like school.	44%	42%
I feel safe at school.	74%	70%

There was also a reduction in the difference between perceptions among African American students and their white peers concerning liking school and feeling safe at school. As these data points represent only one year's change, they do not indicate a trend. However, the team felt they were important to consider as it considered the next steps. While office referral data was not an outcome measure due to concerns over reliability and the impact of confounding variables, the research team felt it was important to continue to monitor office referral data since its initial connection to the problem of practice. Based on a comparison of the 2020–2021 school year to the previous three school years, office referral data also demonstrates a similar improvement with the racial disparity being significantly reduced and the overall number of office referrals, ISS, and OSS drastically dropping for all populations. My team and I were very hopeful that, in time, the student perceptions of school climate and the office referral data will continue to improve and demonstrate a trend. However, we know that it is too soon to tell.

Self-reflection journal responses to driver measure questions from both cohorts indicated that participants found the majority of their students liked school and felt safe, which was consistent with earlier perceptions. However, through this professional learning series, teachers began to implement quick, formative assessments of student perceptions from week to week to gauge how students felt regarding liking school and feeling safe. During the study, a few participants noted a small discrepancy between the perceptions of liking school and feeling safe among their African American students in comparison to their white students. When participants dug a bit further with students about why they liked or disliked school, they noted that students felt it was "boring," "too hard," or "too much time."

Results from the CRTSE were similar between both cohorts. The average score among participants in the first cohort rose from 75 points to 86 points, and the average scores among participants in the second cohort rose from 75 points to 84 points. The growth among specific indicators varied between both cohorts, but there were some indicators for which participants in both cohorts experienced very high growth. Specifically, both cohorts expressed high growth in being able to teach students about their students' cultures' contributions to science and their ability to critically examine curriculum to determine whether it reinforces negative cultural stereotypes. These two common indicators aligned with the discussions and work the cohorts did during the PD series centered on finding ways to be more inclusive in how we teach, what we teach, and what we use to teach.

Post-PD survey data from both PDSA cycles indicated participants felt they increased their knowledge of and ability to meaningfully incorporate culturally responsive practices outlined in Ready for Rigor Framework in their classrooms. The average response for participants in the first PDSA increased from 2.96 to 3.54 and the average response for participants in the second PDSA moved from 2.91 to 3.41. Across both cohorts, there were three common components from the Ready for Rigor Framework in which participants report high growth or very high knowledge of or ability of the culturally responsive teaching indicator. Participants reported high growth in their knowledge of and ability to help students process new content using methods from oral traditions and their ability to use formative assessment feedback to increase intellective capacity. This consistency across PDSA cycles aligned with the design of the first two PD sessions for each group. In both cases, a discussion of incorporating oral tradition was included as part of building awareness, learning partnerships, and learning community. Each cohort had additional areas of high growth that were unique to the cohort. Upon analysis of the data and reflection on the PD series for each cohort, the differences made sense with changes that were made between each cohort. Adjustments to the second series were made based on data from the first PDSA cycle. As a result, different aspects of culturally responsive teaching were focused on, and we included more opportunities for them to share their experiences and reflect as a group in the second series. Accordingly, this group received less specific culturally responsive teaching strategy support in follow-up professional learning sessions than the first cohort.

Walkthrough data noted similarities between cohorts that included having anchor charts, positive messaging, routines and procedures, and moderate to high levels of student talk within classrooms. Despite the high levels of student talk being incorporated into lessons, there were very few instances observed of students talking through how new information fit into what they already knew. It was observed that teachers made these connections, but it was not consistently something students incorporated into discussions. To stretch students' intellective capacity and equip them with tools to access information with independence, students benefit from being able to verbalize and understand how what they are learning fits into their schema, background knowledge, and life experiences. With teachers mainly being the ones to explain how the new learning fits, they miss the opportunity to stretch students and foster independent learner routines, instead of reinforcing dependent learning.

In the self-reflection journals, when participants were asked "How, if at all, is the professional learning series impacting your classroom and students?" and "What, if any, takeaways do you have this week related to culturally responsive teaching and classroom management?" they frequently reported an increase in their awareness of culture and its importance and impact on student learning and the school environment. Participants also noted the importance of self-reflection and setting intentions around fostering culturally responsive practices in their classrooms and being aware of culture. One participant shared, "Being mindful that there is a bias, and understanding why students do what they do has a lot to do with their culture." A second shared that her takeaway was, "Observing all the different levels of culture every day in the classroom and trying to use it to reach each of my students. I have also been taking the different parts of a learning partnership to build it with my students." Additionally, participants expressed a need to spread change and offered to be a part of spreading that change. Furthermore, participants recognized the importance of building relationships and expressed their commitment to doing so.

Feedback from the balancing measure questions in the self-reflection journals and post-PD surveys was favorable, with participants expressing being thankful for taking part in the series. One participant shared, "I absolutely enjoyed participating in this study and learning the framework/big idea behind cultural competency in education." This participant also shared, "In the future, I would like to learn more about strategies and action steps I can take in order to be able to increase my impact in the classroom setting." Another participant shared, "It was nice to be with like-minded professionals talking openly about education in such a raw form. I think it would be nice to do something like this every so often to meet a professional growth need, spend time with colleagues in a way that is not after-school or overly student-centered, and led by our own people." Additionally, as the series wrapped up, five of the eight participants offered to help facilitate future series.

LESSONS LEARNED

Throughout my three-year study of this problem of practice and doctoral endeavor, I learned many lessons about my problem of practice, myself, my school, and how to impact change. As I reflect on this, I am struck by how much has changed across my division, the state, and the world during this time. I began this study before a pandemic, before a reckoning, and before a full change in state and division leadership. However, the problem was there all along and needed to be examined, and I am so thankful my team and I did. We are now prepared to continue moving forward and furthering equitable outcomes for all our students, refining our approaches to problem-solving through the use of improvement science, and building the leadership capacity among our staff to be stewards of justice and change.

The first lesson I learned was that, while our study had a positive influence among our study participants, the engagement of the team in studying the problem, employing the tools of improvement science, and developing a change idea tailored to our context had a far greater impact on my school than I could have imagined. Since beginning our study, my school's culture changed significantly as evidenced by our discipline data, school climate survey data, and academic achievement data. It can also be felt when you walk in the door and speak to students, teachers, staff, and parents. Slateville Elementary has developed its sense of place. That place is grounded in doing what is right for all of our students. While I had not expected it, I find that the change makes sense. When you bring key stakeholders together who are willing to engage, who will investigate and invest in a problem despite the barriers, and, despite the political landscape, who begin to build awareness and leadership capacity. For my team, by engaging in the study of racial disparity and the different perceptions of safety and liking school, we started to reflect on our own implicit bias. We also started to build our awareness that is critical to culturally responsive teaching. The team members were leaders among their colleagues already, which is, in part, why they were invited to join. As we became more comfortable owning the problem rather than denying it, we became more aware of our actions, the messages we sent, spoken or unspoken, and the perceptions of our students and their families. As we changed, our leadership among our colleagues changed, our actions changed, and our conversations changed. We became more brave and more willing to talk about difficult things. Three years ago, much of this work was done quietly with a small group of people. I remember being so fearful to meet with my research team for our first meeting. I was scared that I would do something wrong, say something wrong, and demonstrate that I had no idea what to do to make things better; however, this fear shifted as we worked together and dove into the problem. For many months, we continued to quietly work for fear of being pulled into the political debate across the state and within our division; we also began to test the waters and touch upon difficult conversations and discuss race, inequity, our racial disparity in discipline, and the opportunity gap that Slateville struggled to overcome. Nonetheless, after we concluded our final PDSA and examined our results, we felt more confident and ready to be bold. In the fall of 2022, as part of our Comprehensive Needs Assessment, I met with the full faculty one afternoon and, for the first time, I named the problem of practice outright to all of them, "Students of color feel less safe and like school less than their white peers and, in years past, [Slateville] has had a historical trend of racial disparity in office referrals, ISS and OSS among African American students as compared to their white peers, and, while we saw improvement last year, we know there is still work to be done." As I led this meeting with my research team embedded throughout, I was not scared, I was impassioned. I was honest. I was confident that, as a school, we were finally ready to do the work together. During this meeting, all members took part in preparing a fishbone diagram to tackle aspects of our problem of practice in teams. The groups were facilitated by key members of my research team and the PD cohorts. It was magnificent to step back, snap photos to capture the moment, and see that with purpose, with commitment, and with a team, we can enact change.

The second lesson I learned was that incidental change, as we experienced by engaging in the study of the problem and using the tools of improvement science to develop our PDSA cycles, is not enough. We need to continue to expand the work and spread change with purpose, or we will not see sustainable change over time. My research team and the participants of the PD cohorts helped solidify this as they shared reflections about their participation. Initially, they were scared; then they felt their own culpability in the problem. Finally, they felt driven to be a part of spreading change. If we are to truly create more equitable environments for all of our students, we must continue to pull the curtain back. We must not simply examine but engage with the problems and develop meaningful change ideas tailored to our school context. Addressing racial disparity in discipline and the inequities within the school experience that our African American students face must remain at the forefront of our efforts because, without equity in the school environment, our students will not and cannot thrive overall.

One last lesson learned through the work my team and I did in this project and the subsequent efforts to apply the tools of improvement science in the context of my school is that we must find ways to operationalize improvement science in the authentic school context. This means that time frames will be shorter, pressures will be multifaceted, and some aspects of the problem and resulting solution will be constrained by outside factors such as division or state initiatives and mandates. However, these are challenges, not insurmountable barriers. To operationalize improvement science, I believe we need to remember that PDSA cycles can and should be small in scope and short in length. Data must be meaningful, useful, and easily able to be analyzed. Using a consistent improvement science toolkit will help to build capacity and tools. As more and more teachers and staff understand the why, what, and how behind the improvement science practice, collectively your school team and key stakeholders will become more efficient and focused in their efforts to enact change and improvement for their students, schools, and community. To work within real-life constraints and shorter time frames, I see that there are critical components for leaders. You must be willing and driven to:

- Understand the problem beyond numerical data by incorporating causal analysis and considerations of the system.
- Research evidence-based interventions and the problem efficiently before selecting a change idea.
- Consider broad change ideas before driving to one through driver diagramming or a modified approach.
- Plan for implementation on a small or short-term scale.
- Include monitoring for outcome, driver, process, and balancing measures with data points that are relevant, accessible, and authentic.
- Set short-term cycles to make small adjustments throughout.
- Adapt the tools and process to meet the needs of your team.
- Take your time to develop trust and open discussion among your team and incorporate strategies to foster high engagement and reflection as you study the problem.

Engagement and reflection are critical, and they cannot be rushed.

If we strive to build a routine of improvement in science in our decision-making as leaders, we can build a culture of true, continuous improvement within our schools and divisions. However, persistence and consistency are necessary to avoid falling into the decision-making habits engrained in much of education. It is imperative to firmly ground yourself in the belief that by responding differently and thoughtfully with purpose we will ultimately be more successful in meeting the needs of all of our students and families.

Chapter 2

Leading Change in Enrollment of Black and Brown Students in Gifted Programs

Kelly A. Huff, EdD, and Tracy Kwock, EdD

THE CONTEXT

Mountain Vista Governor's School (MVGS) is an Academic-Year Governor's School (AYGS) for Math, Science, and Technology serving seven school divisions, 13 high schools total, in the Northern Virginia region. MVGS has two campuses housed on Virginia Community College complexes in Fauquier County and Frederick County. The mission of MVGS is "to present a research-based, technology-enhanced, integrated program in mathematics, science, and the humanities. The program will challenge students to reach their full potential as independent thinkers capable of assuming leadership roles in a constantly changing global society" (Mountain Vista Governor's School, 2020). According to the Virginia Department of Education (VDOE), a Governor's School gives students "academic and visual and performing arts opportunities beyond those normally available in the students' home schools. Students can focus on a specific area of intellectual or artistic strength and interest and to study in a way that best suits the advanced learner's needs. Each program stresses non-traditional teaching and learning techniques" (Virginia Department of Education, 2023). In short, MVGS is listed as a gifted program for students, and according to the VDOE, all school divisions are required to meet the needs of gifted learners by providing instructional services. MVGS fulfills this for the seven divisions that it serves. Tenth, 11th, and 12th grade students come to MVGS in the mornings for their specialized instruction then return to their base high schools in the afternoons to complete other graduation requirements not offered at MVGS, such as fine arts classes, career and technical education classes, social studies (10th and 11th grade), English (12th grade), and world languages. The enrollment at MVGS for the 2022–2023 was 207 students on both campuses.

As additional background, AYGSs in Virginia date back as early as 1973, but MVGS is a newer program, having opened in 2006. Three types of Governor's Schools exist in Virginia. There are Academic Year, as discussed earlier, as well as Summer Residential and Summer Regional Governor's School programs. MVGS is labeled by the VDOE as a half-day, Academic Year program operating with students on campus from 7:30 a.m. to 10:50 a.m., five days per week. Most AYGS programs are part day with only two being full-day programs. Students do not need to be labeled as gifted to join MVGS, but they must apply and be accepted to the program through their local school divisions.

THE PROBLEM

Currently, there are 19 AYGSs in Virginia, and one historic challenge to gifted programs has been a lack of diversity within the student population, most notable being the disproportionality of Black and Latinx students. This problem is not unique to Virginia. Since the federal government defined "giftedness" in 1972, there have been wide discrepancies in the state's identification, funding, and accountability to gifted students and gifted programming, which has led to many inequities. In Virginia, this is reflected in the screening, identification, and access of students to gifted programming. "Universal screening has been shown to have a significant positive effect on the identification of Black and Latino gifted students" (Woods, 2016, p. 6). However, there are no statewide requirements for universal screening. "Underserved students are also less likely to be identified as gifted because most states emphasize academic achievement in identification" (Woods, 2016, p. 6). This is problematic in that underserved students typically attend underserved schools, which are more likely to have less qualified staff and other funding disparities, or "lower social and financial capital" (Woods, 2016, p. 6). This lack of capital translates to decreased access to information about gifted services and support for gifted programming for Black and Latinx students. For this reason, individuals such as Donna Ford (2010) and organizations such as the National Association for Gifted Children continue to conduct extensive research and advocacy work to level the gifted playing field. Ford (2010) states that "[t]he barriers to increasing the participation of Black and Hispanic students in gifted education, as noted earlier, have remained pretty much similar to those that I have discussed 20 years ago, 15 years ago, 10 years ago, and 5 years ago" (p. 32). Ford (2010) continues,

> The underrepresentation of Black and Hispanic students in gifted education is meaningful and statistically significant. . . . The most recent data for which federal statistics are available, Black students are underrepresented by 48%; more specifically, 253,000 more Black students should be identified as gifted. Likewise, Hispanic students are underrepresented by 38%. . . . Hispanic and Black students are not being challenged to reach their full potential in schools nationally. (pp. 31–32)

Today, the issue has not gotten better. Card and Giuliano (2016) confirm that "minority students are substantially underrepresented in gifted education programs. The disparities persist despite efforts by many states and school districts to broaden participation" (p. 13678). "Nevertheless, the fractions of Black and Hispanic students in gifted programs remain far below the fraction of Whites and Asians" (Card & Giuliano, 2016, p. 13683).

Table 2.1 shows the six-year enrollment demographic trend at MVGS before the intervention work of the MVGS Equity Team, formed in the summer of 2021.

Table 2.1. Six-Year MVGS Enrollment Demographics

Subgroup	21–22	20–21	19–20	18–19	17–18	16–17
Asian	11%	12%	5%	7%	9%	10%
Black	3%	2%	1%	2%	2%	1%
Hispanic/Latinx	6%	7%	3%	3%	4%	4%
White	71%	76%	80%	80%	82%	82%
Unspecified	9%	3%	1%	1%	3%	3%

What are the primary reasons why so few Black and Latinx students are applying to and enrolling in MVGS from its 13 feeder high schools? This question was generated in the early winter of 2021 by us, the two authors, one of which is the director at MVGS and the other is a project coordinator for a Training and Technical Assistance Center (T/TAC) in Southwest Virginia. The common threads that initially connected us were our fervor about student inclusion and equity and our pursuit for our doctorate degrees in education.

THE TEAM

Kelly

I am drawn to this work, not merely because of my position at MVGS, but because of my firm belief in providing access to educational opportunities to all students. This originated during my time as a K–12 public school teacher and administrator at the secondary level in an extremely rural division in Southwest Virginia. Over 50% of the division's students were and are identified as economically disadvantaged based on the Free and Reduced Lunch Program as determined by the National School Lunch Program (NSLP). Watching the dropout rate increase, attendance rates fall, and student apathy grow, these lived experiences ignited a passion in me to find pathways for students into key, nontraditional service areas, such as students who identify as female enrolling in welding, carpentry, and automotive courses and students identifying as male enrolling in early childhood education, culinary arts, and nursing programs. I learned quickly that providing students with access to desired programming yields positive outcomes on graduation rates, attendance rates, income rates, and employment rates. Opportunity means success.

Tracy

I am a multiracial woman of Asian and European descent and have always worked in educational settings where I have been within the ethnic minority. I have often used my positionality of "otherness" to see larger systems of inequity at play. My belief that the educational system should work for *all* students has led me to explore more progressive styles of teaching and learning, such as place, problem, and project-based learning. My philosophy lies in empowering students to work on challenges within their own communities and providing learning opportunities in a real-world context. According to the history of the Polaris Charter Academy (2023), of which I was a founding member, I believe in providing learning environments in which students and teachers are both active, equal participants in the learning process—who use their strengths and learn from their failures to improve themselves and their world. I believe in using this same approach to address more systemic inequities within educational systems—supporting and empowering stakeholders to work with educators to examine problems and enact change.

The Coleman Report of 1966 suggested, among other things, "that socioeconomic school integration could increase academic achievement more than any other school strategy" (Wells et al., 2016). This report affirms that student diversity, whether socioeconomic or ethnic, has lasting educational benefits for all learners. A report by *The Century Foundation* (Wells et al., 2016), as well as other research since the Coleman Report, emphasizes "the important educational benefits—cognitive, social, and emotional—for all students who interact with classmates from different backgrounds, cultures, and orientations to the world." We agree and recognize that schools must reflect the diversity in America to tap into it to transform learning and education today. Moreover, we believe in "the positive relationship between student learning and exposure to peers of different backgrounds" (Wells et al., 2016). Thus, the MVGS Equity Team was born.

In late summer of 2021, we formed a collaborative school-based team, or MVGS Equity Team, to bring about effective change to improve student diversity at MVGS that was more aligned with the demographics of the school's feeder divisions. The team was, and continues to be, comprised of volunteer members from multiple stakeholder groups including parents, guardians, students, MVGS teachers, MVGS service school teachers, MVGS service school counselors, and MVGS service division administrators. The team started with 13 members and has grown to more than 20 members in less than two years. We formed the team by promoting its purpose via email and word of mouth with the idea that "if you build it, they will come," and they did. Membership remains open to any wanting to join; however, invitations to partake were, and continue to be, extended to some members to ensure diversity of voice and perspective.

The team, which meets virtually once or twice per month, utilizes Improvement Science (IS) as a systematic approach to diversity challenges at MVGS (Bryk et al., 2015). According to Bryk and colleagues (2015) in *Learning to Improve: How America's Schools Can Get Better at Getting Better*, IS is the key to moving beyond the old practices of schools "going fast and learning slow" and promotes a systematic approach to "learning fast to implement well" (pp. 6–7). IS has six principles to its approach:

1. Make the work problem-specific and user-centered.
2. Focus on variation in performance.
3. See the system that produces the current outcomes.
4. We cannot improve at scale what we cannot measure.
5. Use disciplined inquiry to drive improvement.
6. Accelerate learning through networked communities. (Bryk et al., 2015)

Improvement Science in Education: A Primer, by Hinnant-Crawford (2020), expands on the Bryk and coauthors' (2015) text yet acknowledges that IS "is not extremely robust since the field is still blossoming" (p. 27). Although IS is still a newer problem-solving method, definitions are emerging quickly. However, "while there are a multitude of definitions with the literature delineating Improvement Science, there is general agreement on the ultimate purpose of Improvement Science, that being continuous improvement through systematic study" (Hinnant-Crawford, 2020, p. 29). The systematic study, which is the six principles listed earlier, drives improvement, not so much as a methodology but more like a framework.

Before holding the first MVGS Equity Team meeting in July 2021, we realized that we needed a mindset, not just a framework, to tackle such a complex and emotionally charged topic. Liberatory Design, according to the National Equity Project (n.d.), "is an approach to addressing equity challenges and change efforts in complex systems . . . [and] is both a flexible process that can be used by teams and a set of equity leadership habits that can be practiced daily." This mindset has several consistent practices, or rather meeting habits, ranging from understanding personal knowledge gaps or limitations to placing all team members at the center of the work to embracing uncomfortable moments (see NationalEquityProject.org). Overall, Liberatory Design aims to enhance capacity for equity leadership, empowering participants to bring about tangible change within the communities that hold significant importance to them. Both the process and the results of this approach work together to advance collective liberation on a larger scale (Robalewski, 2021). In a sense, IS provides the framework for teams to implement continuous improvement through systematic study, and Liberatory Design provides the meeting practices to "generate self-awareness to liberate designers from habits that perpetuate inequities" (Stanford University, 2023). By aligning the processes of IS with the philosophy of Liberatory Design (see Figure 2.1), we felt this would help ensure not only equitable outcomes for MVGS students but would be done in a way that empowered historically marginalized voices at each stage of the process, instead of perpetuating further oppression.

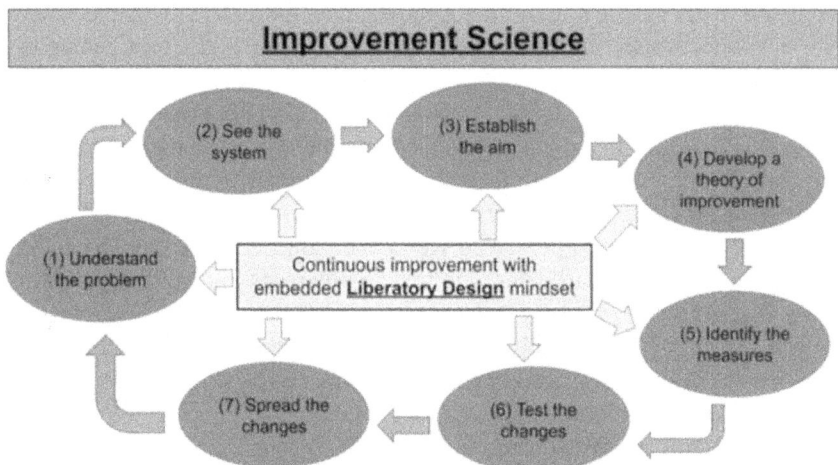

Figure 2.1. MVGS Equity Team IS Flowchart with Liberatory Design

PROBLEM INQUIRY AND ANALYSIS

To better understand the specific problem, in July 2021 the MVGS Equity Team started reviewing and analyzing existing secondary quantitative data consisting of annual MVGS demographic reports and published literature on ethnic disproportionality in gifted programs. The MVGS Equity Team used the data to construct a primary problem statement that addressed the "three *core improvement questions*: what is the specific problem I (we) am (are) now trying to solve? what change might I (we) introduce and why?, and, how will I (we) know whether the change is actually an improvement" (Bryk et al., 2015, p. 9). By exploring the data, the team felt comfortable stating that the total number of Black, Latinx, white, and Asian students who apply or enroll at MVGS was disproportionate to the total number of students in the same racial and ethnic categories from the MVGS feeder schools with Black and Latinx students being underrepresented, and white and Asian students being overrepresented. While the ratios have fluctuated slightly, the disproportionality has remained consistent for at least the past three years, with no signs of sustainable leveling.

To best understand why MVGS might be getting these disproportionate outcomes, the team utilized an initial root cause analysis exercise, five whys, to dig a little deeper. They partnered up and took turns being both the interviewer and interviewee. The activity began by the interviewer asking, "Why are Black and Latinx students applying to MVGS at a disproportionate rate?" The interviewee then stated a potential reason. The interviewer reframed the reason stated into a why question, and the interviewee then had an opportunity to answer the reframed question. This was repeated five times. This exercise allowed participants to explore multiple casualties and think beyond the surface explanations. The only "whys" participants were cautioned to avoid was placing blame or a perceived inherent fault ("Because they're lazy"). Not only does this type of thinking perpetuate negative stereotypes, but it stymies or derails the problem-solving process. Figure 2.2 is a sample of one of these exchanges as relayed back to the group. After the completion of the exercise, participates combined their individual ideas into a general group hypothesis.

While the MVGS Equity Team had a general hypothesis as to why the school was getting disproportionate outcomes in enrollment, they knew the best people to shed light on the problem were the people closest to it—the students who had decided to apply or not apply. In mid-Fall 2021, the team moved to collect and analyze primary, qualitative data using student interviews (see Appendix A). The interviews were conducted, and then the results were thematically coded using Quirkos. The whole process was designed to help gain more targeted insights and perspectives as they pertain to students' experiences and perceived views and values toward applying to MVGS. The interview also sought to determine potential barriers and selling points for the program. The students who were selected to be interviewed were recommended by the MVGS director, MVGS service school counselors, and/or MVGS service division administrators. These were predominantly Black and Latinx students, along with other ethnicities, who did or did not apply to MVGS (although eligible to do so), and who did or did not enroll at MVGS based on a variety of factors.

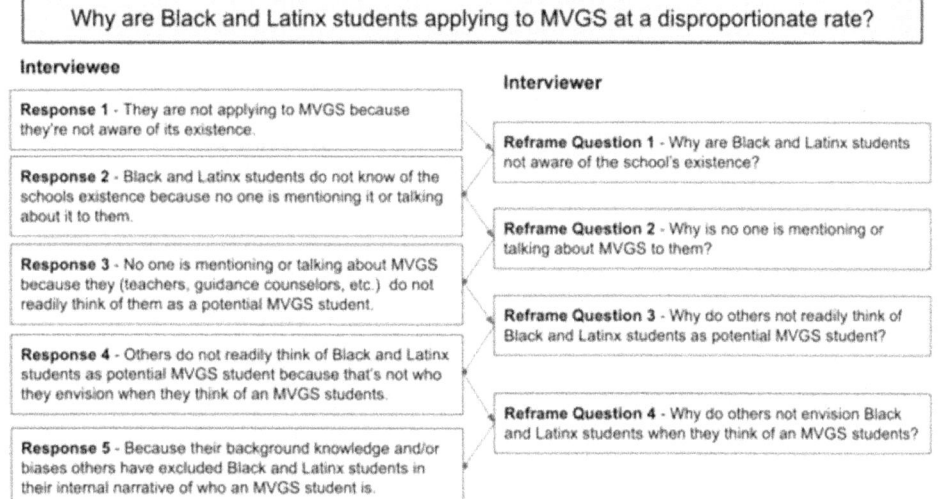

Figure 2.2. MVGS Equity Team Five Whys Analysis

Before the student interviews, the prevailing thought of the MVGS Equity Team was that students were embarrassed to go to MVGS because they did not want to be seen as overly academically focused or negatively labeled as a "brainiac." After completing the interviews, the team discovered that the students' primary concern was not about stigma. It was centered around self-efficacy in that students needed more information about the program to determine if they felt as though they had the necessary behaviors or skills to perform well in the program. They wanted more information communicated to see if it was a good fit for them. They also felt that having an adult who could help them identify and recognize those qualities within themselves would increase their self-efficacy and increase their confidence in applying. Overall, the interviews showed that prospective students were not well informed on MVGS and had trouble seeing or imagining themselves there. With a firm grasp of the overarching problem, with some key root causes investigated, and with an established IS team up and functioning, the MVGS Equity Team felt it could move from IS Step 1 (understand the problem) to Step 2—fully see the system. To aid in the analysis of potential systems impacting the problem, the team utilized an IS tool called a fishbone diagram (see Figure 2.3; Bryk et al., 2015, p. 69). According to Bryk and coauthors (2015), "A tool called a *fishbone diagram* assists in working through this problem analysis and visually representing the product of these discussions. Each major bone represents a key factor thought to contribute to the unsatisfactory outcomes. The smaller bones capture the details that emerge from conversations about these factors" (p. 68). When reviewing the diagram in Figure 2.3, one can see that the MVGS Equity Team selected four "major bones," or key factors, contributing to student disproportionately: (1) awareness/communication, (2) misconceptions/perceptions/attitudes, (3) internal/external student barriers, and (4) acceptance process.

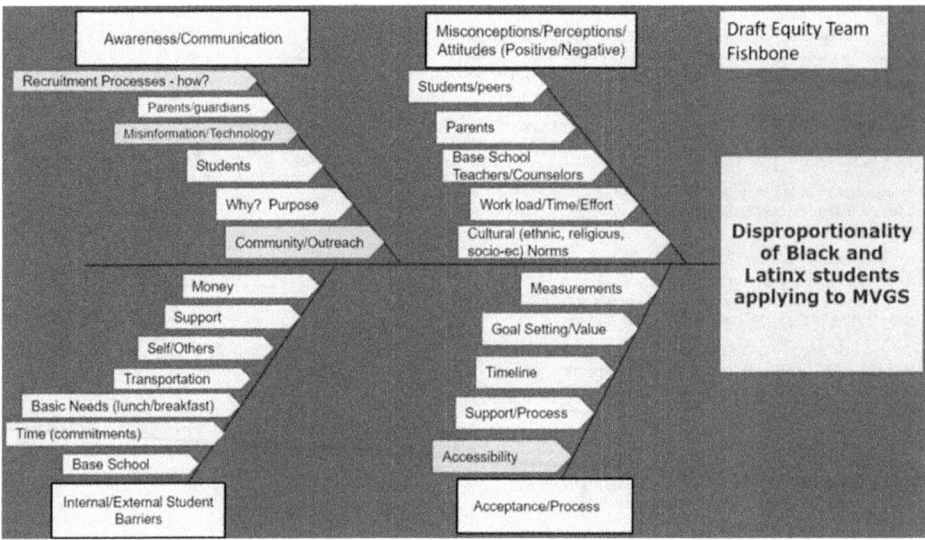

Figure 2.3. Fishbone Diagram

To broaden the fishbone diagram, the team moved on to another IS tool called a system improvement map (see Figure 2.4; Bryk et al., 2015, p. 71). According to Bryk and coauthors (2015), "Whereas the fishbone diagram facilitates brainstorming, the system improvement map . . . represents what we learn through these discussions about how the institution is organized to carry out work in a particular area" (p. 70).

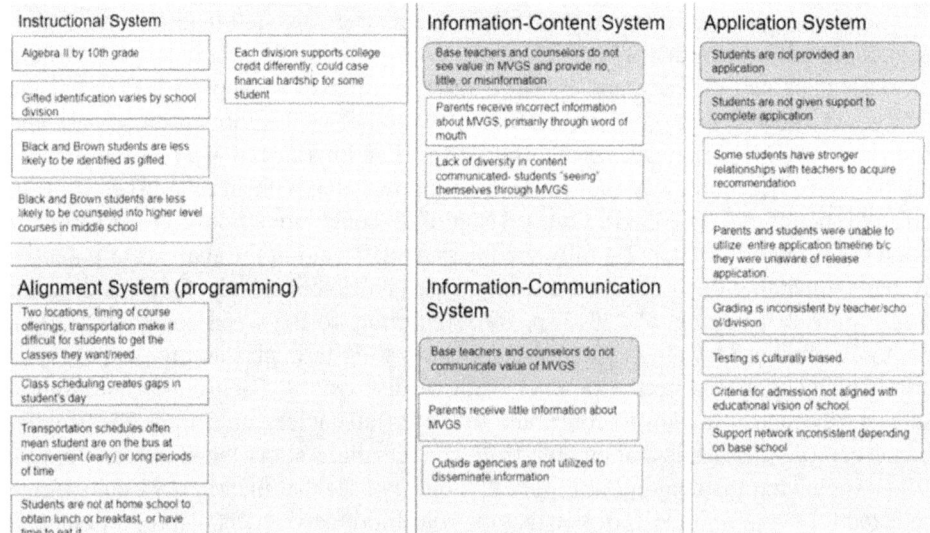

Figure 2.4. System Improvement Map

The purpose of the map is to see the organizational features within MVGS, or any organization, that may be impacting the problem and may need to be addressed for improvement to occur. In short, the map "provides a conceptual bridge for moving the study of root causes to identifying tactical starting points for change" (Bryk et al., 2015, p. 72). When reviewing Figure 2.4, one can see the five organizational systems that may be impacting student disproportionality, which are: (1) instructional, (2) alignment, (3) information—content, (4) information—communication, and (5) application.

CHANGE IDEAS AND INTERVENTION

Moving into IS Steps 3 and 4, establishing an aim and developing a theory of improvement, the MVGS Equity Team started a driver diagram (Bryk et al., 2015, p. 73) to continue aligning and solidifying a potential theory toward improvement (see Figure 2.5). This "organizes the various changes the network is trying out. It gives participants a common language as they build toward a solution to a shared problem" (Bryk

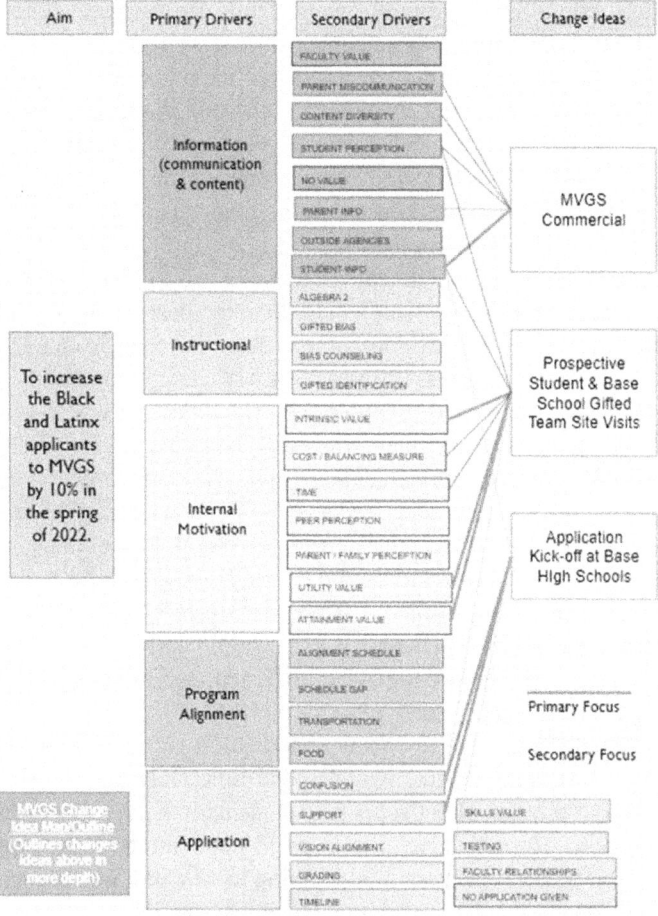

Figure 2.5.   Driver Diagram

et al., 2015, p. 73). The key improvement hypotheses, or primary drivers, correlated to the five major systems, which were *information, instructional, internal motivation, program alignment,* and *application.* As the team progressed from the fishbone diagram to the systems map and then to the driver diagram, the word *barriers* kept arising as a common term. The team focused on what *barriers* Black and Latinx students might be facing and causing them to not apply to MVGS. These *barriers,* or drivers or systems, became the focal point with the team belief that if a primary barrier were addressed and potentially removed, then improvement would be actualized.

As Bryk and coauthors (2015) point out, "The approach is explicitly designed to accelerate learning-by-doing. . . . The overall goal is to develop the necessary *know-how* for a reform idea ultimately to spread faster and more effectively" (p. 8). Given this, the MVGS Equity Team started to dig deeper into the primary drivers, moving the discussions more toward *how* rather than *why,* thus fleshing out the secondary drives and change ideas on the driver diagram, as noted in Figure 2.5. During the finalization of the driver diagram, the team revisited the quantitative data (enrollment), qualitative data (interviews), the published literature on ethnic disproportionality in gifted programs, the five whys activity, the fishbone diagram, and the systems map. The team's discussions quickly turned toward, "How can the team address the primary and secondary drivers?" During these conversations, we ultimately selected *information* as the primary driver. This did not imply that the other drivers were not barriers, but the team had substantial data, as generated through the IS process, to understand the nuances of the information barrier and felt that it provided potential change ideas that could be developed, tested, and refined quickly and were within the team's immediate locus of control. Based on the team's understanding of *information* as the primary driver, they set increasing Black and Latinx applicants to MVGS by 10% in the spring of 2022 as the measurable aim. Next, we had to tackle which change idea, as part of our theory of improvement, would yield the best results toward this aim.

As seen in Figure 2.5, we developed three potential change ideas to address the information driver. The first was to create an MVGS commercial, a visual media piece highlighting key features of the program. The objective was to present a realistic portrait of being an MVGS student, including benefits, challenges, and challenge supports to combat current communication gaps. The commercial could potentially be distributed to all divisions and feeder schools for showing in classes, faculty meetings, school board meetings, and more. A version of the video would also be available in Spanish for greater accessibility. Both would be posted to the MVGS website and promoted on social media. It was discussed by the MVGS Equity Team that this change idea be implemented, but in a school year there was not enough time to produce a quality piece before the 2021–2022 application period, which runs from January through March each year.

The second change idea was to conduct application kick-off site visits. A team of MVGS faculty, staff, and students would spend time (full day or half day) at each base high school to provide direct support to students to help guide them through the application process. The objective was to build application skills, knowledge, and understanding for students interested in applying to MVGS. We discussed as a team that this change idea be implemented immediately at the discretion of each base high school. It should be noted that no measurements of this strategy were taken, as it was not deemed to be the primary change idea but a supplemental strategy to immediately assist students; however, the team has considered collecting this data in future years to inform continuous improvement. MVGS faculty, staff, and students were invited to 11 of the 13 service schools to conduct an application kickoff in December 2021 and January 2022. Two schools declined the event stating that they would conduct their own sessions within their buildings.

CYCLES OF IMPROVEMENT

As the MVGS Equity Team moved into late fall of 2021, we took on IS steps 5 and 6 to identify the measures and test the change. The third and chosen change idea was for prospective students to visit MVGS and experience the program in person before deciding on whether to apply or not. The team "used disciplined inquiry to drive improvement" (Bryk et al., 2015, p. 113) by answering three questions:

1. What specifically are we trying to accomplish?
2. What change might we introduce and why?
3. How will we know that change is actually an improvement (Bryk et al., 2015, p. 114)?

We initially brainstormed that students from base schools be invited to MVGS to get a chance to interact with students and teachers during a typical school day. The objective was to provide pre-application students with a realistic portrait of being an MVGS student, including benefits, challenges, and challenge supports to combat information barriers. Providing pre-application students with an opportunity to feel and experience life as an MVGS student may help them to form a better decision-making process aligned with their own expectations and values.

According to IS, a Plan-Do-Study-Act (PDSA) cycle (Bryk et al., 2015, p. 121) was the applied course of action that we, as the MVGS Equity Team, collaboratively planned.

> The heart of the cycle is articulating hypotheses, based on a working theory of improvement, and then gathering data to test them. Predictions are made about the results expected. When the predictions are compared to what actually happens, gaps in understanding are revealed. . . . PDSA cycles are needed to develop a change idea that actually works. (Bryk et al., 2015, p. 121)

Given this, the key features of this change idea expanded as follows:

- Invite students from two different service divisions, creating two opportunities to have two cycles of improvement, specifically those who have high disproportionality application rates of Black and Latinx students as well as similar base school structures and overall enrollment.

- Work through the service division administrators and service school counselors to encourage, recruit, and send students who exhibit qualities of a successful MVGS student, not necessarily just ones identified as gifted or enrolled in honors or accelerated course work. A list of these qualities was created by current MVGS students, faculty, and staff to align with the MVGS mission and vision. This document is now called the *Profile of an MVGS Student* (see Appendix B). Administrators and counselors were asked to give consideration and extend invitations to Black and Latinx students who exhibit these qualities.
- Provide visiting students with time to socialize and ask questions of current MVGS students, faculty, and staff while touring the campus. Participation in hands-on activities (ones similar to what MVGS students do within their classes) that involve problem-solving and critical thinking and opportunities to experience a mock schedule were kept at the forefront of the planning.
- Engage students in an application workshop so that they have the information and skills necessary to complete an MVGS application.

The site visits were conducted in January and February at the discretion of MVGS and the service divisions. Factors, such as transportation, testing, and permission forms, were discussed and considered. There was a one-week offset between the two divisions' visits to allow for appropriate analysis of measures and cycle changes by the MVGS Equity Team.

The first PDSA cycle occurred on January 26, 2022, and the second on Wednesday, February 2, 2022, which was a change in the original date of January 12, 2022, due to inclement weather. For both cycles, an itinerary was developed by us and MVGS faculty and staff, then approved by the MVGS Equity Team before the visits. This itinerary was shared with the visiting schools well before the visit for final acceptance. The primary driver/system (information) was the focal point in the itinerary development.

With IS, improvement can only occur with accurate measurements to promote further learning. Understandably, there must be multiple measures to evaluate the PDSA progress and inform decision-making for the MVGS Equity Team. We tracked and shared four types of measurements, including outcome, driver, process, and balancing.

Outcome measure directly correlates to the aim, which for the MVGS Equity Team was to increase Black and Latinx applicants to MVGS in spring 2022 by 10% or more. This data was collected and finalized by the end of May 2022. As the MVGS director, I worked with service division administrators to gather this information once the application process concluded.

"Driver measures let you know if you are moving in the right direction before you have the data from the outcome measure" (Hinnant-Crawford, 2020, p. 140). For the MVGS Equity Team, the driver measure focused on students broadening their information base/knowledge of MVGS during the site visit. This was conducted via a student pre- and post-survey, which had similar questions, on the day of the visit (see Appendices C and D). The survey was constructed on a Likert scale to accurately scale responses to statements, such as: How familiar are you with the MVGS program? How much do you understand about the MVGS program? How confident are you in potentially attending MVGS? The prediction for this driver measure was that students would increase one unit or more from the pre-survey to the post-survey. One difference between the pre- and post-survey was a free response ending, which included: What do you hope to learn during the MVGS site visit? What information or experience would you like to have had during the MVGS site visit? These driver-measure questions would provide the team with data to adjust the site visit from the first PDSA cycle to the second.

Process measures ensure that the planned change has been implemented with fidelity. It ensures that the system and processes work as designed to deliver the outcomes intended. This was best achieved by the MVGS Equity Team through a task-specific checklist along with a reflection component. This tool helped track and drive the MVGS Equity Team during the study phase of the PDSA (see Appendix E for sample rubric). Balancing measures reveal unintended consequences of the change idea. As an early prediction, the Equity Team hypothesized that MVGS may see a decrease in other demographic applicant groups as enrollment numbers are relatively fixed. Another potential problem area was that students would become less interested in applying to MVGS after the site visit. Overall, the question remains: Did the site visits improve the information system or cost the information system?

THE RESULTS

The first PDSA cycle site visit, consisted of 23 prospective students with 22 participating in the pre- and post-surveys (see Appendices C and D). The second PDSA cycle, site visit, consisted of 15 students with 13 participating in the pre- and post-surveys. All students were selected to attend the visits based on the "Profile of a MVGS Student," and the feasibility of MVGS program completion prerequisite, which is Algebra II or higher before their sophomore year. Research field notes showed ethnic and racial diversity among the student attendees in the first PDSA with very little diversity in the second PDSA.

The results of a small portion of the descriptive statistics from question one and five only on the pre-survey and post-survey are reported next, with results from a paired-sample t-test included too. Note that a Likert scale was used on the survey ranging from 1 to 5 with 1 being little to no knowledge, familiarity, understanding, or beliefs, and 5 being excellent knowledge, familiarity, understandings, or beliefs. Comparisons should not be made from the first and second PDSA cycle driver measurements.

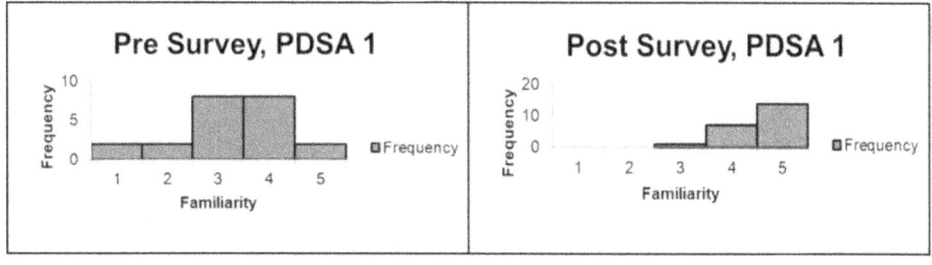

Figure 2.6. Question 1, Histogram of Students' Familiarity with MVGS Program, PDSA 1

Table 2.2. Question 1, Descriptive Statistics of Students' Familiarity with MVGS Program, PDSA 1

	Pre/PDSA 1	Post/PDSA 1
Mean	3.272	4.590
Median	3	5
Standard Deviation	1.077	0.590
Minimum	1	5
Maximum	5	5

Note: Likert scale ranges from 1 (I do know not anything about the MVGS program) to 5 (I know a lot about the MVGS program)

In the first PDSA cycle, a paired-sample t-test (see Figure 2.6) was conducted to compare students' familiarity with MVGS at the start of the site visit and the end of the site visit. The results of the paired sample t-test for the first PDSA indicated that there was statistically significant growth in the students' familiarity with MVGS before the site visit (M = 3.272, SD = 1.077) and after the site visit (M = 4.590, SD = 0.590); t(21) = −6.918, p = 0.000. It is important to notice that the standard deviation of the students' familiarity with the MVGS program decreased from 1.077 to 0.590 indicating that there was less variation in the students' familiarity after the site visit compared to before the site visit (see Table 2.2).

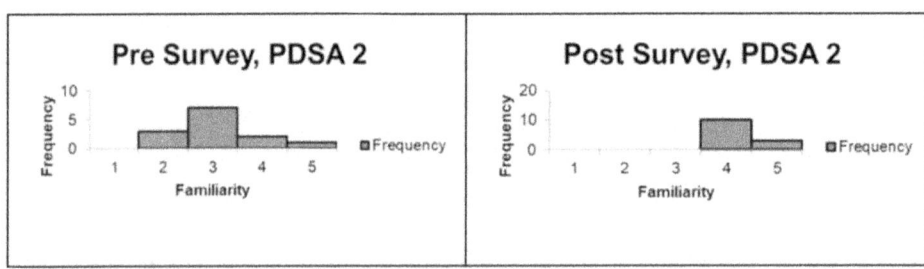

Figure 2.7. Question 1, Histogram of Students' Familiarity with MVGS Program, PDSA 2

Table 2.3. Question 1, Descriptive Statistics of Students' Familiarity with MVGS Program, PDSA 2

	Pre/PDSA 2	Post/PDSA 2
Mean	3.077	4.231
Median	3	4
Standard Deviation	0.862	0.439
Minimum	2	4
Maximum	5	5

Note: Likert scale ranges from 1 (I do not know anything about the MVGS program) to 5 (I know a lot about the MVGS program)

In the second PDSA cycle, a paired-sample t-test (see Figure 2.7) was conducted to compare students' familiarity with MVGS at the start of the site visit and the end of the site visit. The result of the paired sample t-test indicated for the second PDSA that there was statistically significant growth in the students' familiarity with MVGS before the site visit (M = 3.077, SD = 0.862) and after the site visit (M = 4.231, SD = 0.439); t(12) = −5.196, p = 0.000. It is important to notice that the standard deviation of the students' familiarity with the MVGS program decreased from 0.862 to 0.439 indicating that there was less variation in the students' familiarity after the site visit compared to before the site visit (see Table 2.3).

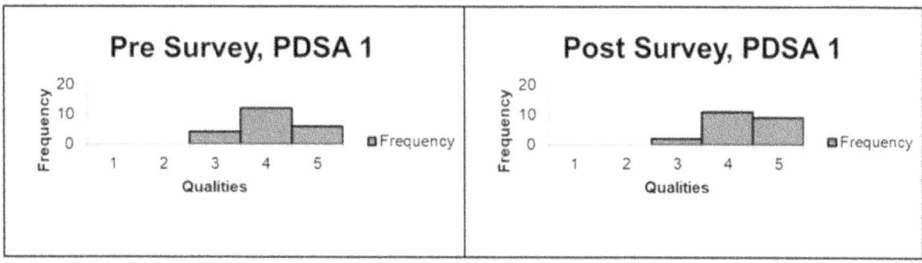

Figure 2.8. Question 5, Histogram of Students' Beliefs in Their Qualities to Achieve Goals at MVGS, PDSA 1

Table 2.4. Question 5, Descriptive Statistics of Students' Beliefs in Their Qualities to Achieve Goals at MVGS, PDSA 1

	Pre/PDSA 1	Post/PDSA 1
Mean	4.091	4.318
Median	4	4
Standard Deviation	0.684	0.646
Minimum	3	3
Maximum	5	5

Note: Likert scale ranges from 1 (I do not have the qualities) to 5 (I possess all the qualities)

A paired-sample t-test (see Figure 2.8) was conducted to compare students' beliefs in their possession of qualities to obtain their goals at MVGS at the start of the site visit and the end of the site visit. While the result of the paired sample t-test for the first PDSA cycle indicated that there was not a significant difference in the students' beliefs in their possession of qualities to obtain their goals at MVGS before the site visit (M = 4.091, SD = 0.684) and after the site visit (M = 4.318, SD = 0.646); t(21) = −1.742, p = 0.048, the mean opinion of the students' opinions did increase (see Table 2.4).

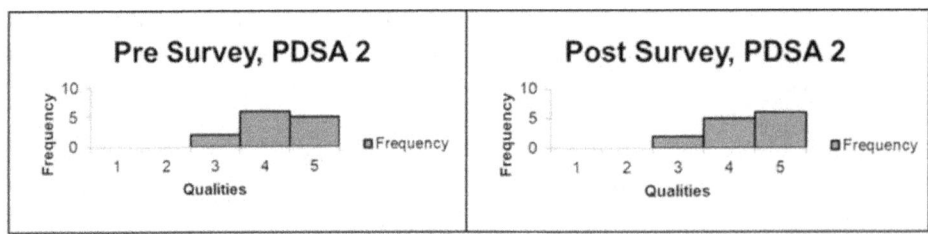

Figure 2.9. Question 5, Histogram of Students' Beliefs in Their Qualities to Achieve Goals at MVGS, PDSA 2

Table 2.5. Question 5, Descriptive Statistics of Students' Beliefs in Their Qualities to Achieve Goals at MVGS, PDSA 2

	Pre/PDSA 2	Post/PDSA 2
Mean	4.231	4.310
Median	4	5
Standard Deviation	0.725	0.751
Min	3	4
Max	5	5

Note: Likert scale ranges from 1 (I do not have the qualities) to 5 (I possess all the qualities)

A paired-sample t-test (see Figure 2.9) was conducted to compare students' beliefs in their possession of qualities to obtain their goals at MVGS at the start of the site visit and at the end of the site visit. While the result of the paired sample t-test for the second PDSA cycle indicated that there was not a statistically significant growth in the students' beliefs in their possession of qualities to obtain their goals at MVGS before the site visit (M = 4.231, SD = 0.725) and after the site visit (M = 4.310, SD = 0.751); t(12) = −0.562, p = 0.585, the mean opinion of the students' opinions did increase (see Table 2.5).

Notably, the fifth multiple-choice question on the pre- and post-survey required additional analysis as it revealed little growth as compared to the other questions, such as question one. However, upon further discussion in the MVGS Equity Team, it was concluded that the prospective students most likely came in with a high confidence level, having been invited to attend the site visit, and left with the same or slightly higher confidence level having learned more about the program. Although studies on the impact of giftedness on students' self-efficacy offer mixed results, there are a multitude of studies to confirm the Equity Team's hypothesis. "High self-efficacy reflects confidence in the ability to exert control over one's own motivation, behavior, and environment, and allows students to become advocates for their own needs and supports," according to Transforming Education (2020), a national, nonprofit organization dedicated to the academic development of all students with an emphasis on underserved populations. "Studies also have shown that students with high levels of self-efficacy participate more" (Transforming Education, 2020), as evidenced by the prospective students' willingness to attend and participate in the MVGS site visit.

The pre- and post-surveys also consisted of open-ended questions. There were two in the pre-survey, which were: What are your goals for high school and directly following high school? And, what do you hope to learn or do during your MVGS field experience? There were four in the post-survey which were: What did you find beneficial or learn from your visit to MVGS? What else would you have liked to have done, experienced, or learned from your visit to MVGS? What concerns or barriers do you still see in applying to or attending MVGS? And, do you have any additional thoughts, comments, or questions? We, like with the student interviews, identified themes during the qualitative coding process using Quirkos related to these six questions: academic goals, learning expectations, benefits, additional needs, barriers or challenges, concerns, and general comments.

First, during the pre-survey, students provided information on their academic goals. The most recurring responses were to attend college, graduate high school, graduate high school with a high grade point average, earn an associate degree while still in high school, and focus on a major either in engineering, medicine, computer science, or law. This emphasized that the students selected to attend the site visit were academically motivated with postsecondary aspirations, confirming that MVGS could facilitate these students in their educational endeavors. It also validated that districts consider the use of the Profile of an MVGS Student, the process measurement tool that outlines some qualities of gifted learners as shared previously in the chapter.

The second pre-survey question focuses on students' learning expectations for the site visit. The most recurring responses were programmatic design, learning opportunities, and dual enrollment options or college preparation.

During the post-survey, students led off with a question focusing on the benefits of the site visit. The most common responses were that they learned about MVGS classes and curriculum, the faculty and staff, the program climate and culture, the day-to-day MVGS schedule and operations, and current MVGS students, thus addressing their pre-survey questions about learning expectations for the day.

The second post-survey question asked students to identify any topics that they wanted to learn about or have additional time exploring. The top response was none. The other top responses were STEAM (science, technology, engineering, arts, and mathematics) groups and classes.

Third, students were asked about any potential barriers or challenges they could identify in applying to or attending MVGS. Workload concern was the major response. The other concerns were after-school activity participation and scheduling conflicts with the base high schools. In speaking with students at both site visits, both of us were able to garner that the true concern was time. The prospective students were worried about being able to do the things they enjoy, like sports and after-school jobs, and keep up with the rigor of classes at MVGS and their base high schools. Would they be able to balance it all? Will they be able to have a life?

Finally, the last open-ended, post-survey question centered around collecting general comments/insights from the prospective students. The top result was none with a few statements that the visit was fun and exciting.

After examining all of the data collection from the pre- and post-surveys, or driver measures, it was revealed that prospective students at each site visit increased their knowledge of MVGS, as predicted. The open-ended responses in the pre- and post-surveys assisted the MVGS Equity Team in making achievable changes between the first site visit/PDSA cycle and the second site visit/PDSA cycle. The noted changes that were discussed and implemented centered around easing prospective students' minds regarding the overall commitment to attending MVGS. This was accomplished through meaningful seminar time with current MVGS Student Ambassadors as well as MVGS faculty and staff. The MVGS Student Ambassador program was started by and is facilitated by the MVGS program counselor in the fall of 2022. Students apply to be the voice of MVGS and to be the people that students, parents, or guardians, whether at MVGS or not, turn to with questions about the program.

Specifically, the second PDSA cycle when compared to the first PDSA cycle incorporated a lower MVGS Student Ambassador to prospective student ratio to provide more time for visiting students to engage current students in both informal discussion to formal sessions with teacher-facilitated question and answer moments. The ratio during the first PDSA cycle was approximately 6:1 with the second PDSA cycle having a ratio of 3:1. Prospective students were also provided more time with MVGS instructors to talk about STEAM groups and classes. Both were data-driven changes as approved by the team.

After both PDSA cycles, the MVGS Equity Team revisited the process measurement standards that were developed in the late fall/early winter (see Appendix E). Out of the 34 processes measured, three were not achieved for a 91.2% rate of adherence. The process measures that were not met trended toward challenges within the school district and were largely beyond the control of us and the MVGS Equity Team. Some considerations for scaling the process that came from the process measures were the timing of the event(s) and the use of the Profile of an MVGS Student document. It was unclear as to how readily the document was used to select participants for the site visits and might require additional process measures to ensure its successful application moving forward. Plus, site visits during the winter months were subject to inclement weather challenges. These were not realized by us but need to be a consideration in the future.

The outcomes measure, as seen in Table 2.2, shows that the aim of the MVGS Equity Team was not realized, which was to increase Black and Latinx applicants to MVGS in spring 2022 by 10% or more.

However, the applicant pool did show a minor increase in Black and Latinx applicants, thus moving the equity needle. Black applicants moved from an average of 4.79% in the 2020–2022 school years to 7.84% in the 2022–2023 school year showing a 3.35% increase. Latinx applicants moved from an average of 8.81% in the 2020–2022 school years to 9.80% in the 2022–2023 school year showing a 1.72% increase. MVGS did see a decrease within the demographic of multiple ethnicities. The 2022–2023 applicant pool did not have any students identified as being two or more ethnicities, whereas the year prior had 6.68% of the applicants identify as such. The data cannot confirm if the multiple ethnicities included Black or Latinx (see Table 2.6).

Table 2.6. Three-Year MVGS Enrollment versus Applicant Demographics

Subgroup	Enrolled 2022–2023	Enrolled 2021–2022	Enrolled 2020–2021	Applicants 2022–2023	Applicants 2021–2022	Applicants 2020–2021
American Indian/Alaskan	0.48%	0.52%	0%	1.96%	3.57%	0%
Asian	12.56%	10.82%	10.4%	9.80%	8.47%	11.6%
Black	5.80%	3.09%	1.9%	7.84%	5.08%	4.5%
Latinx	8.70%	6.19%	6.6%	9.80%	8.47%	7.7%
Native Hawaiian	0.48%	0.52%	0.5%	0%	0%	0%
White	70.05%	71.13%	72.5%	70.59%	67.80%	71.6%
Multiple	1.93%	7.73%	8.1%	0%	6.68%	4.5%

MVGS did not experience any students becoming less interested in applying to MVGS after the site visit given the unit increases with each question. Communication to students enhanced enrollment with MVGS having 194 students enrolled in the 2021–2022 school year and increasing to 209 students enrolled in the 2022–2023 school year. If anything, it can be concluded that providing students with in-depth information about the program resulted in more students applying and being accepted.

Balancing measures address the question, are the changes designed to improve one part of the system causing new problems in other parts of the system? More specifically, did the site visits (PDSA cycles) improve the information system at the cost of another system or subgroup? As mentioned earlier, the subgroups that saw a dip were multiple ethnicities, as well as American Indian or Alaska Native. However, it is unclear as to whether this decrease was a result of the site visits or a change in the way students are self-identifying. Although the site visits or PDSA cycles might be seen as a disruption to the school day for prospective students and MVGS students due to the time and attention spent on them, there was no cost to the learning system. Actually, there was an increase in learning because of the high level of student participation. Both MVGS students and prospective students took ownership in and of the visits, engaging in meaningful conversations and discussions ranging from academics to mental health to executive functioning skills to post-secondary plans. The PDSA cycles did cause an imbalance in the allocation of time and resources for the MVGS director, MVGS faculty and staff, gifted coordinators, and district transportation departments. Both spent additional time and resources to plan and implement the site visits to benefit all students. However, it is the job of MVGS to communicate its purpose to the community, allowing potential students, along with their parents, to understand MVGS as an educational option. So, although the site visits took up time that might have been spent on other school-related tasks, it was not outside the scope of the MVGS personnel's work.

SPREADING THE CHANGE

Today, the MVGS Equity Team continues its work on the initial problem of applicant disproportionality by scaling up the site visits to include more schools and more students for future PDSA cycles. As outlined, IS is a continuous method of improvement that MVGS will adhere to moving forward for years. MVGS will always work to create opportunities for underserved students so they can overcome disadvantages and find success, as establishing fairness and inclusion never ends. Therefore, we and the MVGS Equity Team started to address IS Step 7 by actively designing a process module, via Weebly, to spread the change to other organizations to assist them in uncovering, addressing, and improving access to their programs for historically underserved students. The process module, which was started in August 2022 and continues today, provides workable documents, assessments, strategies, metrics, research, sample plans, frameworks, videos, and more to address what specific programs may need to implement change based on the findings from this research. Of note, the module is more about supporting others in using the IS process with Liberatory Design mindsets than it is about following what the MVGS Equity Team did and does. We decided to do this based on the positive and inquisitive reaction of so many school and division leaders as we conversationally shared our work in emails, meetings, and conferences. The module acts as a roadmap to help other specialty programs in public education, such as regional technical programs, prioritize their diversity needs and work toward practical, hands-on, active, viable improvement beyond mere theoretical work. The process module at https://improvementscience.weebly.com/ assists and supports specialty academic programs to utilize IS methodology with a Liberatory Design mindset. Currently, two other AYGSs are using the module to grow and improve their program.

LESSONS LEARNED

One key learning, and a limitation at the same time, for us, was the impact that the political climate can have on research. We want to start by addressing the shift in Virginia as it pertains to equity from the start of this research to the publication of this chapter. As a brief overview during the time of this research, the Commonwealth transitioned through three governors from McAuliffe to Northam to Youngkin, and five state superintendents from Staples to Constantino to Lane to Balow to Coons. On May 19, 2022, the entirety of the VDOE's EdEquity website, finalized under ex-Superintendent Lane, had been removed from the internet. Earlier in the spring, the OneVirginia website was also removed in its entirety from the internet. This was an initiative from ex-Governor Northam, as a result of House Bill 1993, to build a statewide strategy to advance diversity, equity, and inclusion (DEI) initiatives across the state in services, systems, and operations. The intent was to use the inclusive excellence framework to create collective impact, sustainable change, innovation, and productivity across state government and other sectors of the Commonwealth. When Governor Youngkin took office in January 2022, he published a slew of Executive Orders with the first one addressing "Ending the Use of Inherently Divisive Concepts,

Including Critical Race Theory, and Restoring Excellence in K–12 Public Education in the Commonwealth." This order states, "Political indoctrination has no place in our classrooms," thus implying that schools and teachers in America were conspiring to brainwash children on topics such as slavery, segregation, and the Civil Rights Movement. The order continues to state, "Inherently divisive concepts . . . instruct students to only view life through the lens of race and presumes that some students are consciously or unconsciously racist, sexist, or oppressive, and that other students are victims." On February 23, 2022, Dr. Balow, the then state superintendent submitted an interim 30-day report on inherently divisive concepts, which contained rescissions and modifications of programs, policies, and materials, which included rescinding the EdEquityVA project, a DEI Audit Tool per Dr. Lane, and all resources on the VDOE website on culturally responsive practices. The pendulum continues to swing, creating an unclear pathway moving forward to equity in education and continued work as noted in this study.

We acknowledge another large system, beyond the information system that was selected in this study, which impacts student disproportionality at MVGS and potentially other educational programs is transportation. In the Commonwealth, it is up to each school division to determine policies regarding transportation to and from educational programs. For some divisions, this may mean picking students up near their homes via school division transportation vehicles or buses. It may mean expecting students to get to designated locations through the county to catch a school division transportation shuttle, which may require private transportation to get to the shuttle pick-up location. It may even be students using public transportation to get to and from home, the program, the base school, and back home again. Inequity exists with the latter two models when students are not able to get themselves to district shuttle or public transit locations. The inconsistency of how each division addresses transportation indicates a need for reform at the state level. Students may or may not apply or attend special programming based on the fact that they cannot overcome the barriers of transportation.

More than anything, a huge takeaway for us was that involving students in the entire process is crucial. Before the student interviews, the prevailing thought of the MVGS Equity Team was that students were embarrassed to go to MVGS because they did not want to be seen as overly academic and studious. But, with student input and insights, the team learned that their concern was not about stigma. It was centered around self-efficacy in that students needed more information about the program to determine if they felt as though they had the necessary behaviors, skills, and supports to perform well in the program. They wanted more information about the program and communication from the program to see if it was a good fit for them. In tandem, student voice and advocacy on the MVGS Equity Team concreted these affirmations proving that student representation is key to IS and educational success no matter the change idea.

For us, the entire process enhanced our work as social justice leaders (SJL). Although there are tremendous barriers that students face within the educational setting, SJLs make it the forefront of their work to strive toward equitable practices for marginalized students. It is critical that SJLs "not hide from the data" but "that facing the statistics was essential to the task of accountability" (Theoharis, 2009, p. 3).

The MVGS Equity Team does not hide from the data but embraces it and follows it to alleviate the challenge of injustice in education and takes steps to decrease these injustices. "At its core, this challenge recognizes that not only are schools failing many historically marginalized students but also the causes of failure that are known and remediable. Thus, it is a matter of will and commitment" (Theoharis, 2009, p. 1), which we possess.

APPENDIX A

MVGS Student Interview Script Outline

MVGS Student Interview Script Outline

1. Initial welcome - must include review and submission of parent consent/student assent form. Focus - make student feel comfortable and at ease.

2. Basic demographic information:
   Name
   Grade
   Current base high school
   Current Status as it Pertains to MVGS

3. How did you learn about MVGS? (Or. are you familiar with MVGS?)

4. Why did you choose to apply or not to apply (or why will you choose to apply or not apply) to Mountain Vista Governor's School?

5. Why do you think high school students choose to apply or not apply to Mountain Vista Governor's School?

6. What do you see as the benefits or added value of applying to and/or attending MVGS?

7. What do you see as some of the challenges of applying to and/or attending MVGS?
   - Schedule
   - Transportation
   - Peer influence/ perception
   - Family influence / perception
   - Cost
   - Base school (counselor, teacher, etc.) influence
   - Application
   - Student representation of the program
   - School perception (What's the information / feel floating around about MVGS?)

8. Potential Follow Up Questions, as listed below with correlation to main questions listed above:

   (Correlation to question #2) Did you, or will you, apply to MVGS this year? Please tell us more about why you chose to apply or not apply.

   (Correlation to question #5) Why do you think Black and Latinx students choose to apply or not apply?

   (Correlation to question #4 or #6) What are your current hopes and goals for your high school career and after high school? What do you need (opportunities, skills, etc.) to achieve your goals?

(Correlation to question #7) What is getting or has gotten in your way of achieving your goals?

(Correlation to question #7) What would make MVGS, or any gifted program, a better place to attend classes?

(Correlation to question #7) What would make your home school a better place to be?

(Correlation to questions #3 & #7) Is your base high school assisting you in achieving your goals?

(Correlation to questions #4 & #7) What are you most worried or concerned about in terms of reaching your goals?

(Correlation to question #7) When you were applying to MVGS, was transportation a concern?

(Correlation to question #7) When you were thinking about applying to MVGS, was money a concern?

(Correlation to question #3) In what ways did your friends and family respond when you mentioned applying to MVGS?

(Correlation to questions #4 & #7) What criteria should students be judged for admittance at MVGS?

(Correlation to questions #4 & #5) What is the best way to showcase your talents to a committee for admittance at MVGS?

(Correlation to question #7) What is the reputation of MVGS among your peers?

APPENDIX B

Profile of an MVGS Student

What does an MVGS Student Look Like?

DETERMINED, AMBITIOUS, HYPERFOCUSED, HARD WORKING
- ☐ Deliberate with goals and tasks.
- ☐ May be annoyed with interruptions.
- ☐ Might have issues transitioning from one topic to another.
- ☐ Can dig in when motivated.
- ☐ Can be very attached, specialized to a topic.

PASSIONATE, CURIOUS, OPENMINDED, LIKES TO ASK QUESTIONS
- ☐ Enjoys enrichment opportunities for the sake of learning.
- ☐ Has diverse interests that can differ from peers.
- ☐ Takes things apart, challenges how things are "supposed" to work.
- ☐ May appear to challenge authority.
- ☐ Loves to understand "why".
- ☐ Makes strong inferences, likes it when the answer isn't "too easy".
- ☐ If bored with the standard curriculum might want to graduate early or drop out. Might be frequently absent from class.
- ☐ May need to be reminded that learning can be joyful.

UNIQUE SOCIAL EMOTIONAL NEEDS
- ☐ Under enormous pressure to succeed. May have anxiety or panic attacks. May have perfectionist tendencies with adaptive and maladaptive behaviors.
- ☐ May not be used to being challenged/failing. Have strong reactions to "bad" grades.
- ☐ Enjoys interacting with other gifted peers in an inclusive environment; might struggle in relationships with non-gifted peers. May seem standoffish.
- ☐ May be hypercritical towards self and others. Can be highly competitive.
- ☐ Sometimes hesitant to share their interests or intellect for fear of criticism.

INDEPENDENT, INTERNALLY MOTIVATED
- ☐ May not be used to asking for help.
- ☐ Time management can be a struggle.
- ☐ May forgo sleep to study/work.
- ☐ Won't turn anything in that isn't "perfect".
- ☐ May overcommit themselves.
- ☐ May score high on tests but underachieve in other academic tasks.
- ☐ Get good grades because they are scholars, but grades are not the primary motivation for learning. (typically salutatorian, not valedictorian)

APPENDIX C

PDSA Pre-Survey

Mountain Vista Governor's School Prospective Student Pre-visit Survey

The purpose of this survey is to gather information on your familiarity with MVGS. The information gathered from this survey will be used to help MVGS understand recruiting practices from the student perspective. Participation in this survey is completely voluntary, and you may opt out an anytime by closing this window or shutting down your device. There is no penalty for not participating in this survey. Your answers will be completely anonymous, and no one will be able to connect you to your responses to any of these questions.

*required

khuff@mvgshome.org (not shared) Switch account

* Required

I have read the description of the MVGS survey that is printed above. My parent/guardian and I received prior notice of this survey, and I know that I can quit the survey at any time. I know that my participation, as a student, is voluntary and will help MVGS plan for the future*   Mark only one circle.

○ I agree to participate in the survey. Skip to next question.
○ I DO NOT agree to participate in the survey. Simply close this window.

Student Number/Identifier *

Your answer

I am familiar with the Mountain Vista Governor's School Program *

  1 2 3 4 5
I do not know anything about ○ ○ ○ ○ ○ I know a lot about the MVGS
the MVGS program.   progam

I understand what it takes to be successful at Mountain Vista Governor's School. *

  1 2 3 4 5
I'm not sure what it takes to ○ ○ ○ ○ ○ I fully understand what it
be successful at MVGS.   takes to be successful at
                                                    MVGS

I understand what it is like to be a Mountain Vista Governor's School student. *

  1 2 3 4 5
I'm not sure what it is like to ○ ○ ○ ○ ○ I fully understand what it is
be a MVGS student.   like to be a MVGS student

I understand how to complete the Mountain Vista Governor's School application * to maximize my potential for being accepted into the program.

  1 2 3 4 5
I do not understand how to ○ ○ ○ ○ ○ I understand how to complete
complete the application.   the MVGS application to
                                                    maximize my potential for
                                                    being accepted into the
                                                    program.

I believe I posses the qualities necessary to obtain my goals at Mountain Vista * Governor's School.

  1 2 3 4 5
I do not have any of the ○ ○ ○ ○ ○ I posses all of the qualities
necessary qualities to obtain   neccessary to obtain my
my goals at MVGS.   goals at MVGS.

What are your goals for high school and directly following high school? *

Your answer

What do you hope to learn or do during your MVGS field experience? *

Your answer

Submit   Clear form

APPENDIX D

PDSA Post-Survey

APPENDIX E

Process Measurement Tool

Process Measurement Checklist

Process	Yes	No	Date Completed / Notes
Determine participating divisions utilizing selection criteria			
Division's gifted coordinator and/or school counselor has worked closely with MVGS within the past school year.			
Racial demographic make-up of division is disproportionate to the number of students applying to MVGS within the past two application cycles.			
School's Black or Latinx is at least 10%.			
Representation of divisions that feed into the Warrenton Campus and the Middletown Campus.			
Division has seen a decrease in overall enrollment of students to MVGS within the past 1-2 years.			
For dissertation only: Divisions of are relatively equal size; # of students can be accommodated in one visit but also provide a good sample size (preferably a division with 2 high schools)			
Determine site visit days for 2 divisions (7:30 to 2:30) **Site visit should be scheduled when...**			
There is flexibility within MVGS instruction and causes least disruption to normal schedule (preferably a Wednesday flex day).			
100% of the current MVGS student body is scheduled and expected to be on campus.			
100% of the MVGS staff is scheduled and expected to be on campus, and does not have any conflicting priorities (other PD opportunities or meetings).			
Visit should occur after the current year's MVGS application has been released but 1-2 weeks prior to its due date.			
Visit should not fall on a day when prospective students might miss important instruction or experiences at their base high school such as SOL testing, the 2-3 classes directly at the end or beginning of a semester, the 1-2 days immediately preceding or following a school break, or specialty days within a block schedule.			
Develop or revise MVGS student profile (What are the qualities and characteristics of a successful MVGS student?)			
Faculty, student mentors, and equity team members will collaborate to construct profile.			
Profile should be a collection of qualities to be used as a guide, not a requirement			
Profile should reflect current research about qualities of a gifted learner			
Distribute and support utilization of MVGS student profile to selected divisions			
MVGS director and division GT coordinators will work together to determine how to best teach educators on how to utilize student profile			
Division GT coordinators will meet with base school counselors and GT head instructors to review student profile and construct a list of potential students based on eligibility requirements			
Division GT coordinators, base school counselors and GT head instructors will crosswalk potential student list with profile to determine			

site visit invitation list			
Support recruitment of prospective students for site visit with an emphasis on MVGS student profile and underrepresented populations			
An adult from the base school (counselor, teacher, etc.) will invite prospective students from the list to partake in MVGS site visit. Adult will convey qualities student possess that they believe makes them a good candidate for MVGS and answer any initial questions.			
Adults will follow up with students to determine interest and provide them with necessary paperwork to attend site visit.			
Adults will continue to check in with students until all required paperwork has been collected.			
Provide transportation for site visits			
GT coordinators will secure free district transportation for all students who have returned required paperwork.			
Assess prospective students interest and knowledge of MVGS			
Students will gather together at beginning and end of site visit and be provided with verbal directions on how to complete pre and post surveys.			
Students will be provided with pre and post survey either digitally (that they can access on their personal device) or a paper copy			
Students will be provided time (at least 5 minutes) to complete pre and post surveys.			
Implement STEAM group activities with prospective students.			
Hands-on and participatory			
Further the work of the STEAM group			
Group will be small enough to ensure that every prospective student has the opportunity to participate meaningfully			

As much as possible, prospective students will choose the STEAM groups they wish to participate in.			
Implement seminar group with prospective students			
Provide prospective students with new content.			
Interact with a stated topic in a small group format			
Potential students will have the opportunity to discuss new ideas with each other and MVGS students			
Broaden potential student's skill set			
Provide and support social interactions between prospective and current MVGS students			
Integrated groups with MVGS and prospective students during morning activities			
MVGS students will discuss what and how to communicate with potential students prior to site visit			
Provide prospective students with class visits			
Prospective students are provided time to ask questions of MVGS faculty and staff			
Prospective students are provided a brief (5 minute) overview of key highlights of each class by the class's teacher			
Prospective students will engage with content by participating in a related hands-on activity			
Provide application support to prospective students			
Explain process			
Go through each part; students have a copy to look			
Key things they need for each part			

Review timeline due date / organizer e' notes			
Ask questions of teachers for clarification			

Chapter 3

Leading Change in Teacher Stress and Mental Health

Jessica Cromer, EdD

THE CONTEXT

Our school division sits nestled in the rural Blue Ridge Mountains of Virginia. The greater school community is mostly conservative in its values, although about a quarter of the population has voted Democratic in recent elections. The major economic industries include agriculture, tourism, and the arts. No interstates run through our county, there are no railroads, and all water flows out. However, the community is not entirely isolated as we are within an hour of two major universities and the largest city on the western side of the state. Our local communications provider has done an immense amount of work to secure fiber internet connection to 95% of our homes. This has been a draw for families seeking a rural but connected lifestyle and has allowed for economic expansion in the instructional technology sector.

Approximately 1,700 students are enrolled in our five schools: four preschool through seventh grade elementary schools and one high school with grades 8–12. Our student body is 89% white, 5% Hispanic, 4% multiple races, and 1% Black. All of our students receive free breakfast and lunch. Of the approximately 169 teachers employed by the division, approximately 31 are male. Eighty-seven teachers have a master's degree or higher and the average salary is $48,143.98.

Given our small size, we have a limited number of support positions in our schools. There are five school counselors employed in the division and two school psychologists. The 14% of students with special needs are served by 22 special education teachers and four speech therapists. The division has one behavior specialist, one math specialist, two instructional technology resource teachers, six elementary reading specialists, and one secondary literacy coach. In addition to our superintendent, our leadership team consists of the five school principals, three assistant principals, and our central office leaders in instruction, assessment, special education, and technology.

Each school also receives support from school-based clinicians through the local community service board. These clinicians can offer individual and group counseling services to students within the school day. Therapeutic Day Treatment (TDT) services are also available to students at all of our schools. This more intensive support for students includes intervention and therapy services in the school and in students' homes.

School-based services are available to all students, but those without Medicaid pay based on a sliding scale. The TDT service is available only to students with Medicaid. The work of school-based clinicians and the TDT services are completed with the cooperation of, but not under the direction of, our division.

THE PROBLEM

Before COVID, the division began to see an increase in the number of students who have experienced trauma. To further support these students and their teachers, the division added a behavior specialist in the 2019–2020 school year. This position oversees the implementation of functional behavioral analyses and behavior intervention plans and provides some interventions directly to students. Of the 29 student cases initially staffed by this position, only seven students were identified as needing special education services. The remaining 22 students had previous traumatic experiences that impacted their ability to perform in the classroom.

This increase brought new challenges into the classroom environment that started to impact student learning as well as teachers' physical and mental health. Traumatized students have a difficult time with focus and self-regulation. They may overreact to everyday tasks and can have negative outbursts or aggression. Teachers sought comfort and ways to help their students from the professionals in their buildings. Administrators were at a loss as to how to help these students, support their teachers, and maintain order in their schools.

In 2018, the division began an initiative to learn more about trauma, its impact on students, and what educators can do to mitigate trauma's negative impact on learning. All staff received training on the basics of trauma, adverse childhood experiences, and the impact of traumatic events on the brain. Principals and guidance counselors had more intensive follow-up sessions to address the factors that might be barriers to our efforts and plan for how we could support both our students and teachers.

The division administrative team, which consists of all building principals and central office administrative personnel, participated in a book study of *The Trauma-Informed School* (Sporleder & Forbes, 2016) during the fall of 2019. Monthly reading assignments and discussions have helped principals and assistant principals change their mindset as it relates to student behavior, discipline, and the lasting impacts of adverse childhood experiences on staff wellness.

We also partnered with the local community services board to provide two focused professional development sessions at each of the five schools in the 2019–2020 school year. The sessions reviewed the impacts of trauma from previous training, shared strategies for responding to trauma in the classroom, and introduced the importance of educator self-care.

In a Spring 2019 division survey of teachers and administrators, approximately 93% of the 118 respondents indicated they have experienced one or more symptoms of secondary traumatic stress (STS) when working with students who have experienced trauma. Thirteen percent of survey participants reported experiencing one or more symptoms very often.

The fall of 2020 brought changes in Medicaid regulations, which resulted in the loss of therapeutic day treatment services for many of our students. The COVID-19 school closure in the spring of 2020 brought more reductions in these services as many students were dropped from caseloads. As a result of the loss of services, more responsibility for supporting the mental health of students fell on classroom teachers, school counselors, and building administrators.

We began to see this added stress impact our teachers both mentally and physically. As Stamm (1999) first noted, "The process of empathizing with a traumatized person helps us understand that person's experience of being traumatized, but in the process, we may be traumatized as well" (p. 20). Our teachers' exposure to students who have experienced trauma manifested into signs of burnout, compassion fatigue, and STS.

Symptoms of secondary traumatic stress mirror those of post-traumatic stress disorder (PTSD) and can include physical ailments such as fatigue, digestion issues, and trouble sleeping as well as emotional and behavioral symptoms such as detachment, anxiety, and an increased use of self-destructive coping mechanisms such as drugs or alcohol (Hydon et al., 2015). Beginning in 2013, the American Psychiatric Association (2013) considered STS a valid criterion for diagnosing PTSD if the exposure "causes clinically significant distress or impairment in the individual's social interactions, capacity to work or other important areas of functioning" (p. 1).

THE TEAM

The initial survey responses highlighted the need for more research on the problem. We established a division research team with representation from a variety of stakeholders. This team included an elementary teacher, a high school special education teacher, an elementary school counselor, the division behavioral specialist, the division school psychologist, an elementary assistant principal, and the director of special education and student services. All members of the team were purposely selected for their specific knowledge base, experience in the division, credibility with staff, and work with students that have experienced trauma.

PROBLEM INQUIRY AND ANALYSIS

The team created a fishbone diagram to help identify the major causes of STS within the division. The conversation and experience of the team members helped develop a comprehensive view of the issue in the division. Teachers did not receive pre-service training on trauma or on the impact it can have on professionals offering assistance. In some cases, teachers felt that excessively worrying about their students was a natural result of their job, a sentiment that is also a common stereotype of educators in their role as caregivers. Teachers in the division also felt that they needed more classroom resources in the form of strategies and support personnel to help the students and in turn improve their own well-being. The team also noted that there was a stigma associated with wellness and that certain people may not have felt comfortable asking for

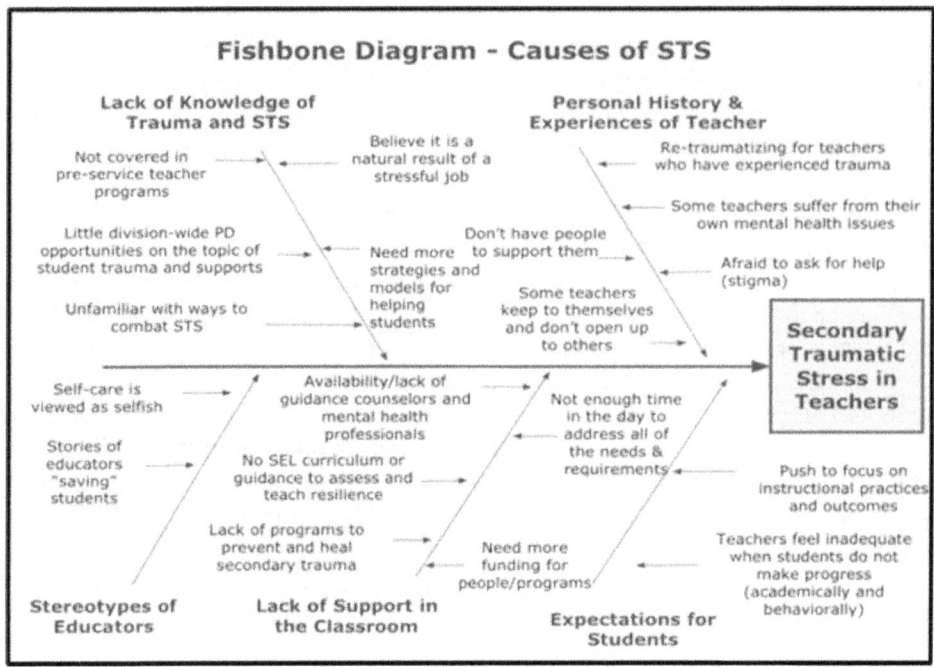

Figure 3.1. Fishbone Diagram: Causes of STS

help or reaching out to others for ideas. Figure 3.1 shows a more detailed description of all five causes and their supporting details as outlined by the division research team.

Empathy interviews related to the problem were conducted with four teachers at our largest elementary school to gauge their knowledge of STS and to gather information on common self-care practices. The teachers were selected using a random name generator and asked questions related to the challenges and rewards of teaching students who have experienced trauma, the impact on teaching performance, and helpful self-care strategies.

Several themes emerged from these interviews regarding the impact of STS on teachers in the division. First, all four teachers indicated their lack of training and instruction in supporting students who have experienced trauma. Two of the respondents identified their lack of confidence in handling trauma disclosures and challenging mental health issues in their classrooms. Second, the teachers noted the reward of helping students who have experienced trauma find success socially and academically. Each teacher mentioned student success as a motivator for their work as educators.

Three of the four teachers interviewed felt that teaching students who have experienced trauma has made them better teachers and open to trying new strategies in the classroom that benefit all students. All four teachers indicated that they engaged in self-care activities on their own to help deal with stress. These activities included realizing they need to step away for a break, healthy eating habits, exercise, talking with colleagues who understand, and therapy sessions with licensed counselors.

This work found early success as there was high interest in the topic and exploring ways to better support our teachers. As we moved through the COVID-19 pandemic, it became more challenging to focus on the work of lowering STS in teachers when so many other issues demanded our time and attention. The importance of team member selection cannot be understated. The individuals on our team were committed to the work and the improvement of teacher well-being. Their desire to support teachers kept them focused and moved the process forward.

CHANGE IDEA AND INTERVENTION

While a large amount of research could be found on the impact of trauma on the classroom environment, empirical research on the impact of trauma-exposed youth on educators had only recently begun to be published at the time of our planning. Multiple researchers (Borntrager et al., 2012; Caringi et al., 2015; Essary et al., 2020; Hydon et al., 2015) described the increasing prevalence of STS among educators and the occupational hazards that result from this exposure. Molnar and coauthors (2017) completed a comprehensive review of STS literature and noted that approximately 18–33% of individuals who respond to and support victims of violent crimes against children are at risk of STS.

Research supported our initial beliefs that certain factors influence STS in public school educators such as class load and size, characteristics of students, access to community resources and support systems, as well as the teacher's own mental health status and personal trauma history (Borntrager et al., 2012; Caringi et al., 2015; Essary et al., 2020). Specifically, larger class sizes and caseloads, intense classroom behavior incidents as a result of experienced trauma, and a history of personal mental health issues could cause some teachers to be more susceptible to STS. Alfuqaha and Alshra'ah's (2018) comparison study also found that unmarried female teachers experienced higher levels of burnout than their male or married female counterparts.

Interestingly, despite the STS challenges to physical and mental health, educators report higher than average levels of job satisfaction than other professions that are exposed to the traumatic experiences of others (Borntrager et al., 2012; Koenig et al., 2017). This fulfillment is also called compassion satisfaction and is explained as a protective factor that builds resilience and buffers some effects of STS (Caringi et al., 2015). Other protective factors include feeling successful with students, self-care techniques, and having a social support network (Kulkarni et al., 2013; Samios et al., 2013).

Although the research on STS interventions for educators is sparse (Bercier & Maynard, 2015), available research shows training on the impacts of STS, instruction in and the practice of mindfulness, and supportive peer and supervisory cultures can mitigate the impacts of STS. These are the specific areas we decided to focus our research on given their previous success in the research and the ease with which we could implement related change ideas.

Workshops on relevant issues are a simple and common intervention for addressing a problem. Gentry and coauthors (2004) used the concept of "training as treatment" to address the impact of STS in professional settings (p. 135). Specifically, providing staff with training on stress management and burnout prevention has been shown to reduce PTSD and STS symptoms and develop an optimistic professional attitude (Berger et al., 2016; Molnar et al., 2017; Wald et al., 2016). In addition, training that utilizes evidence-based practices for addressing STS increased the self-efficacy of participants, which seems to moderate the impact of their symptoms (Ortlepp & Friedman, 2002; Prati et al., 2010; Sprang et al., 2007). Thus, the more qualified a person feels in their work responsibilities, the more resilient they may be when faced with professional challenges.

However, not all training is beneficial. Bober and Regehr (2006) found that time spent learning about self-care activities such as physical activity, reading, and participating in a hobby does not translate into time spent engaging in those activities. Killian (2008) corroborated those findings and concluded that only one personal resource, emotional self-awareness, seemed to impact the effects of STS.

One strategy for emotional self-awareness is through the practice of mindfulness. Mindfulness-based stress reduction is a specific type of self-care approach that uses meditation to bring awareness to thoughts and feelings without judgment (Ludwig & Kabat-Zinn, 2008). Recent studies have documented the ability of mindfulness to offer protection from the effects of STS by reducing psychological distress, decreasing burnout symptoms, and improving the compassion satisfaction of those in helping professions (Anama-Green, 2020; Goodman & Schorling, 2012; Molnar et al., 2017; Sharp-Donahoo et al., 2017; Thieleman & Cacciatore, 2014). There is promising evidence that mindfulness is not only beneficial to the professionals who are practicing it but also for the clients and students they serve. Grepmair and coauthors (2007) found that clients of clinicians who practiced mindfulness and meditation had better outcomes than clients of clinicians who did not.

Training experiences can also bolster the social and peer support of those at risk of STS. Studies have concluded that these social connections can reduce the stigma associated with seeking help and provide professionals with a safe environment to vent and share emotions (Alisic, 2012; Molnar et al., 2017; Sharp-Donahoo et al., 2018). Although a beneficial intervention, peer support has mainly been used for primary trauma exposure and has been cautioned as a stand-alone, long-term treatment for secondary trauma exposure (Molnar et al., 2017; Rose et al., 2003; Ruzek et al., 2007).

Despite a lack of research on specific STS interventions for educators, the literature reviewed suggested a wide range of research-based interventions from the individual to the system level. Efforts to address the impact of STS focus more on the general health and wellness of professionals rather than addressing the specific effects of indirect trauma exposure. Our division research team wanted to build interventions that mitigate the immediate impacts of secondary trauma exposure and also serve as preventative or protective factors. We used the research and our knowledge of the school division to develop an aim statement: By the spring of 2022, teachers will report a decrease in rates of self-reported secondary traumatic stress symptoms.

The team then identified primary drivers that could be a catalyst for influencing that outcome. We felt that the main drivers of this problem were the awareness of STS, professional support systems for teachers, teacher self-care, and a socio-emotional learning curriculum. Figure 3.2 illustrates these primary drivers as well as the secondary drivers that could be made actionable. We also brainstormed change ideas that

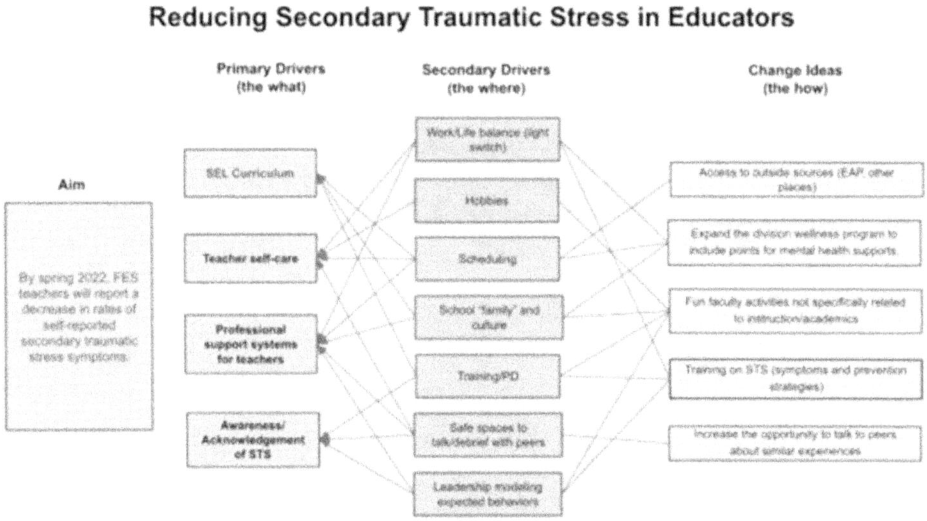

Reducing Secondary Traumatic Stress in Educators

Figure 3.2. Driver Diagram: Reducing STS in Division Educators

could be implemented through Plan-Do-Study-Act (PDSA) cycles to improve the primary drivers of this problem.

We chose to focus our improvement efforts on the change ideas of professional support systems for teachers and awareness and acknowledgment of STS. After consulting the research literature, the team identified specific change initiatives that we thought would impact the two selected primary drivers, including teacher training, opportunities for peer support, and instruction in mindfulness practices.

Specifically, staff would receive instruction on STS signs and symptoms and the importance of self-awareness. Professional skills training would also be offered to teachers to ensure they had the strategies to effectively address students who had experienced trauma. Staff would also be offered education on the practice of mindfulness. Community organizations and nonprofit mindfulness organizations could assist in the training of staff.

CYCLES OF IMPROVEMENT

Given the context and demographics of our division, the PDSA cycles implemented the change ideas of staff training and support that aimed to reduce the impacts of STS on teachers. A detailed timeline of the initial PDSA cycles which includes training session topics, feedback opportunities, and data analysis opportunities is detailed in Figure 3.3.

This timeline allowed for two full PDSA cycles that addressed the primary drivers of STS awareness and professional support systems. Data on participant knowledge and follow-through was collected during each cycle and analyzed by the division research team. The success of the change ideas was measured throughout each cycle

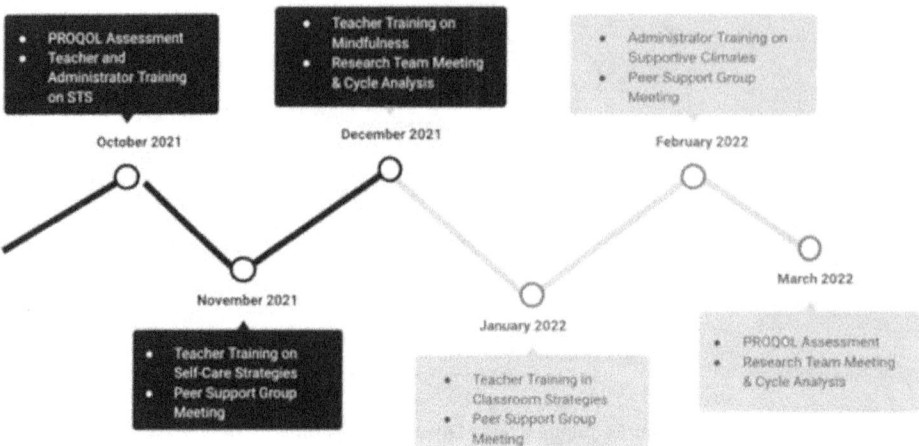

Figure 3.3. Initial Timeline of PDSA Cycles

by the outcome, driver, process, and balance measures to determine if improvements have been achieved and to alter the interventions for the next cycle if needed.

Outcome Measures

The overall aim of our research was for teachers to report a decrease in STS symptoms. This outcome was measured by the Professional Quality of Life (ProQOL) self-assessment tool. The ProQOL measures the experiences of professionals as they work with others who have experienced trauma (Stamm, 2010). The 30-item self-assessment contains three subscales: Compassion Satisfaction (CS), Burnout (BO), and STS. ProQOL is not a diagnostic tool but one that allows individuals to assess their balance between positive and negative experiences within their work. The assessment was given at the beginning of the first PDSA cycle in October and again at the end of March when the second PDSA cycle wrapped up. The results determine if the implementation of the change ideas decreased the STS symptoms experienced by teachers in the division.

Driver Measures

The research team hypothesized that if teachers were engaging in training, self-care activities, and support, they would in turn experience fewer symptoms of STS. To determine if teachers were engaging in the activities, the team designed a weekly log for teachers to track their participation. These electronic logs were short and specific for teachers to easily complete and provide the team with the necessary data to gauge the effectiveness of the change ideas. Teachers used a checkbox to indicate their choice of recent self-care activities and rated their stress level for that week on a scale of 1 (low stress) to 5 (high stress).

Process Measures

The team needed to gather both qualitative and quantitative data on how the change ideas were working. Process measures consisted of data related to teacher participation in the training and support activities. Training sessions were set up to take place during scheduled faculty meetings that staff were expected to attend. The peer support sessions were optional, but the research team needed to consider how many teachers were participating in both opportunities.

At the end of each training episode, the team asked participants to complete an anonymous exit survey with questions related to training content and the implementation of new skills. The exit survey questions asked teachers to share the benefits of the training, additional pieces they would have liked to have seen, and how they saw themselves applying the knowledge they gained. The team used these exit survey responses from the training to determine if the content objectives were being met and if teachers were receptive to implementing the ideas presented.

Balance Measures

Several systems and processes had the potential to be impacted by the implementation of our change ideas. First, our focus on STS could have triggered stress responses in teachers. The extra attention on trauma, mental health, and resilience had the potential to cause anxiety and stress for teachers who may have experienced their own trauma or have their own mental health issues. Reviewing data from the exit surveys, activity logs, and training data was instrumental in determining if the interventions caused additional stress for staff.

Second, acknowledging the importance of self-care could have led to issues with staff performance through attendance or engagement on the job. By learning about the impacts of stress on their physical and mental well-being, staff could establish personal boundaries that began to impact their work performance. Staff attendance data was easily tracked through the division's attendance platform, Frontline. School administrators also tracked data from classroom walkthroughs and observations that would show any performance issues related to the instruction of students who have experienced trauma.

These factors were discussed in weekly meetings with the school administrators. Discussions in these meetings focused on staff attendance and performance as well as areas of staff concern and positive happenings from the week. Similar to the weekly teacher log, conversations in these meetings also included a ranking of the week's stressors to be sure that the implementation of the change ideas was positively impacting the school staff.

Successes and Challenges

We finalized plans for the first PDSA cycle in late spring of 2021. The division experienced a higher-than-normal teacher turnover rate that summer, including two school principals. In addition to the major staffing changes, two days before the start of the 2021–2022 school year, the governor announced a mask mandate for all schools in the state as a result of the COVID-19 pandemic. Hopes had been high that the pandemic would have a decreased impact on the upcoming school year since all students were in-person and attending full time, five days a week. This last-minute change in a highly conservative electoral district created challenges for students and families as well as staff at every level in the division. School board meetings became filled with public comments on the issue and social media was rampant with negative posts directed at our schools and staff.

COVID continued to impact student and staff attendance during the 2021–2022 school year, which caused stress on several systems due to the lack of available substitute teachers. The division experienced an average of 114 absences of teaching staff each month. This frequently led to the reassignment of instructional assistants to fill these vacancies. Teachers felt the impact of this daily as they lost support from the assistants in their classrooms. These challenges led the research team to reconsider the initial timeline and adjust the first round of change ideas to better accommodate the new climate. Figure 3.4 illustrates the actual PDSA timeline that was planned and implemented by our team. Despite the societal changes and edits to our initial plan, the team itself was a measure of success. We had established a trusting, safe environment to share thoughts and ideas which allowed us to pivot our plans and still provide beneficial interventions. Members offered candid feedback on the data which allowed us to cater our improvements to the context of the pandemic.

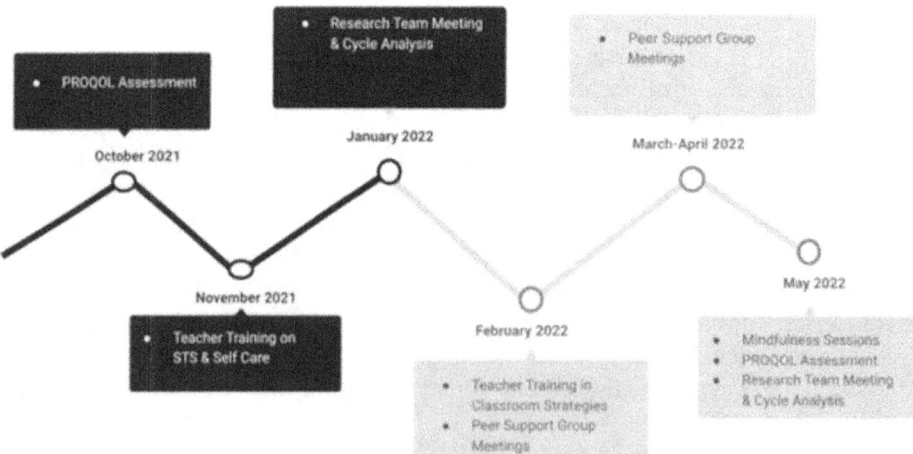

Figure 3.4. Actual Timeline of PDSA Cycles

FINDINGS

PDSA Cycle 1

The project began with a short overview at an early fall faculty meeting. All teaching staff were briefed on the reasons for tackling this problem in the division as well as on the training and optional survey opportunities to inform the work of the research team. After the meeting, staff were emailed the consent form as well as a link to the anonymous ProQOL that would provide a pre-assessment of their self-reported STS levels before engaging in the interventions.

The first training on self-awareness and secondary traumatic stress was held at a subsequent virtual faculty meeting in front of all staff and was conducted by a local therapy provider. The training included a reference to the ProQOL as well as a detailed description and rating scale related to teachers' compassion satisfaction, burnout, and secondary traumatic stress. Following this initial training event, anonymous exit surveys were delivered to staff via email, and the results were analyzed by the research team to help inform the next cycle.

Findings from Cycle 1

The initial ProQOL results, shown in Table 3.1, indicated that the majority of participants were experiencing moderate to high levels of both burnout and secondary traumatic stress. The majority were also experiencing moderate to high levels of compassion satisfaction with their work, which research indicates can be a protective factor against secondary traumatic stress (Borntrager et al., 2017; Caringi et al., 2015; Koenig et al., 2017).

Table 3.1. Fall 2021 ProQOL Results

	High	Moderate	Low
Burnout	4%	88%	8%
Compassion Satisfaction	63%	29%	8%
Secondary Traumatic Stress	50%	42%	8%

The research team also analyzed the exit survey data to determine the effectiveness of the first training session. Generally, the feedback on the training was positive and the majority of respondents noted their appreciation for the knowledge and strategies that were provided. Many teachers also expressed their interest in more tools for supporting their mental health and noted that they could see themselves implementing the activities that were presented. As one participant stated,

> I am going to start making myself a priority and setting professional boundaries. I have gotten better at this but I still struggle. The PD just helped me realize that it is acceptable to do this. I really liked the self-love portion of the PD as well. It helped me come up with some things that may help me at school.

There were a handful of comments that were more critical of the experience and helped the team understand that one training was not going to be beneficial for everyone. Those responses focused on the problems in the education system as a whole and indicated that teachers did not find value in being told to take care of themselves. One participant stated, "Bringing to light issues we feel every second of every day did not feel beneficial; if anything it further highlighted the gap between how we feel and the problems not being addressed in the first place."

As a result, the research team concluded that there was most definitely a continued need for this work but that we would need to shift some factors for the next cycle, including the use of the term "wellness" in place of the term "self-care."

PDSA Cycle 2

Using the information from the first PDSA cycle, the research team decided that future work would be better received at voluntary sessions, not the pre-established faculty meeting dates where all staff would be forced to participate. The second cycle of interventions followed the research recommendations on peer support groups and the practice of mindfulness. Both opportunities would be held at regularly scheduled times over several months so that teachers could join as their schedules allowed.

The peer support sessions were designed with our local community service board to provide an opportunity for teachers to receive support from licensed professionals, as well as their colleagues, in a safe and informal setting. The sessions were named "Teacher2Teacher: Caring for Ourselves, Caring for Each Other" and were held virtually, every other week for three months in the spring of 2022. Counselors from our local community service board led the sessions, which were only open to instructional staff. Administrators were asked not to attend so that the teachers and instructional assistants could feel comfortable speaking freely about topics that were causing them stress.

In the past, we had offered a free mindfulness class for staff each fall through a partnership with a local nonprofit organization. The class required a large time commitment, including several half-day retreats. The research team wanted to offer staff a less formal way to learn about the practice of mindfulness and its benefits to personal wellness. Working with the local organization, the research team planned weekly mindfulness sessions over six weeks to introduce the concept of mindfulness as well as assist staff in developing a personal practice.

During this second cycle, the research team also began collecting regular data from staff and administrators to measure the overall impact of these sessions. Every two weeks, instructional staff were emailed the short wellness logs described in the driver measures section above. While the team initially planned to distribute these anonymous logs each week, informal reflection on the current state of teacher well-being resulted in distribution every other week.

In addition to gathering feedback from instructional staff, the team was also interested in how these activities were impacting the overall operations of the school. These check-ins were held in person and allowed the administrators to rate the weekly stress level in the building and also reflect on the highs and lows of the week. For comparison, these administrator check-ins were conducted every two weeks along with the distribution of the teacher wellness logs.

The cycle concluded with another administration of the ProQOL scale to determine the change in self-reported levels of STS after being exposed to the training and wellness opportunities. Teachers were once again emailed the consent form with a link to participate in the anonymous rating scale.

Findings from Cycle 2

The second PDSA cycle provided the research team with ample amounts of data to analyze and study. Overall, the feedback on the Teacher2Teacher sessions was particularly positive and several teachers even returned for multiple meetings with the group. After each session, the facilitators and research team debriefed the feedback they received. There was some concern that the sessions were taking a negative tone, so an agenda was developed for the third session that included time for teachers to share a struggle and success as well as time for the staff from the local organization leading the sessions to share specific behavior research and strategies for discussion. Data from the exit surveys show that this change made a positive impact on the participants and their overall experience for the remainder of the sessions. Participant comments centered on the opportunity to affirm that they were not the only ones struggling with the school year. Several participants noted appreciation for the classroom strategies that were shared while remarking on the continued need for more specific ideas to help them cope with the daily stressors of teaching. Participants also seemed grateful for the strategies that were shared in the sessions. One participant stated, "They shared a chart of the 'whys' behind some behaviors with suggestions on how to respond to those behaviors. I've already printed it. I also want to try some of the kindness activities they shared." While no identifying information was collected from the participants of these sessions, session leaders shared that the majority of educators were from early childhood and primary grade levels.

Although fewer teachers participated in the mindfulness sessions than participated in the Teacher2Teacher meetings, their feedback was also generally positive and appreciative of the knowledge that they gained during the experience. The research on mindfulness as a stress reducer and resilience builder was confirmed by participants in the exit surveys as many noted their renewed focus and excitement to learn more. One participant shared their "renewed focus and awareness; excitement for more."

Data from the biweekly wellness logs indicated that 60% of staff completed the logs, and, of that percentage, 93% reported that they were engaging in some type of wellness activity. The top three activities logged by staff were watching a movie or television show, spending time with loved ones, and going for a walk. Interestingly, the average stress rating scales reported by staff on the logs mirrored the rise and fall noted by administrators in their check-ins, although it was slightly higher than the score given by the school administration as noted in Figure 3.5.

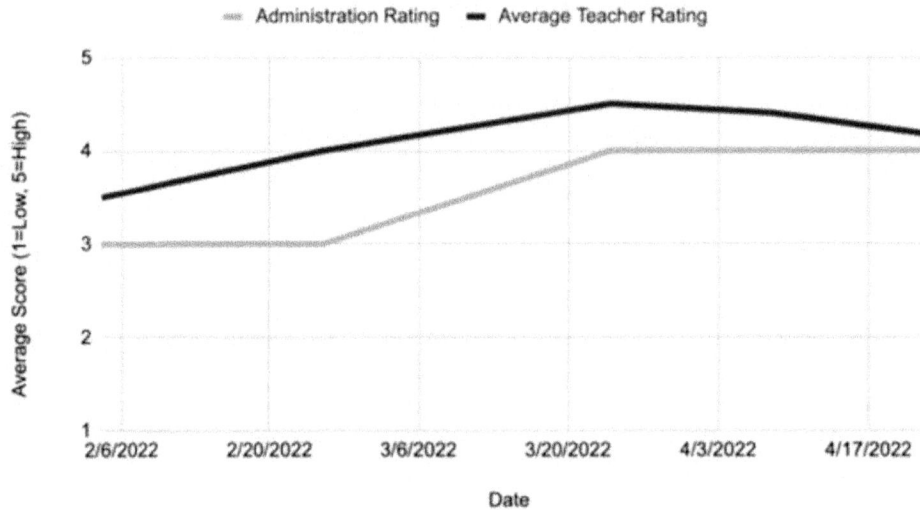

Figure 3.5. Average Teacher and Administrator Weekly Stress Rating

The research team concluded that the rise in stress toward the end of March could not be attributed to any single activity but rather multiple factors including the long stretch of school days without a break, the oncoming state testing window, the removal of the mask mandate, and some ongoing issues staff were reporting with the new administration.

Staff engagement with the activities was a challenge in this work. No more than 12 staff members attended a Teacher2Teacher session and no more than six attended a mindfulness session. Participation in the wellness logs also saw a decline with approximately 30 staff members participating for the first two surveys and about half that number participating after that data collection. The research team felt this may be the result of the optional nature of the intervention activities, but we felt that the personal nature of the intervention offerings was best served to a voluntary audience at the time.

The outcome data from the May 2022 administration of the ProQOL, shown in Table 3.2, shows that none of the staff reported high levels of burnout or STS and that all of the participants in the survey reported moderate or high levels of compassion satisfaction in their work as an educator. In comparison to the fall data, there was a large decrease in the level of STS reported by teachers, which was a primary goal of the PDSA cycles. The levels of burnout were also reduced throughout the year, but the research team concluded that this may be reflective of the fact that teacher stress level in May is naturally lower with summer break on the horizon. There is some concern that the level of compassion satisfaction fell throughout the year for the participants as this indicates fewer staff members are deriving pleasure from their work or feeling effective in their job as an educator.

Table 3.2. Fall 2021 and Spring 2022 ProQOL Results

	October 2021 (24 Participants)			May 2022 (15 Participants)		
	High	Moderate	Low	High	Moderate	Low
Burnout	4%	88%	8%	0%	73%	27%
Compassion Satisfaction	63%	29%	8%	47%	53%	0%
Secondary Traumatic Stress	50%	42%	8%	0%	87%	13%

LESSONS LEARNED

Our view of educator mental health and wellness is much sharper than it was when this work began several years ago. Our work has affirmed the initial belief that teachers are impacted by not only STS but by various other physical and psychological stressors as they fulfill their daily responsibilities. The research team learned quickly to classify our work as "teacher wellness" or "teacher well-being." Other terms such as "self-care" and "self-help" seemed to trigger more negative responses from our teachers and imply that the burden of care fell on individuals rather than the system. We also felt that a general wellness approach could encompass more than just interventions for STS in the future. We want our teachers to be healthy, happy, and effective both inside and outside their classrooms.

In addition to the importance of word choice, we learned that one size does not fit all in the approach to teacher wellness. Feedback on each training session or opportunity was scattered between strong positive and strong negative feelings. What works for some teachers clearly will not always work for all. Just like our students, we will need to differentiate our strategies and offer a variety of options for their well-being. Most importantly, our team learned that this work must continue. The variety and intensity of responses to our work illustrate that this is a topic that needs continued focus and effort.

The research team also walked away with a renewed appreciation for the improvement science approach to problem-solving. The tools and processes used in this project allowed us to examine the problem and plan interventions during the uncertainty of the COVID-19 pandemic. The ever-changing context and unique perspectives of educators made it challenging to simply move from one planned step to the next during this time. Rather, it was more beneficial to slow down and let the data speak to when staff were ready for the next steps and to inform what those next steps should be. By moving slower, thoroughly examining the problem, engaging with stakeholders, and working within the context of our division, we brought about sustainable changes to the way we support our teachers.

Chapter 4

Leading Change in the Overrepresentation of Students of Color in Special Education

Shanice Harrington, EdD

The disproportionate representation of minoritized students in special education and their overrepresentation in more restrictive placements and in discipline are important and unresolved issues in our system of public education (Albrecht et al., 2011). According to Frattura and Capper (2021), intra-school segregation has perpetuated the marginalization of, and inappropriate educational service delivery to students and families of color, families living in poverty, and those who are linguistically diverse. Students who are identified with a disability, as homeless, as in need of addiction services, as second language learners, or as "at-risk" students are more likely to be removed from the core of teaching and learning where students who identify with the characteristics of the dominant group (e.g., white, middle to upper class, nondisabled, English speaking) are taught (Frattura & Capper, 2021).

The public school system is centered on whiteness around a socially constructed white norm. In the *Journal of Educational Supervision*, *whiteness* is defined as "an assemblage, a racial discourse or perspective supported by material practices and institutions, which exists as a historically and socially developed construct based on oppressions, power, and falsehood" (Lynch, 2018). The *white norm* casts out those who do not assimilate to it or meet its expectations. These outside spaces—many of which are structured under the guise of special education—include remediation programs, intervention programs, and ability grouping within classrooms. Although research has shown that segregated learning spaces have not improved academic outcomes, educators continue to provide educational services in these spaces because they assume it is best for the students assigned to those spaces. Students of color (SoC) are often overrepresented in these contexts, because those assigning educational services are often white female educators who view student differences (attributes outside of the socially constructed norm) as disabilities or disorders (Frattura & Capper, 2021). In doing so, they reinforce both a white and a nondisabled normative.

Research has also shown that students receiving special education services are often denied access to high-quality teaching and learning afforded to their nondisabled peers (Griner & Stewart, 2012). Access is denied when students are removed from the core of teaching and learning and sent to an outside space to learn. A lack of access to high-quality instruction is detrimental to student success in education and, consequentially, in life. Specifically, as noted in *Schools Are Still Segregated, and Black Children Are Paying the Price*, denying SoC access to high-quality instruction perpetuates a cycle of depressed outcomes, which can include involvement in the criminal justice system and reliance on public support (Garcia, 2020). Depressed outcomes for SoC have been linked to disproportionate representation in special education programs. Depressed outcomes include the school-to-prison pipeline (Frattura & Capper, 2021), higher school drop-out rates (Losen & Orfield, 2002), and the ever-growing racial academic achievement gap (Garcia, 2020).

THE CONTEXT

Southeast Elementary School (SES) is in the Hope School District. The district lies within a larger county, but it stands independently. The majority of the residents in Hope School District are affluent and either Asian or white. SoC, for this study, make up 34.2 percent (Black 11.2%, Hispanic 16.4%, multiracial 6.6%) of the total student population in the district. Figure 4.1 provides a chart to visualize student demographics in the district during the 2017–2018 school year.

Teachers of color have been disproportionately represented in this district for several years. Between 2012 and 2019, teachers of color represented between 13–14% of teachers in the district, while white teachers represented between 86–87%. Figure 4.2 illustrates the representation of white teachers and Black teachers from 2012 to 2019.

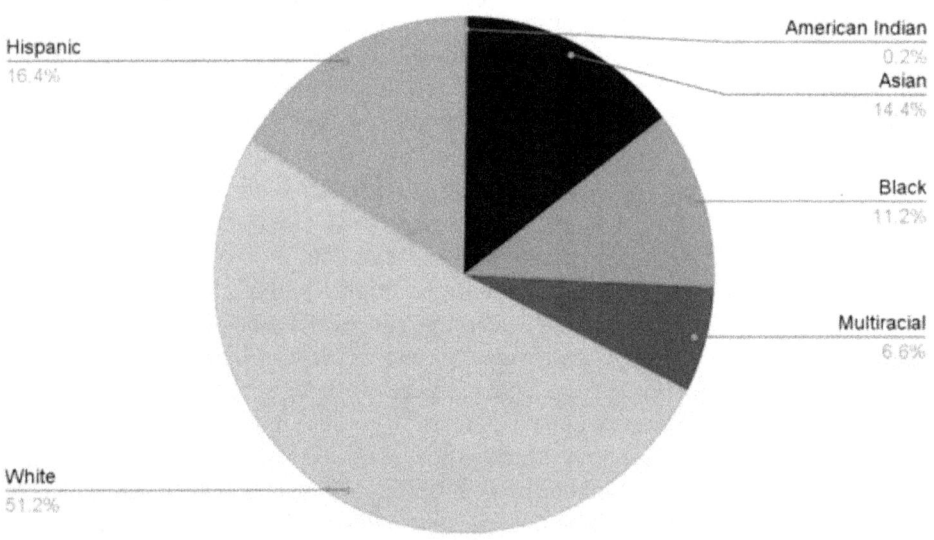

Figure 4.1. Student Demographics in 2017–2018

Leading Change in the Overrepresentation of Students of Color in Special Education 81

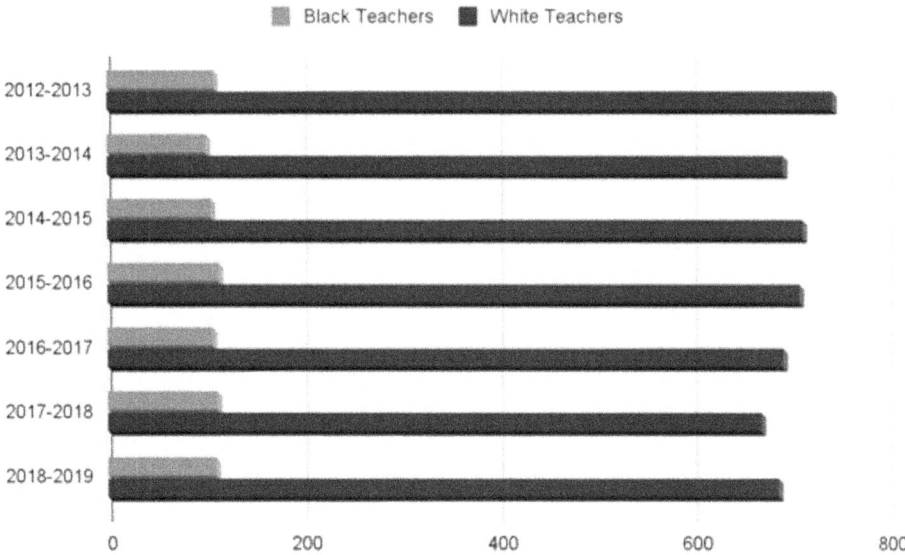

Figure 4.2. Comparison of Black and White Teachers in Hope School District

The disproportionate representation of teachers makes one wonder whether it is connected to the district's high achievement gap between white and Black students. Could the lack of understanding of cultural differences by white teachers have led to the overrepresentation of SoC in special education? Studies have shown that in affluent school districts with fewer African American children, the percentage of African American children labeled as needing special education was reported to be higher or disproportionate. Similar concerns have been reported for Latinos (Zamora, 2007).

To determine if there's a disproportionate representation of SoC, a school psychologist of Hope School District compiled a list of students who had been receiving special education services during the 2017–2018 school year at Southeast Elementary School. When the data were compiled, no names were used, only the date of referral and racial identification. The data were disaggregated, focusing only on racial groups that had two or more students represented. Specifically, the data were disaggregated by categories of Hispanic/Latino, Black, and white for comparison purposes. While Black and Hispanic/Latino students both represent SoC, the team separated them to analyze the data to see if there was a disproportionate representation of both groups separately.

In column A of Table 4.1, the racial identities of SoC (Black, Hispanic/Latino) and white students are listed. In column B, the numerical value and percentage of the total population for each racial identification is listed. Next, column C provides the numerical value and percentage of students represented in each racial identification. Column D represents the numerical representation and percentage of students if representation were proportional. It is important to note that students who are not accounted for in the total of students identified as needing special education services do not identify as white, Black, or Hispanic/Latino. For this study and investigating a problem of practice, only the SoC and white students were identified for comparison purposes.

Table 4.1. Southeast Elementary School's Special Education Population

Column A	Column B	Column C	Column D
Racial Identification	Makeup of the Total Population	Identified as Special Education	Target Proportional Representation
Black	67 students or 12%	18 students or 27%	8 students or 17%
Hispanic/Latino	51 students or 10%	8 students or 16%	6 students or 13%
White	235 students or 43%	20 students or 9%	28 students or 10%

Note. Total population of students = 551 students; total number of students receiving special education = 46

Figure 4.3 illustrates the data in Table 4.1 in the form of a graph to provide a visual representation of the data. As it can be concluded by the data represented in both Table 4.1 and Figure 4.3, a disproportionate representation of SoC in special education does, indeed, exist as compared to their white peers. The data shows that, of the 67 Black students (12%) enrolled at Southeast Elementary, 18 students received special education services, which is 27% of the total population. For Hispanic students, of the 51 students (10%), 8 students received special education services, which is 16% of the population. Last, for white students, of 235 students (43%), 20 students received special education services, which is only 9% of the population. To maintain proportionality, subgroup populations should be less than or equal to 12–13% of the total population. Figure 4.4 provides a representation of what the subgroup population representation should have been if representation was proportional.

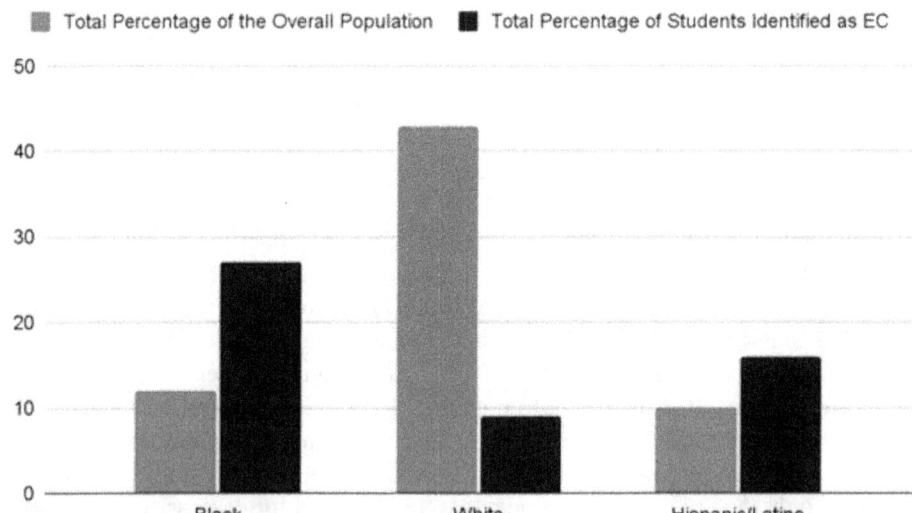

Figure 4.3. Southeast Elementary School Special Education Student Representation 2017–2018

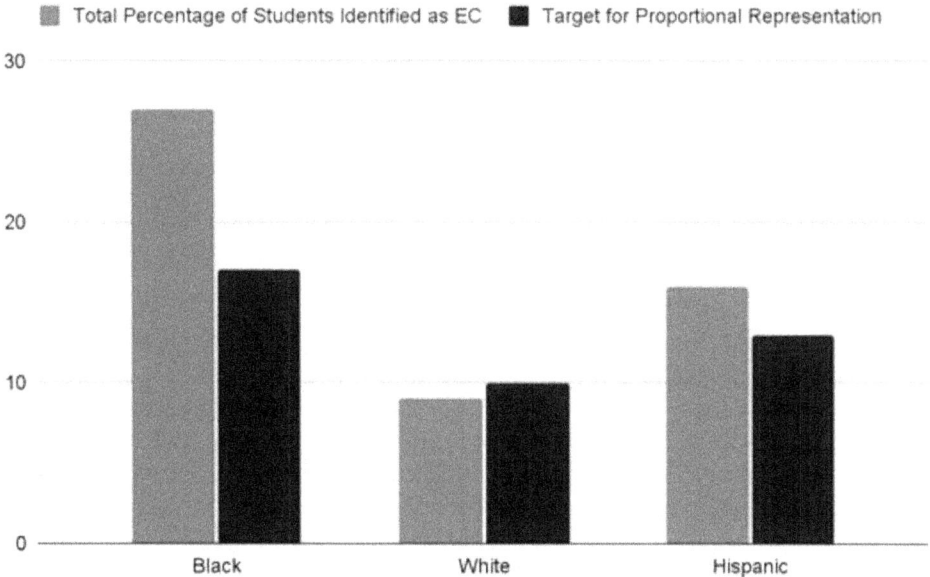

Figure 4.4. Proportional Representation for Southeast Elementary Special Education Students 2017–2018

Equity Initiatives in the District

The school district has made intentional efforts to address inequities that are often faced by historically marginalized students. The district has an Office of Equity and Engagement, which has a mission to "work to eliminate inequities by disrupting systems that have historically marginalized students through empowerment and district support." Among the department, there is an Equity Advisory Council, which has a mission to engage, inspire, and empower parental participation and collaboration with the district's Board of Education and district administrators to improve the quality of education for traditionally underserved students district-wide (Equity and Engagement/Equity and Inclusion Overview, n.d.).

As a part of the district's work to address racial disparities for SoC, they have adopted the incorporation of the *Students' Six* (Meyer & Davis, 2012). The Students' Six process took shape when a troubling trend became apparent: the overall performance on standardized tests and other achievement measurements was high. However, when the data were broken down by race and ethnicity, SoC were left behind (Schwartz, 2014). The overall goal was to create more culturally sensitive classrooms for students and teachers. Students' Six was not developed to be a product or resource but, instead, a process built on facilitating open communication between students and teachers. Furthermore, the strategies have a central idea that students have a lot to teach teachers when it comes to addressing issues like race, racial justice, racial dynamics, and cultural sensitivity in the classroom. The Equity Collaborative (2021) upholds the following pillars as The Students' Six:

1. Be visible
2. Proximity/create a safe space
3. Connect to students' lives
4. Connect to students' culture
5. Address race and racial dynamics in the classroom
6. Connect to students' future selves

THE PROBLEM

In my earlier years as an educator, I served in the role of a general education teacher. In this role, I had the privilege of working with a diverse population of students. One of the observations that I made was that many of my SoC entered my classroom either being served under the provisions of an individualized education plan (IEP) through special education or they were identified as requiring tier 3 intervention; the most intensive support a student can receive within the Multitiered System of Support (MTSS) Framework. Within my classroom setting, I provided core instruction that ensured every student could find their entry point to access the general curriculum, aligning with my philosophy that all students can learn. Though this was my belief in my small sector of the overall school and district, it was apparent to me that SoC continued to enter my class, each year, disproportionately represented in special education. Being in a district where SoC represented a small fraction of the overall population, I realized that this was a potential problem. I began to serve as a mentor to SoC in affinity groups and made an intentional effort to make SoC feel like they had a community within the school in which they felt valued and successful. Building relationships with students and celebrating their successes, within school or outside of school, was one of my most effective approaches. Despite my efforts to support students and encourage colleagues to do the same, the cycle of overidentification for SoC in special education was continuous. Even as a special education resource teacher after five years in the general education setting, I worked tirelessly to help SoC achieve their goals and exit from needing special education services.

After 10 years in education, I see this cycle continuing in my local context, though I know, wholeheartedly, that SoC are capable of success, just as their white peers. I have arrived at the point of wondering, is it that the students are not able to access the curriculum, or is it that the teachers that are serving the students have a perspective that sets a barrier for students before they even have a chance?

PROBLEM INQUIRY AND ANALYSIS

In an attempt to dig deeper and understand the potential causes of the overrepresentation of SoC in special education at Southeast Elementary School, I met with a team of eight elementary school teachers. There was a representative from all grades (K–5), as well as an exceptional children's (EC) teacher, PE teacher, and art teacher.

I interviewed them in a group setting, posing the question, "Based on your experience and observations, what do you believe to be the potential causes of the overrepresentation of SoC in special education?" I captured their responses on the fishbone diagram. According to Bryk and coauthors (2015), a fishbone diagram is a tool that assists in visually representing causes for analysis. Each major bone represents a key factor thought to contribute to the problem (located in the head of the fish). The smaller bones capture the details that emerge from conversations about these factors (Bryk et al., 2015). Figure 4.5 illustrates the fishbone diagram theorizing six possible contributing factors to the disproportionate representation of SoC in special education, including (1) classroom management, (2) quality instruction, (3) professional development, (4) MTSS infrastructure, (5) parent-school engagement, (6) trauma-sensitive awareness. Although six potential causes were identified in the fishbone diagram, I will focus on the cause most closely related to the improvement initiative: culturally relevant teaching and professional development to support it.

There are two intersecting problems at the heart of this problem of practice: (1) special education, as it presently operates, often denies students identified with disabilities access to high-quality teaching and learning through the provision of segregated service delivery or removal from the core; and (2) SoC are often inappropriately and disproportionately assigned to special education services, denying them access to high-quality, culturally relevant teaching and learning.

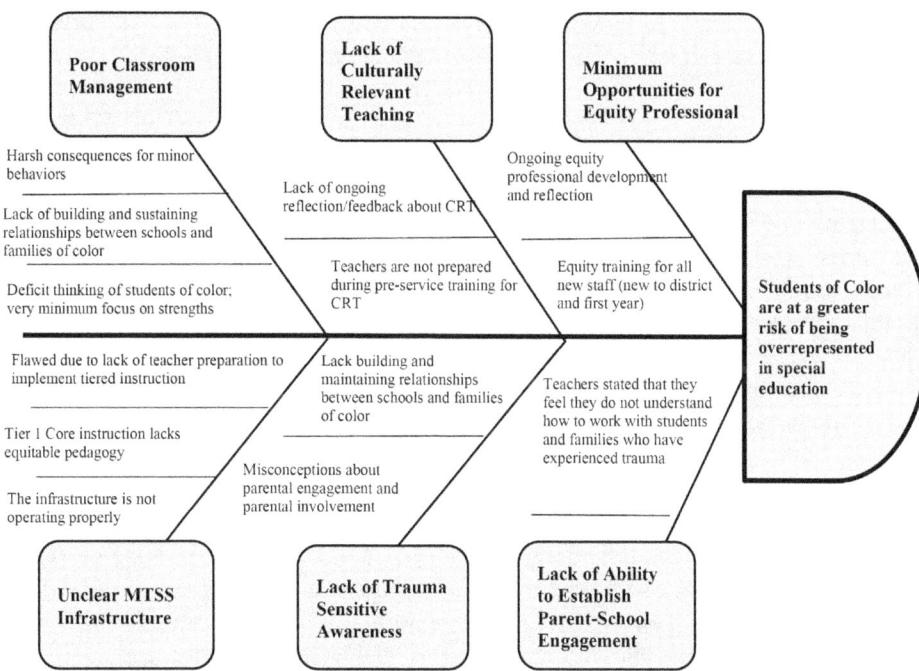

Figure 4.5. Fishbone Causal Analysis

CULTURALLY RELEVANT TEACHING

In education, culturally responsive teaching is often used interchangeably with culturally relevant teaching. There are varying definitions of each term and though they have similarities, there are differences (Muniz, 2019). Each approach strives to achieve the same goal: to defy the deficit model and ensure SoC see themselves and their communities reflected and valued in the content taught in school. Preeminent scholars in the field of equity in education; Gloria Ladson-Billings, Geneva Gay, and Zaretta Hammond, all uniquely define culturally relevant or culturally responsive pedagogy in their literature.

Ultimately, I wanted to focus on building teachers' capacity to enact culturally relevant curriculum and pedagogy, which is aligned with the works of Gloria Ladson-Billings. Culturally relevant pedagogy is described as more of a way of being or thinking that then manifests into ways of doing (Escudero, 2019). It is not something that has a prescription or a "box to check off" when one claims to be culturally relevant. Instead, it is a perspective, or mindset, that builds the foundation for how educators approach every aspect of their instructional practice. Furthermore, it cannot be simplified to "a set of specific strategies, a checklist for lesson planning, or specific curriculum because all of these must be directly connected to and informed by a teacher's specific set of students who they are as people and as learners, their communities, their history, and their context" (Escudero, 2019). Before this work can be done with fidelity, educators have to reflect on their own identity, culture, biases, and privilege to critically assess and strengthen their instructional practice (Escudero, 2019).

A Lack of Culturally Relevant Teaching

When schools and classrooms lack culturally relevant teaching practices, it becomes detrimental for SoC. It also supports the notion that schools are not designed to meet the needs of all children. According to Capper and Frattura (2021), historically, schools have been designed to teach to a normed group of students (e.g., white, nondisabled, English-speaking, middle to upper class). Not only does a normed system identify what is normal, but it also designates what is not normal. If students do not share the identities or assimilate with the normed group, they are treated differently and often denied the access and opportunity offered to their normal peers (Capper & Frattura, 2008). Since assimilation to the normed group was a widespread expectation in schools, tracking became a means of sorting through growing numbers of students according to race, disability, class, or language. When students were not able to assimilate to the norm of their white, nondisabled, and English-speaking peers, the perception was the child had deficits beyond what could be addressed in the core of teaching and learning (Gorski, 2011). Furthermore, Capper and Frattura (2021) state that "marginalized students who are at risk of being identified for special education are often students who are experiencing societal poverty. Due to a perception of schools that poverty is a challenge outside of the school's control, schools often become complicit in generating and perpetuating societal poverty."

Research findings have identified the root causes for overidentification in special education as the lack of culturally competent teachers, low socioeconomic status, curriculum that is not culturally relevant, and a need for professional development on equity (Ford, 2012). Specifically, when educators cannot implement culturally relevant teaching practices, there's a potential risk of minimizing SoC maintaining cultural integrity (Ladson-Billings, 1995). This often leads to schools being perceived as a place that is hostile as SoC feel they cannot be themselves as their culture (i.e., style of dress and vernacular) is looked upon as inappropriate since it does not fit within the white norm (Hollins, 1994; King, 1994).

When teachers' perceptions include implicit biases toward SoC's learning abilities, they often lean toward their beliefs that they cannot learn, leading to lower expectations. This ultimately leads to the notion that SoC need something extra, the notion that core instruction is impossible for them to access without the support of an intervention or specially designed instruction from special education services.

SERVICE DELIVERY MODELS: MULTITIERED SYSTEMS OF SUPPORT

In addition to the design of programs to separate students of marginalized populations, there was the formation of the Response to Intervention (RtI) Framework. This framework, now replaced with the MTSS, is a process of systematically documenting the performance of students as evidence of the need for additional services after making changes in classroom instruction. MTSS promises to change the way schools support students with learning and behavioral problems by systematically delivering a range of interventions based on demonstrated levels of need (Park et al., 2016).

To ensure students are receiving instruction to best meet their needs, there are clearly defined tiers of instruction. For MTSS, tier 1 instruction is the core curriculum that is taught, what "all" students get. Tier 2 instruction takes place when students have challenges with tier 1 instruction. Under tier 2, students meet with teachers, for example, in a small group within the classroom setting to support their progress toward goals in tier 1 instruction. Tier 3 instruction is more intensive support. It can take place in very small groups or individually and usually with one of the school's interventionists. When students do not respond to additional support provided at the tier 2 level, they are referred to the tier 3 team. At this point, the MTSS team collaborates to determine the best-fit interventions for the student to be able to overcome significant barriers to be able to achieve tier 1 proficiency.

The term "tier 1" refers to core instruction that is offered to all students. Effective tier 1 core instruction is generally understood as instruction that is supported by research evidence (Shapiro, n.d.). It is usually provided in a classroom setting where the standard course of study is delivered. Unfortunately, tier 1 is often a place reserved for students who fit the norm. Teachers in these spaces may not see themselves as responsible for (or capable of) teaching students who are not thriving in these spaces. This can be reinforced by the existence of other tiers, especially if they are associated with separate instructors and spaces. Research supports keeping students in the classroom (Siegal, 2007). Removing them often communicates who is a competent learner and who is not (Steele & Aronson, 2018). Research suggests that what we seek is a heterogeneous classroom where students are not removed and teachers can teach to a wide range of learners given support and continued learning from other educators and specialists (Capper, 2018). Continued learning topics should include pedagogical practices like culturally relevant teaching.

CHANGE IDEAS AND INTERVENTIONS

This problem of practice is informed by three primary theoretical frameworks: critical race theory, whiteness studies, and critical disabilities theory. All three theoretical frameworks demonstrate the challenges faced when race and disability intersect for individuals, specifically for SoC in public school, which is centered on white norms. They collectively illuminate the complexity of oppressions that lead to the disproportionality of SoC in special education. Each theory presents a unique perspective on the impact that race plays on how opportunities differ for students in education. The intersectionality of disability and critical race theory, also known as DisCrit, explores how racial identification can impact the likelihood of being identified as disabled. Furthermore, in a system where teachers are predominantly white females, Matias (2015) emphasizes that they should begin to shoulder some of the burden of race to increase the likelihood that they will stop emotionally projecting their feelings of guilt or discomfort onto SoC.

Design Team

The design team was a team at McHill Elementary, another elementary school in the Hope School District which was impacted by a disproportional representation of SoC in special education. During the time of implementation of the improvement initiative, I served in two different roles. Initially, I served in the role of a special education resource teacher (at SES) during the time that I collected data to determine if the problem of practice was indeed a problem of practice. Shortly thereafter, I transitioned to the role of EC (Exceptional Children's) Program Facilitator at McHill Elementary. Though I was serving in a new role at a different school within the district, after inquiring into the problem at SES, I noticed similar problems at McHill Elementary. Therefore, the improvement initiative was implemented at McHill and not SES.

After careful exploration of leadership teams, committees, and grade-level professional learning communities at McHill Elementary, as the researcher, I decided to inquire with the equity committee about designing the improvement initiative. These individuals were selected to participate on the design team due to their knowledge of the equity goals of the school district, their extensive training related to having courageous conversations about race, and their capacity to apply an equity lens to bring forth change for SoC. There were a total of 12 members on the team. The members of the equity committee included: one pre-K teacher, two kindergarten teachers, one second grade teacher, two third grade teachers, one fourth grade teacher, one fifth grade teacher, one special education teacher, one Spanish teacher, one English as second language teacher, and the school social worker.

The role of the design team was to coordinate the specific dates for which the professional development (PD) sessions would take place and gather baseline data (via surveys) from teacher participants before the beginning of the improvement initiative. Specifically, the design team focused on the three fundamental questions of the model for improvement to guide their work (Langley, 2014):

1. What are we trying to accomplish?
2. How will we know that the change is an improvement?
3. What change can we make that will result in improvement?

Using these questions supported efforts to ensure clarity about the specific problem we were trying to solve (question 1), demanded some reasoned explanation about the particular changes to be attempted and what we expect these changes to accomplish (question 2), and last, to ensure that we relied on data to know if changes introduced were an improvement, not relying on our own ideas (question 3) (Bryk et al., 2015).

The design team met to define the purpose of the work of strengthening core instruction. The team also determined the portion of the district's instructional framework that is aligned to addressing culturally relevant teaching practices. In addition, the team identified the equitable practices that were connected with the specific instructional framework that was focused on. The instructional framework addresses environment, planning, instruction, and assessment. See Appendix A for each instructional framework.

Participants

Participants were general education teachers at McHill Elementary School in Hope School District—recruited at the beginning of the 2021–2022 academic school year. The term "general education" teacher refers to the teacher responsible for providing instruction in the core curriculum. The general education teacher is also responsible for collaborating with the special education teacher to provide an inclusive learning experience for both students with disabilities and students not identified with disabilities. Participants were willing, noncoerced volunteers. Consent was obtained from participants via a digital informed consent document embedded in a recruitment email. The number of participants in the improvement initiative was proposed to be no more than ten participants. This was an intentional approach to establish a professional learning community amongst participants with the focus of student learning (for all students) at the core of the improvement initiative. Through the improvement initiative, participants were provided with an opportunity to work collaboratively with one another to share ideas and brainstorm how they can improve their practices for SoC to access the general curriculum. As the researcher, I shared how the initiative aligned with the work of the school district, Student Success Goal, see Figure 4.6, so that the team acknowledged how this work is supportive of a larger goal to move our district forward.

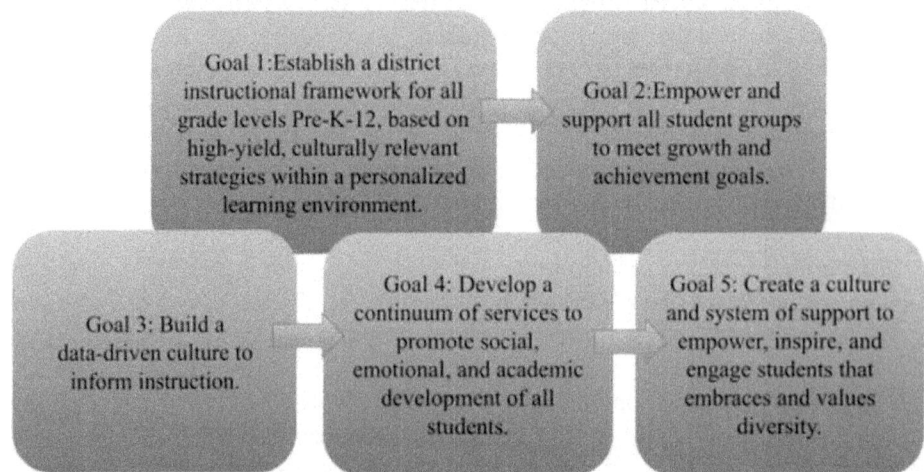

Figure 4.6. Hope School District Strategic Plan: Student Success Goals

IMPLEMENTATION TEAM

The purpose of the implementation team was to gather diverse individuals who collectively have the expertise and a wide range of experiences and perspectives necessary to implement the evidence-based practices of the initiative. In addition, they served the purpose of developing and maintaining the system and infrastructures to support effective and equitable implementation (Frank Porter Graham Child Development Institute, n.d.). The implementation team was composed of select members of the equity committee. On the implementation team, there was one member from each grade level (preK to fifth grade), as well as one special education teacher, one ESL teacher, a school counselor, a school psychologist, and the school social worker.

The purpose of designing the implementation team in this way is to have a representative from each grade level and a representative from multiple departments. With representation from various departments within the organization, we can incorporate a variety of perspectives. Table 4.2 includes the improvement initiative implementation schedule. The schedule captures each initiative, task, and the month that it was implemented. Initiatives included design team meetings, gathering of baseline data, targeted professional development, reflection, and impact of professional learning.

My theory of improvement holds that raising awareness about disproportionality and providing teachers with formalized professional development on culturally relevant teaching, will increase teacher capacity and efficacy to enact culturally relevant practices throughout core instruction thus reducing the likelihood of referrals of SoC to special education. At the beginning of this improvement initiative, I posited that such professional development would keep more SoC in the classroom thus ensuring access to the core and higher quality teaching and learning.

Figure 4.7 illustrates the ultimate and immediate aim of the proposed improvement initiative as well as primary and secondary drivers in the form of a driver diagram.

Table 4.2. Improvement Initiative Implementation Schedule

Change Initiative Implementation & Evaluation Timeline

Initiative	Task	Sept.	Oct.	Nov.	Dec.	Jan.	Feb.
Design Team Meeting 1. The design team will meet to define the purpose of the work of strengthening core instruction	Define the "why"	X					
Gather Baseline Data 1. Assess participant knowledge of Culturally Relevant Teaching and Implicit Bias/Disproportionality prior to the targeted professional development	Baseline Assessment Outcome Measure	X					
Targeted Professional Learning 1. Participants will engage in professional learning, raising awareness about the disproportionality of SoC in special education 2. Participants will engage in professional learning, acknowledging bias 3. Participants will engage in professional learning focused on strengthening core instruction to be culturally relevant	Plan, Do, Intervention Component		X				
Reflection 1. Participants will reflect on their own bias 2. Participants will reflect on aspects of their own teaching practices that can be improved to incorporate culturally relevant teaching practices in their core instruction	Study Process Measure			X	X	X	
Impact of Professional Learning 1. Participants will complete a post-survey to assess their learning before and after implementation of the change initiative 2. Participants will utilize a CRT checklist to monitor their implementation of culturally relevant teaching in their core instruction 3. Participants will monitor their referrals to intervention and special education teams	Act Outcome Measure, Balancing Measure			X	X	X	

Bryk and colleagues (2015) define a driver diagram as a tool that organizes the various changes a network is trying out. It gives participants a common language as they build toward a solution to a shared problem. The diagram focuses on a small set of hypotheses about key levers for improvement, specific changes that might be attempted for each, and the interconnections that may exist among them. The driver diagram consists of a measurable improvement aim, primary drivers, secondary drivers, and change ideas (Bryk et al., 2015).

It was my immediate aim for teachers to increase their capacity to deliver tier 1 instruction with culturally relevant practices to meet a wide range of needs in the classroom and reduce referrals (support services or discipline) for all students. Primary drivers are a set of small improvement hypotheses that are the best initial bets for what to target in the context of improvement (Bryk et al., 2015). Specifically, for strengthening core instruction, the primary drivers are teacher accountability, school culture and climate, school-community connectedness, and human resources. Primary drivers are too general to guide change; therefore, each primary driver is associated with a secondary driver. For this improvement initiative, the secondary driver is professional development that focuses on culturally relevant teaching. Griner and Stewart (2012) stated that culturally relevant practices in schools and classrooms are an effective means of addressing the disproportionate representation of racially, culturally, ethnically, and linguistically diverse students in programs serving students with special needs.

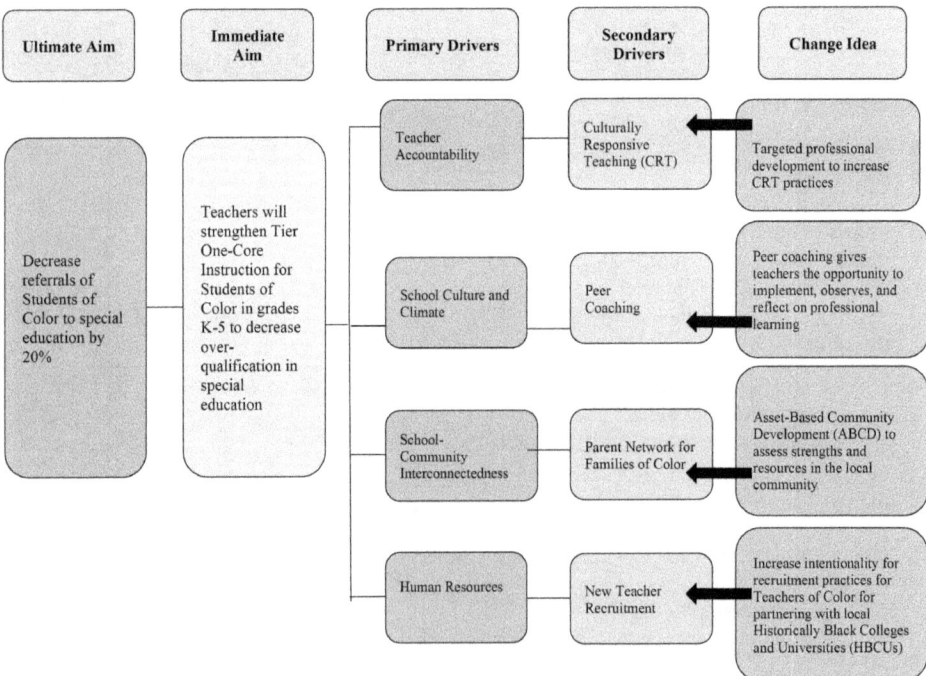

Figure 4.7. Driver Diagram

I chose to focus on the intermediate goal of building teacher capacity to implement culturally relevant teaching as some studies have concluded that "the root causes for overidentification in special education are the lack of culturally competent teachers, low socioeconomic status, curriculum that is not culturally relevant, and a need for professional development on equity" (Ford, 2012). I hypothesized that building teacher capacity to enact culturally relevant teaching practices has the potential to reduce the number of referrals of SoC to special education thus disrupting the cycle of poor outcomes associated with such an identification.

CYCLES OF IMPROVEMENT

The Improvement Initiative: Professional Development for Culturally Relevant Teaching

In the following section, I provide descriptions of the two interrelated components of this improvement initiative with relevant research support. There were two interrelated components of this improvement initiative. They include (1) professional development and (2) culturally relevant teaching. Figure 4.8 provides a visual of the expectations of the improvement initiatives.

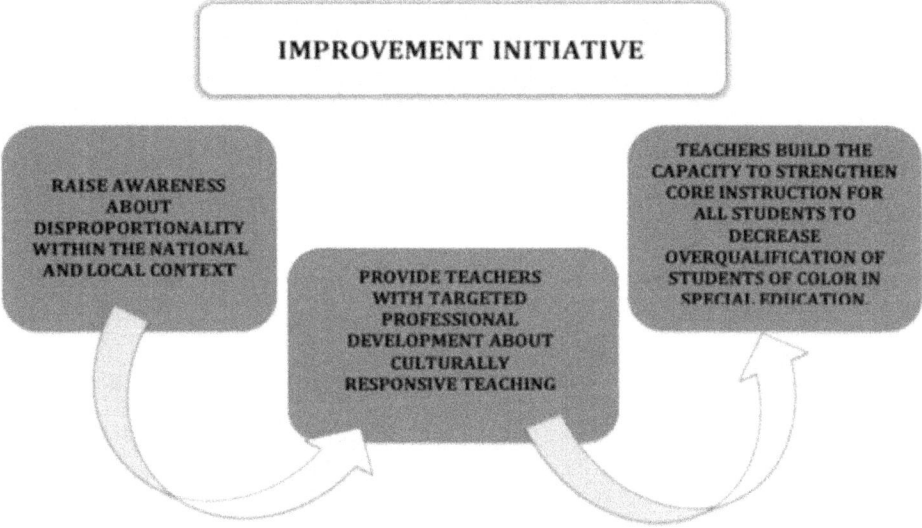

Figure 4.8. Improvement Initiative

Goals/Outcomes

The long-term goal of strengthening tier 1 core instruction with culturally relevant practices was aimed at reducing the overrepresentation of SoC in special education. This will reduce the representation from being disproportionate to a proportionate representation instead. It is also a long-term goal of this work that teachers will begin to gain clarity and progress on teacher evaluation standards focused on teachers establishing a respectful environment for a diverse population of students. We focused our professional development content on addressing contributing factors to disproportionality, such as implicit bias, and collaboratively reviewed how it can be dismantled through self-reflection and utilizing initiatives that are already being implemented in our district.

The intentionality of the design was based on the understanding that learning designers consider how to build knowledge, develop skills, transform practice, challenge attitudes and beliefs, and inspire action. For this improvement initiative, professional development content focused on addressing contributing factors to disproportionality, such as implicit bias, and collaboratively reviewed how it can be dismantled through self-reflection and utilizing initiatives that are already being implemented in the district.

Formative Evaluation of the Improvement Process

To measure the effectiveness of the improvement initiative, I used Plan-Study-Do-Act (PDSA) cycles. A PDSA cycle is a model for improvement that provides a framework for an efficient trial-and-learning methodology (Langley, 2014). The specifics of each component of the PDSA cycle for the study are provided in Table 4.3. Table 4.3 provides an overview of the practical evaluation measures that will be described in the following sections.

FORMATIVE EVALUATION RESULTS AND ANALYSIS

Driver Measure

A driver measure is a measure associated with primary drivers. Since these drivers are intermediate outcomes in the working theory of improvement, they play a key role in the testing of a working theory of improvement (Bryk et al., 2015). The driver measure was originally proposed to be a culturally relevant teaching self-monitoring checklist. The implementation team decided to utilize the tools from the district as they would be relevant to participants and could reinforce what was already expected. Specifically, for the driver measure, an adapted version of the 27 Equitable Practices Classroom Visit tool was utilized. Participants focused on equitable practices 1, 2, 3, 6, 7, 8, 9, 15, and 19. Though participants did not formally observe each other, or themselves, the tool was utilized to self-assess and reflect. Of the 27 Equitable Practices, nine aligned with the purpose of the study included in Appendix B.

Table 4.3. Practical Evaluation Measures

Type of Measure	Instrument	What it measures	Frequency of Administration
Practical Evaluation Measures			
		Summative Measures	
Outcome Measure (Quant/Qual)	Pre- and Post-surveys	1. Teacher beliefs about implicit bias and disproportionality	Beginning of the study and end of the study
		2. Teacher self-assessment of their knowledge and use of culturally relevant teaching practices	
Outcome Measure (Qual)	Focus Group	Participant learning over the course of the intervention	End of the study
		Formative Measures	
Driver Measure	Modified, 27 Equitable Practices	Participants would self-assess their use of CRP in the classroom	Post-PD on the topics of implicit bias and CRT
Process Measure (and benchmark outcome)	Reflection journals: participants reflect on the knowledge gained from each PD session.	1. This information will be used by the design team to inform subsequent PD sessions (Intended use)	Results analyzed by the team midway through the study
		2. It also revealed additional teaching learning data	
Balancing Measure	Referrals to MTSS and Special Education (EC) referrals for SoC	1. Number of referrals of Students of Color to special education	Measured at the end of the study
		2. Number of referrals of Students of Color to MTSS	
	Focus Group	1. Participant implications for next steps in their work to continue to dismantle disproportionality for their school	Measured at the end of the study

Process Measure

For the process measure, we chose to implement the use of journal reflections. In the journal reflection, participants responded to the question, "What do you believe to be some of the contributing factors to the disproportionality of SoC in special education?" This question was proposed and reflected upon during the first PD session and again midway through the study. The design team's intended purpose of utilizing journal reflections was to inform subsequent PD sessions. In addition, it revealed additional teacher learning data related to the concepts being covered. The data were collected midway through the implementation of the study.

Balancing Measures

We chose to use referrals to special education and MTSS for SoC as a balancing measure. We were concerned that after participants learned about disproportionality and the harm it can cause, they would stop referring or significantly reduce their referrals to special education. Although a reduction is the goal, there is a risk of under-identification for services, which would cause an injustice for some students who could benefit from identification and additional support. Referrals to MTSS and special education were monitored by the implementation team throughout the study.

During the last session of the professional development, participants shared their next steps in the form of a focus group upon completion of the series of professional development. These data were collected to gain an understanding of what participants perceived to be the necessary next steps for themselves and their school to continue to dismantle disproportionality. They responded to the following questions from the instructional framework related to incorporating Students' Six in the instructional framework for the district:

- How do you build relationships with your students?
- How do students know your expectations?

OTHER PROCESS AND OUTCOME MEASURES

For this study, there were two outcome measures: pre- and post-surveys measuring teacher beliefs about implicit bias and disproportionality as well as their knowledge and use of culturally relevant teaching practices. See Appendix C for the surveys. The surveys included Likert statements such as, "Rate your understanding of each of the Students' Six strategies." It also included true or false questions such as, "Implicit bias is linked to disproportionality." There were also efficacy scales in which participants captured their overall sense of SoC's ability to access the general curriculum. This included responses to the following statements, "Based on my experience, I believe that Students of Color are less likely to access the general curriculum without extra support from me as compared to their white peers," "Based on my experience, I believe that Students of Color are less likely to access the general curriculum without intervention from tier 3 intervention as compared to their white peers," and "I implement Students' Six strategies in my classroom." There was an open-ended question, as well, which required participants to share what they believed to make them culturally relevant educators.

The purpose of this initiative was to attain an intermediate goal of building teacher capacity to implement culturally relevant core instruction. I used data collected during professional development as well as pre- and post-surveys to measure effectiveness. After the intermediate goal is achieved, teachers will be encouraged to monitor their culturally relevant teaching practices. They will also be encouraged to engage in critical conversations among their professional learning communities (PLCs) about referrals to the intervention team or special education for all students.

The COVID-19 Pandemic

During the implementation of the improvement initiative, schools were impacted by the global COVID-19 pandemic. Initially, as a result of the pandemic, schools operated on Plan C, 100% virtual learning starting in March of the 2019–2020 school year. One hundred percent virtual learning continued into the 2020–2021 school year until March 2021. Schools began to slowly reopen, first offering a hybrid model in which students had the option to return to school in person or continue to engage with instruction remotely.

During the implementation phase of the improvement initiative, starting in September 2021, schools were operating on full in-person learning. There were options for an alternative learning arrangement in which families could choose to keep their child at home to learn virtually, but, for the most part, the majority of students returned to in-person learning. Students with significant health needs typically opt for the alternative learning arrangement. Reopening schools required very strategic planning with the priority of taking every precaution to minimize the spread of the COVID-19 virus. Minimizing the spread meant that teachers and students were back in person, but things were very different. Everyone in the building would be required to wear a mask at all times (except during lunch while students eat or during scheduled mask breaks), and social distancing continued to be strongly encouraged. The COVID-19 pandemic impacted the initiative as it had to be conducted virtually to minimize the risk of spreading the virus. After implementation, other impacts were revealed; they will be discussed later in the findings.

FINDINGS

Upon completion of implementing the improvement initiative, there were several findings based on the data collected. One finding of the outcome measure pre- and post-surveys was that teachers had high levels of understanding before the PD based on their ratings being high on the pre-surveys. With the understanding that participants could have inflated their self-assessment scores, it is important to consider that the responses may not be an accurate report of the true baseline knowledge for evidence-based practices for culturally relevant practices (Students' Six).

Another finding upon completion of the implementation of the improvement initiative was the difference between the perceptions of general education classroom teachers and nonclassroom teachers (physical education teacher and school social worker) to implement the equitable practices. While classroom teachers' reports indicated that they felt competent to implement the equitable practices, the nonclassroom teachers indicated that they could continue to reflect upon and improve their practices.

Reflection journals were originally intended to inform subsequent PD sessions. Upon review of the journal entries, it was determined that participating teachers were understanding disproportionality and the impact that implicit bias has on it. Therefore, it was appropriate to proceed with the subsequent sessions in the PD plan. Teachers were learning the concepts and it was appropriate to continue with the subsequent PD plan.

Other findings included a demonstrated mindset shift for participants regarding how they contribute to disproportionality and how they can be more intentional about dismantling it. This was found during the focus group at the end of the PD sessions when participants demonstrated an eagerness to move the work forward of dismantling disproportionality within their school. They brainstormed equity events and peer observation cycles that they felt inspired to establish in partnership with the school's equity team.

While this improvement initiative did demonstrate a shift in the mindset of participants, I believe that there is more work to be done to build teacher's capacity to have conversations that isolate race. Often, when having discussions, even with framed questions about race, the conversation would shift, for example, to a discussion about girls versus boys or the proper use of pronouns.

During the final focus group discussion, one major theme that emerged was the reference to mask-wearing and how it has presented challenges in building relationships with students. Terri, a first grade teacher, expressed some of the ways that she is breaking the barrier of building relationships despite mask-wearing. She shared that she steps outside on her class porch and pulls her mask down when she needs to have critical conversations with students. She expressed that this allows her to show students (with facial expressions) that she cares about them and wants the best for them. Also, when students are outside in larger areas, it was shared that it is important to just have conversations with students to connect with them and know them on a personal level.

Lynn, a fourth grade teacher, shared that since the implementation of the improvement initiative, she decided to take individual pictures of each student with their mask off (outside), and she created a walk with their pictures that she titled, "Who We Are Behind the Mask."

Sherlisa, the social worker, expressed that, with all the things that are going on in school buildings daily, it has become very easy to be distracted by things that she has to do, even when being present with a student. She stated that she has had to sharpen her active listening so that students feel that she is fully present.

Molly, a third grade teacher, shared that she has an "I am" mirror in her classroom. She and her students use the mirror daily to recite affirmations. This supports the work of ensuring students are connecting.

Linda, another third grade teacher, stated that expectations have morphed over the year. Due to what students have faced over the past two years as a result of COVID, learning from home, and other challenges, once students returned to the building this year, they needed to feel like they were back together. They needed time to "relearn school" and the confirmation that their classroom is a safe space to make mistakes and always give their very best. It is after this that learning could happen now that they feel safe in their space with their teachers and peers. Also, demonstrating and acknowledging to students that teachers are not perfect and they are also always learning.

Because responses did not specifically address building relationships with SoC, the question was restated to include SoC.

(Restated) Reflection question: How do you build relationships with your SoC? How do students know your expectations?

Lynn shared that one of her students stated to her, "I don't know what you expect from me, I am a Black boy in a mostly white school." She described the student as very sharp but struggles with some of his social-emotional needs. Connecting with this student and building a trusting relationship with him has been particularly important, especially being a "warm demander."

Linda expressed that one issue at McHill is that some classes are not diverse. This makes it awkward when having critical conversations about diverse cultures, as it seems to put certain students on the spot (e.g., all of the kids look at the two Hispanic students when the class has conversations about Hispanic culture).

During the focus group, the team also shared ideas about what they could do to continue moving the work forward. One idea that emerged was to have an equity event with stations sharing the 27 Equitable Practices, Instructional Framework, and Students' Six. This could be an in-person event in which other staff members have the opportunity to learn about these district initiatives to address issues of equity. Though participants did not observe each other using the tools, they suggested including an opportunity for teachers to walk around and complete peer observations using the district initiatives.

Another idea shared was to create a "resource bank" with the great things that are happening across the school to establish a sense of community, trust, and belonging for students within classroom settings. Having a resource bank could give teachers ideas of what is already working so that they do not always have to recreate it.

One finding after the initiative that could raise concern is the fact that no participants made referrals to MTSS or special education for their SoC. While this was not addressed directly with participants, it could be assumed that there were no referrals as participants' new knowledge discourages them from making referrals to not contribute to the problem of disproportionality. Though dismantling disproportionality is the goal, the negative impact of not making referrals increases the risk of under-identifying SoC who may actually have learning difficulties that need to be addressed.

LESSONS LEARNED

Challenges

Number of Participants

Limitations of this study include the number of participants and measures taken to minimize the spread of COVID-19 such as mask-wearing. The number of participants was proposed to be a maximum of ten. After recruitment via email with a flyer in the school's morning message, only seven participants expressed interest on the electronic interest form and ultimately provided consent for their participation. During the implementation of the study, Hope School District placed a moratorium on professional developments. There was a large emphasis on the mental health of district employees, therefore they were not required to participate in PD beyond required school and district-level training. Also, due to COVID (social distancing) and an attempt to have more buy-in to participate, the PD sessions were offered virtually. Though research does not lean more toward online or in-person learning being more effective over the other, there are advantages to in-person training versus online. Continu Team (2013, October 18) report the following advantages of in-person learning versus online learning:

- More fluid exchange of ideas
- Social interaction during training
- Good retention due to decreased likelihood of multitasking
- Improved hands-on training
- Faster response to questions and instructor feedback
- Higher satisfaction scores

Mask-Wearing

As teachers self-monitored their equitable practices using the equitable practices checklist, they noticed the limitations of mask-wearing when building relationships with students. For example, as a practice of the Students' Six, teachers noted that proximity looked very different when social distancing is expected, impacting students who benefited from nonverbal praise or visual cues.

Opportunities

Implicit bias impacts an educator's ability to be culturally relevant to their students. This negatively impacts the student learning experience, especially SoC, as it makes it difficult for them to be viewed as capable learners without requiring additional support from their teachers or intensive intervention. This contributes to the ever-growing disproportionate representation of SoC in special education and underrepresentation in gifted education programs. Before an educator can be culturally relevant to their students, they must first acknowledge their implicit bias. Addressing implicit bias lessens the likelihood of perceiving or treating being culturally relevant as a "checkbox" of things to do and increases the chances that it is embraced on a personal level by the practitioner. Ultimately, this will increase access to the general curriculum for all students.

Schools have taken a deficit perspective of marginalized students (i.e., SoC) and their families, believing the students and their families are at fault for underperformance, not the school or its many inappropriately normed systems. Ultimately, the narrative tends to be that these students are less likely to graduate from high school or graduate with lower skills, which severely limits their postsecondary options. As adults, individuals face the possibility of unemployment or lower-paying jobs which starts or continues the cycle of poverty for them and their families (Capper & Frattura, 2008). This is why disproportionality and implicit bias must be addressed on an ongoing basis in public school sectors until it is dismantled.

Studies have confirmed that disproportionality of SoC in special education continues to be a growing problem. SoC are at greater risk of being overidentified for special education than their white peers (Arnold & Lassmann, 2003). In a blog interview, Zaretta Hammond speaks about culturally relevant teaching not being about using a few strategies, but more about an educator's stance. She states:

> It takes time to master but teachers can put core practices into place now. It's really important to not begin this journey alone; do it in community, with other teachers. That is one of my major goals—to build communities of practice around culturally responsive teaching so that we can point to classrooms that help culturally and linguistically diverse students leverage their cultural learning tools and accelerate their own learning. (Ferlazzo, 2015)

Though we focused on culturally relevant teaching, the design of the improvement initiative supports Hammond's statement about learning together—in a community. Too often, teachers are required to participate in PD that is loaded with information that can support improving their teaching practices. However, they do not always have the opportunity to implement, receive feedback, and refine their practices accordingly based on the knowledge that they have gained through PD. In addition, to be effective, this type of work cannot follow the format of a "one-shot" professional development. It would be most impactful to adopt a structure in which teachers have the opportunity to implement and self-reflect. The goal should be to provide focused, sustained, and intensive training that is required to bring forth change. With this initiative, we make efforts to ensure collaboration, for opportunities to demonstrate understanding, and to reduce the possibility of failing to account for teachers' new level of expertise (Joyce & Showers, 2002).

As a Black woman, educator, and mother to a Black child, the work of this improvement initiative was sincerely addressing an educational inequity of which I am passionate. This work requires a great deal of intentionality and is not an easy fix that can be done with a checklist. SoC are very capable and deserve to have the space to shine their strengths and abilities without being expected to conform to white norms.

APPENDIX A

District Instructional Framework: Environment

ENVIRONMENT		
Look-Fors: *Learner experiences have been designed to foster safe and inclusive environments, which honor students' unique voices, strengths, interests, and needs.*	**NCEES (Standard II)**	**Equitable Practices**
E6. Adults use the "Student Six" strategies to promote success for every student: visibility, proximity, connecting to students' lives, engaging students' culture, addressing race, and connecting learning to the larger world.	IIa, IIc	1, 2, 3, 8, 19
Key questions to ask teachers/students	**NCEES (Standard II)**	**Equitable Practices**
[TEACHER] How do you build relationships with your students? How do students know your expectations?	IIa, IIc	6, 7, 8, 9, 15, 22

APPENDIX B

District Equitable Practices (used for the study)

CHCCS Equitable Classroom Practices Classroom Visit Tool			
Name	Observer	Subject	Date/Time
Instructional Equitable Classroom Practice: Learning Environmental Strategies		Observed	Not Observed
1. Arranges the classroom to accommodate discussion Arranges seating to facilitate student-student discussion; seating to facilitate teacher-student discussion			
2. Ensures bulletin boards, displays, instructional materials, and other visuals in the classroom reflect the racial, ethnic, and cultural backgrounds represented by students Displays and uses materials (supplemental books) that reflect all students' racial, ethnic, and cultural backgrounds year round; Displays products and props from students' home and community background			
3. Uses a variety of visual aids and props to support student learning. Uses multiethnic photos, pictures, and props to illustrate concepts and content; Uses appropriate technology to illustrate concepts and content			
Instructional Equitable Classroom Practice: Engagement Strategies			
6. Welcomes students by name as they enter the classroom Asks students for correct pronunciation of their names; correctly pronounces students' names			
7. Uses eye contact with all students Makes culturally appropriate eye contact with all students			
8. Uses proximity with all students equitably Circulates around student work areas to be close to all students			
9. Uses body language, gestures, and expressions to convey a message that all students' questions and opinions are important Smiles, Nods head in affirmation, Leans towards students, Turns towards students who are speaking to show interest			
15. Acknowledges all students' comments, responses, questions, and contributions Uses affirming, correcting, or probing to acknowledge all students' responses			

19. Uses students' real life experiences to connect school learning to students' lives Asks students to reflect....			
Comments:			

*Adapted from CHCCS 27 Equitable Practices, 2020

APPENDIX C

Pre- and Post-Survey

Equity PD Pre-Survey

Please complete this pre-survey based on your current beliefs and understandings. Your responses will be confidential.

sharrington@chccs.k12.nc.us (not shared) Switch account

* Required

Chapel-Hill Carrboro City Schools ranks at number two, nationwide, for its racial academic achievement gap. *

○ True

○ False

I have participated in diversity training and/or professional development during my career as an educator *

○ Yes

○ No

Based on my experience, I believe that Students of Color are less likely to access the general curriculum without extra support from me as compared to their White peers. *

○ This has never been my experience.

○ This is sometimes my experience.

○ This is always my experience.

Based on my experience, I believe that Students of Color are less likely to access the general curriculum without intervention from Tier 3 intervention as compared to their White peers. *

○ This has never been my experience.

○ This is sometimes my experience.

○ This is always my experience.

I believe that implicit bias means that a person is racist towards a specific group of people. *

○ True

○ False

Implicit bias is linked to disproportionality of Students of Color in special education *

○ True

○ False

I implement Students' Six Strategies in my classroom. *

○ Always/Daily

○ Sometimes

○ Never

○ What's Students' Six?

I am aware of CHCCS' district initiatives to support effective implementation of culturally relevant curriculum and pedagogy *

○ True

○ False

I consider myself to be a culturally relevant educator *

○ Yes

○ No

List what you believe makes you a culturally relevant educator. (open-ended) *

Your answer

Rate your understanding of each of the Students' Six Strategies *

	1- None at all	I have not heard about it	I sometimes use this strategy	I use this strategy in my classroom everyday
Proximity	☐	☐	☐	☐
Visibility	☐	☐	☐	☐
Connecting to Students' Lives	☐	☐	☐	☐
Engaging Students' Culture	☐	☐	☐	☐
Addressing Race	☐	☐	☐	☐
Connecting to the Larger World	☐	☐	☐	☐

Chapter 5

Leading Change in Onboarding and Support of Novice Teachers

Elisabeth Harman, EdD

THE CONTEXT

This study was designed to explore ways to improve novice special educators' perceived self-efficacy of their knowledge of and ability to implement the High-Leverage Practices (HLP) in Special Education. Special education is widely known as a "hard-to-fill" position in our public education system. Teachers who lack the skill and confidence (self-efficacy) to successfully meet the demands of the position leave the field early, and school divisions are charged with filling these vacancies to ensure that federal, state, and local regulations are met for students with disabilities.

Due to the voluminous need for quality and qualified special educators but a limited applicant pool, it is critical to ensure that hired staff, often with minimal to zero experience, are provided with high-quality, job-embedded, and supported professional learning experiences. This study's aim was that surveyed novice special education teachers in our school division would indicate improved working knowledge of and ability to implement the HLP framework and report increased self-efficacy related to these targeted skills. We hoped that data, over time, would demonstrate that our teachers' engagement in relevant professional learning will result in long-term reduction of stress levels, increased levels of competency and teacher effectiveness, and increased commitment to the field.

Our school division is in southwest Virginia, in a predominantly suburban community with pockets of both rural and urban residents. We are one of the larger school divisions in the Commonwealth of Virginia with almost 14,000 students in 27 schools: 16 elementary, five middle, five high, and one specialty center. Our division reports that its student demographic profile is 76.6% white, 7.3% African American, 6.5% Hispanic, 5.1% non-Hispanic, two or more races, and 4.4% Asian. We serve approximately 2,400 students with disabilities and employ over 200 special education teachers annually. Special education students make up 16.8% of the total student enrollment. Our students with specific learning disabilities, other health impairments, speech or language impairments, autism, and developmental delay represent the most prevalent disabilities in the division, respectively.

As the Director of Special Education and Pupil Personnel Services for this large school division, I am responsible for the hiring and development of new special education teachers in the division. Each year we have some level of employee turnover due to retirements, relocations, and resignations. On average the division has had to replace 15% of its special educators annually. This staff turnover tasks our division with the difficult search for qualified candidates, which are hard to find since there is a significant and chronic shortage of special education teachers throughout the United States. While there are individuals who have "qualifications" on paper, like a license, they often do not come with the needed knowledge and skills to be successful in the school setting. Unfortunately, due to the limited candidates in the field with full licensure, individuals are often hired with a "provisional license." In the Commonwealth of Virginia, this provisional license allows the candidate to teach after taking one special education course and being hired by a school division (Virginia Administrative Code, 2018). This provisional approach allows school divisions to hire employees to fill vacancies, but these individuals are in classrooms while still acquiring the knowledge and skills needed to meet the needs of students with disabilities.

In our division, like many others, we have found that novice teachers, especially those with a provisional license, are generally overwhelmed. Due to their lack of pre-licensure experience, they often have had limited learning opportunities and little to no hands-on experiences with students. Our novice teachers are particularly challenged by the compliance part of special education—the paperwork, the meetings, the legal regulations. These challenges are compiled with learning to co-teach in unfamiliar content areas, learning to time manage, and, for many, learning the required professionalism that is expected with career employment. This "learning stage" can impact the students that are being taught, the co-teaching relationships, and the overall success of the teacher, which can in turn impact future employment.

THE PROBLEM

Teacher Shortage

In 2000, the Council for Exceptional Children (CEC) stated that there were 30,000 special education positions in the United States filled by less than fully licensed teachers (Menlove et al., 2014). The teacher shortage has not improved in two decades; the COVID pandemic has only exacerbated this public education crisis. As a result, there is a vicious cycle in which less qualified teachers, hired due to supply shortage, report higher levels of dissatisfaction and less commitment to their positions and ultimately leave; therefore, the need to rehire teachers continues. Many provisionally licensed special education teachers transfer to general education positions. The rate is 10 times higher than the rate of general education teachers transferring to special education (Muller & Markowitz, 2003). While it may be that some teachers accepted positions to get into the school division and never intended to remain special education teachers, it is also possible that some of the duties required of a special educator are aversive or stressful (e.g., high student caseloads, multiple meetings with educational advocates, balancing content instruction with specially designed instruction that meets the students' needs, or high expectations for students on high-stakes testing) and they leave special education to avoid these less desirable tasks (Menlove et al., 2014).

Professional Development for Novice Teachers

Researchers have hypothesized that special education teachers with limited training and experience may feel overwhelmed and less capable (Berry et al., 2017). Longstanding research and current teachers report that they often leave the profession citing job-related reasons such as lack of clarity about work responsibilities, large caseloads, extensive paperwork, lack of administrative support, and insufficient preparation to handle the job responsibilities (Adams, 2001; Anderson et al., 2001; Brownell & Smith, 1992; Embich, 2001; Wisniewski & Gargiulo, 1997). To support special educators who may feel that they are being asked to teach beyond their training and expertise, additional professional development is one method commonly used by administrators to provide teachers with the knowledge and skills to help them build confidence and commitment to their positions (Billingsley et al., 2004; Brownell et al., 2002; Gersten et al., 2001). By properly preparing and supporting special education professionals before they begin teaching and as they transition into new classrooms, they become more likely to enter and remain in their special education positions (Menlove et al., 2014). Research suggests that quality professional development can support teachers by providing them opportunities to grow as professionals and, thus, have an indirect effect on their intent to stay (Billingsley et al., 2004). In one large-scale study, Gersten and colleagues (2001) explored the factors that influenced the retention of 887 special educators. These educators reported that their participation in relevant professional development resulted in reduced stress levels, increased levels of competency and teacher effectiveness, and increased commitment to the field. If we do not retain qualified special educators, children with disabilities will not have high-quality programs. Understanding the problem of excessive attrition and providing the needed professional development for novice teachers was a critical issue for our study.

The employment of underqualified teachers charged with educating students with learning challenges presents a significant problem for many school divisions, including ours. Accountability standards for school accreditation include specific measures of students with disabilities who are frequently lower achieving than their peers without disabilities. Cheney and coauthors (1992) concluded, "It seemed that the teachers needed to gain confidence in their own abilities and adequacy as teachers before they were able to shift their focus more fully to students" (p. 23). Initial preparation of special education teachers is often insufficient to ensure that they have the skills necessary to provide effective practices (Leko et al., 2015). The lack of employee preparedness and expectation of student performance on accountability measures are an overarching problem that we need to consider when designing professional learning activities for these teachers. Determining what professional development to provide new teachers and how that professional learning should be provided became our primary focus.

Novice teachers need assistance to apply their coursework knowledge and to address problems in their practice while being provided feedback about their instruction for them to improve over time (Billingsley & Bettini, 2017). This assistance and feedback also help to reduce the higher rates of attrition found with special education teachers, particularly new teachers (DeAngelis & Presley, 2011). Leko and Brownell (2011) stated that there is a critical need for novice teachers to have ample opportunities to receive performance feedback to attain and deliver evidence-based practices with fidelity. Novice teachers need a great deal of support because it sets the tone for future years and is critical in the ultimate retention of teachers in the field of special education. Time given to supporting beginning teachers seems to pay off in improving job satisfaction and retaining teachers in the field (Whitaker, 2000).

Teacher Self-Efficacy

Schunk (2020) noted that "an important challenge for pre- and post- in-service teacher education programs is to develop methods for increasing teachers' self-efficacy by incorporating efficacy-building sources" (p. 158). Teacher self-efficacy has been widely researched since it was first introduced in 1977. The concept is based on Bandura's (1977; 1982; 1984; 2004) cognitive theory of social learning and refers to the conviction that a teacher can produce desired outcomes in their students. In comparing special education teachers with high levels of personal teaching efficacy to those with low levels, those with high levels more frequently met their performance goals (Allinder, 1995). Similarly, these teachers with high personal teaching efficacy had higher expectations and goals for their students. Teachers with high levels of personal teaching efficacy were confident about achieving students' goals and tended to motivate students more than teachers with low personal teaching efficacy. They felt more skilled in their teaching practices and were more likely to be problem solvers (Ghaith & Shaaban, 1997; 1999). A significant result of low teacher self-efficacy can be an increased likelihood of teacher burnout and attrition. To increase levels of self-efficacy, school divisions must find ways to support teachers (Lee et al., 2011). Bandura (2004) suggested that self-efficacy is developed through mastery experiences, physiological and emotional states, vicarious experiences, and social persuasion. "Teachers' self-confidence in skills and knowledge as special education teachers seems to be highly related to their perceived teaching efficacy" (Lee et al., 2011, p. 70). Additionally, Schunk (2020) noted that teacher self-efficacy is a significant predictor of student achievement.

High-Leverage Practices

The Council for Exceptional Children (CEC), in conjunction with the CEEDAR (Collaboration for Effective Educator Development, Accountability, and Reform) Center, has established 22 evidence-based, regularly occurring HLP in Special Education that effective special educators should know how to implement (Council for Exceptional Children & CEEDAR Center, 2019; see Figure 5.1). The purpose of establishing these practices was to help define an effective special educator and to outline the instructional practices that are best for fostering student engagement and learning. These HLP

High Leverage Practices					
Collaboration, Assessment, Social/Emotional/Behavioral, Instruction					
Collaboration	Collaborate with professionals to increase student success	Organize and facilitate effective meetings with professionals and families	Collaborate with families to support student learning and secure needed services		
Assessment	Use multiple sources of information to develop a comprehensive understanding of a student's strengths and needs	Interpret and communicate assessment information with stakeholders to collaboratively design and implement educational programs	Use student assessment data, analyze instructional practices, and make necessary adjustment that improve student outcomes		
Social Emotional Behavioral	Establish a consistent, organized, and respectful learning environment	Provide positive and constructive feedback to guide student's learning and behavior	Teach social behaviors		Conduct functional behavioral assessments to develop individual student behavior support plans
Instruction	Identify & prioritize long and short term learning goals	Systematically design instruction toward specific learning goals	Adapt curriculum tasks & materials for specific learning goals	Teach cognitive & metacognitive strategies to support learning & independence	Provide scaffolded supports	Use explicit instruction
	Use flexible grouping	Use strategies to promote active student engagement	Use assistive and instructional technologies	Provide intensive instruction	Teach students to maintain & generalize new learning across time and settings	Provide positive and constructive feedback to guide student's learning and behavior

Figure 5.1. High-Leverage Practices

are divided into four areas: collaboration, assessment, social/emotional/behavioral, and instruction. McLesky (2017) described the development process for identifying the practices and provided definitions and research support for each practice within the areas. These HLP help frame additional questions (and possible actions) for divisions when both hiring and providing professional development for new special education teachers.

Given that the HLP are now widely published, it would seem reasonable to assume that students in special education teacher preparatory programs would be not only exposed to but understanding of and ready to implement these practices. After completion of a staff survey of special education teachers within their first three years of teaching within our division, findings revealed that of the respondents only 54.5% remembered being introduced to HLP during their teacher preparation program. It should be noted that of those who completed the survey 45.5% indicated that they were provisionally licensed, which means they had not completed a program of study and they did not have student teaching experience before employment.

In the absence of an ability to control the teacher preparation programs at the collegiate level, school divisions, including ours, need to be prepared to provide professional development in the areas of HLP. Ideally, if novice special education teachers are oriented toward these same HLP as they begin teaching, they should experience coherence between what they learn in pre-service and in-service learning experiences about effective instruction practices; in contrast, when new special education teachers encounter different sets of practices, they have a harder task, as they must make sense of and reconcile dissonant instructional frameworks (Billingsley et al., 2019, p. 369).

Ensuring that both new and veteran teachers (who are models and mentors for novice teachers) are effectively demonstrating and utilizing the HLP serves many purposes. When the workforce is trained in and effectively implementing the HLP, there are positive outcomes for both the teacher and student. Teachers who are proficient in the HLP demonstrate greater confidence and success in their role, thus reducing the teacher turnover rate. Developing effective special education teachers improves the outcomes for students with disabilities. Aligning professional development and instructional conditions with the HLP ensures that both leaders and mentors provide unified messaging to novice special education teachers, which may in turn help them to make sense of their roles and enact HLP in a manner that should positively impact students' performance (Billingsley et al., 2019). The CEC and CEEDAR promote that the HLP are essential to effective teaching and basic to supporting student learning (Council for Exceptional Children & CEEDAR Center, 2019).

During an introductory series of professional development for new special education teachers in our division during the 2019–2020 school year, it was observed that the framework of the HLP was a relatively new concept to our novice teachers. While each of the 22 skills, or HLP, may not have been completely novel to the novice teachers, there was great variability in perceived understanding of, comfort with, and ability to implement the HLP with fidelity. Survey data of our special education teachers who were within their first three years of teaching indicated that 0% felt "fully knowledgeable and ready to implement all of the 22 HLP when entering their profession." Using a rating scale of 1–5 where 5 equaled "fully knowledgeable and ready to implement" and 1 equaled "never heard of," teachers indicated their comfort level with each HLP when they entered their teaching position. The results indicated 36.4% "had never heard of the HLP"; 9.1% "might have heard something about the HLP"; 45.5% "had heard of the HLP but really had never spent much time on the topic"; and 9.1% were "familiar with the HLP and understood what they meant."

Recognizing the national, state, and local challenges of retaining special education teachers and having to employ teachers who are not fully credentialed and who may also report low levels of self-efficacy warranted our attention. High-quality professional development for new special education teachers should reduce uncertainty of roles and expectations, which should lead to improved teacher self-efficacy. Organizing professional development experiences around a core instructional framework, like the HLP, provides clarity to the special education teachers' role and their instructional practices and provides clear messaging about what, how, where, and when they should be teaching (Billingsley et al., 2019).

Division educational leaders should coordinate professional development activities so that they are coherent instead of random or focused on nonessential instructional skills or knowledge. These leaders need to consider several things including which core practices should be prioritized in the first year of teaching (Billingsley et al., 2019). Organizing professional development around the framework of the 22 HLP helped to focus learners on key concepts to be learned, emphasize the connections among ideas, and link new content to the student's prior knowledge.

THE TEAM

I knew that an undertaking as large as revamping the onboarding of new special educators for our division could not be done alone. Multiple perspectives needed to be considered, extra hands were needed to create learning materials, and, most importantly, I needed "buy-in" for this to be successful. The team for this project included the division's Central Office Special Education Supervisor team, some school-level special education coordinators, and a few novice teachers from the 2019 and 2020 hiring cohorts.

The Central Office team included six supervisors who each have been assigned to division schools that they support in all special education matters. The supervisors assist with the planning and presentation of professional development for all special educators in the division, including the novice teachers.

Each school in our division has a special education coordinator who supports the day-to-day operations of the special education department at the school level. The coordinators act as mentors for new teachers and serve as a coach, when needed, to address teacher development. School coordinators provide valuable input into the "needs" of novice teachers, from their perspective.

Finally, the inclusion of novice teachers from the last two hiring cohorts provided insight into the professional development needs, from their perspectives, of new hires within the division. The input provided by these teachers helped to structure the professional development provided to the novice special education teachers of 2021 who were the cohort assessed in this study.

In collaboration with my team, I determined that, based on observation, novice special education teachers' initial preparation and their lack of experience often resulted in their lacking the skills necessary to implement effective practices (see Figure 5.2). The lack of employee preparedness coupled with the local and state expectations of student performance on accountability measures, expectations for legal compliance, and demonstrations of evidence-based instructional practices was an overarching problem that we needed to consider when designing professional learning activities for these teachers. Determining what professional learning opportunities to provide new teachers and how that professional learning should be delivered was critical. Novice teachers need a great deal of support because it sets the tone for future years and is essential to the ultimate retention of these teachers in the field of special education. According to Whitaker (2000), time given to supporting beginning teachers seems to pay off in improving job satisfaction and retaining teachers in the field.

Historically, the professional learning provided to novice special education teachers in our division was a single day of professional development before the back-to-school teacher workweek. Novice teachers received a half-day of information shared by the Central Office team and spent the other half of the day working in their school with a building-level support person. Novice teachers were generally overwhelmed and frankly "didn't know what they didn't know" so their introductory experience was not very meaningful, nor did it advance their confidence in their ability to be successful in their new role. There was little to no scheduled follow-up or ongoing professional learning that was targeted for these novice teachers. Our team believed that

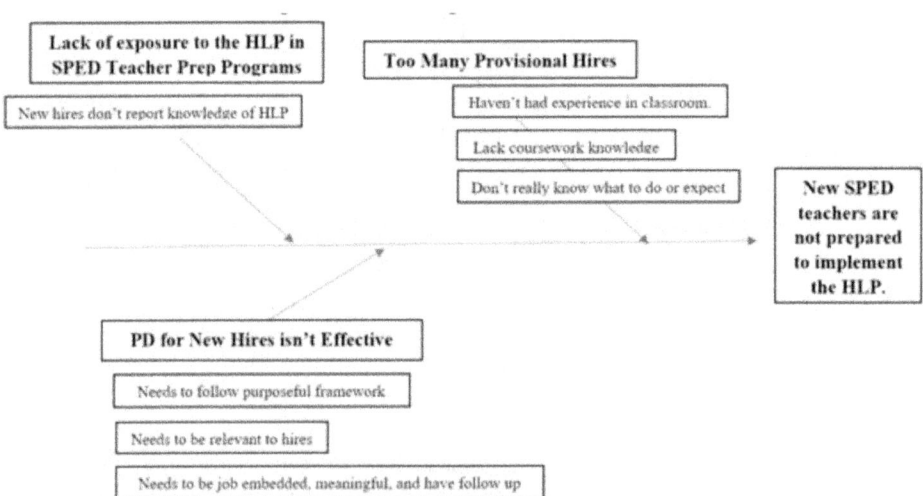

Figure 5.2. Fishbone Diagram for Problem of Practice

providing professional learning in multiple modalities (i.e., in-person, asynchronous online, mentoring) over an extended period, and grounded in a framework, would provide a better first-year experience for novice teachers. The team believed that novice teachers who have professional learning opportunities that improve their knowledge, skills, and self-efficacy in their ability to perform their duties, are more likely to be successful and remain in the field.

After our team came to agreement we began to systematically prioritize topics for learning units/modules, develop an organizational structure that tied all the learning modules together, agree to common language and formatting for our modules, and establish an action plan with timelines (see Figure 5.1). While each team member "specialized" in specific topics and/or modules the team regularly met to review, critique, and revise individuals' work to ensure the cohesiveness that we strived to achieve. We also tried to remain focused on the end-user and to review from their lens.

CHANGE IDEAS AND INTERVENTIONS

A theory of improvement describes how a researcher will advance from problem analysis and hypothesis building to outlining a plan for implementing an action that will result in improvement. After analyzing practical knowledge gained through professional experiences, observations, and review of professional research literature, the team hypothesized a theory of improvement that if novice special education teachers (those in their first year of employment within our division) were provided high-quality professional learning opportunities, grounded in the HLP of special education, both their knowledge of the HLP and their self-efficacy would improve. Improvement of novice teachers' working knowledge of the HLP and their perceived self-efficacy as a teacher are critical to their remaining in the field of special education.

Table 5.1. System Improvement Map: Identification of Sub-Systems Impacting New SPED Teachers' Lack of Preparedness to Implement the HLP

Teacher Prep Programs	Hiring Practices of Human Resources	Finances	Time	Professional Development Plan
Programs may not be introducing the HLP	New hires can be provisionally licensed with one class	Limited ability to pay for substitutes when PD is needed	Limited number of days to provide PD to new hires	Too many "have to cover" issues that may not directly align with instructional practices
If introduced, is there in-depth training and practice implementing the HLP?	Often no student teaching or classroom experience	Only hiring what is "required" to cover staffing in SPED, needs more to be most effective	Limited embedded PD	Must have a framework for which all PD falls (the HLP framework)
	Often new hires are using SPED to get the job they "really want"		Limited time for mentoring that is effective	Need more follow-up after PD is provided
			SPED teachers are covering multiple contents, writing IEPs, having countless meetings	Need more job-embedded PD so that it doesn't feel like "one more thing"
			Limited time for co-planning	

The team designed a professional learning series that included an initial day of in-person orientation and four additional in-person sessions spaced out over the school year, which included structured activities with their mentor. The novice teachers engaged in an asynchronous learning guide that included an introduction, a HLP overview lesson, and 14 topic-specific units or modules grounded in HLP. The learning guide was comprised of curated videos, online resources, division-level specific resources, practices and procedures, and activities that were designed to model HLP and develop the knowledge and skills of the novice teacher. The participants completed the unit activities and engaged with their building-level mentor or Special Education Coordinator through a verification process. A pacing guide was provided to each participant, which was monitored (see Figure 5.3).

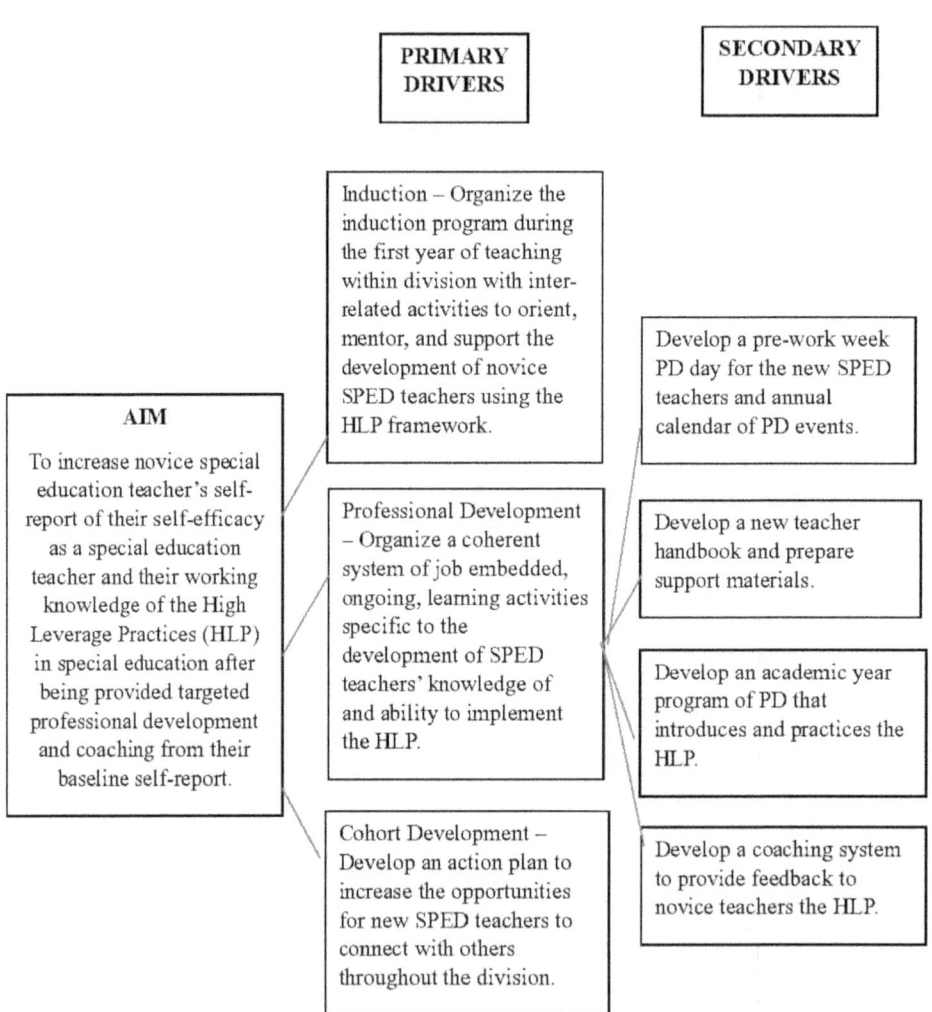

Figure 5.3. Evolving Driver Diagram

Outcome Measures

Outcome measures help practitioners to determine if the change that they introduce is having the desired impact. Outcomes should relate directly to the appropriate improvement outcome (aim) statement (Perry et al., 2020). The aim of this study was that the surveyed novice special education teachers in our school division would indicate improved working knowledge of and ability to implement the HLP framework and report increased self-efficacy related to these targeted skills. If novice teachers complete the professional learning activities and embedded tasks, their knowledge and skills will likely improve. Improved knowledge and skills related to the HLP should result in the successful demonstration of the requirements of the position. If the novice teachers acquired knowledge and demonstrated success in the field, it was hoped that their self-efficacy would improve. It was deemed likely that if improving novice teachers perceived self-efficacy and knowledge, then it would not only help to achieve the aim but also improve the lagging outcome measure of special education teacher retention.

Novice teachers in this study completed a pre-professional learning survey and a post-professional learning survey using a unique ID (of which they were instructed to keep throughout the study) so that comparisons for individuals could be made while maintaining their anonymity. The surveys contained 26 Likert scale questions in which the novice teacher separately rated both their knowledge of and ability to implement the targeted skills from the aim.

Driver Measures

Improvement science is intended to not just improve a problem, but also to improve the system that created the problem (Perry et al., 2020). Driver measures help to demonstrate if the change implemented improves the overall system. If improvement is noted, then progress is being made toward reaching the measurable outcome of the aim.

In the case of this study, the driver measures focused on the professional learning opportunities and mentorship created for the novice special education teachers. The professional learning series included an introductory lesson, an overview of the HLPs lesson, and 14 units. The units include topics that the special education teachers within the division needed to know and to become proficient at demonstrating. The units were all grounded in the HLP. Professional learning occurred through in-person sessions, asynchronous lessons/units of study, and direct mentorship from the novice teacher's building-level support (Special Education Coordinator). Novice teachers were expected to complete specific activities within each unit and to have their Special Education Coordinator verify through observation or review of a product that skills and tasks had been demonstrated and completed. This verification process served as a driver measure and was designed to encourage mentorship between the novice teacher and the mentor, as well.

Process Measures

Process measures inform a researcher by yielding quick and easy indicators about the predicted results of the change introduced. When determining the process measure, the researcher needs to identify the unit of measure from which data will be collected (Perry et al., 2020). After the unit of measure is determined, it must be decided what actual data will be collected. The process measures helped our team to know if what we were doing was working for our teachers, in the way that we hoped it would. We needed to know if our teachers felt like their knowledge and skills were improving.

For this study, in addition to the data that was collected through pre- and post-professional learning series surveys, participants completed a midpoint and exit professional learning validity survey which was used by the team for the next improvement cycles. The learning validity survey engaged the participants in Likert scale and open-ended or comment items about the helpfulness of the professional learning topics covered, additional supports or learning topics that they believed novice teachers would find beneficial, and the support or need for further assistance to be provided by their mentor. These process measures informed the team of the participants' perceptions regarding the effectiveness of the learning activities and supports while also providing their perspective regarding the activity's positive impact on their knowledge and skills. Additionally, the required verifications from mentors/building level support for asynchronous tasks were completed (within a provided pacing guide) by the participants to provide information about the novice teacher's developing skill sets.

Balance Measures

Balance measures inform researchers regarding the change that they have introduced and if it has improved the system or if it has cost the system (Perry et al., 2020). It is important to monitor the change to ensure that it has not negatively impacted the system. It is critical to maintain balance to ensure that progress is not made by creating an adverse impact in an unpredicted way. Adjustments may need to be made to mitigate risks and to maintain balance.

It is important to be mindful of potential problems that could negatively impact the participants, thus jeopardizing the possibility of reaching the aim. Through regular communication with mentors, the team monitored the support school and division mentors provided to novice teachers as they participated in the professional learning opportunities. Mentoring support utilized an "on-demand" assistance approach for questions and concerns while the novice teacher navigated and learned their new role. It was noted that if the professional learning activities became overwhelming, burdensome, or too challenging for the teacher, the teacher's knowledge or self-efficacy would not improve. The mentoring support was deemed critical to the teacher's success. Because mentorship is essential, the in-person sessions included targeted mentor-mentee activities that the team designed to foster communication and collaboration, beyond the "on-demand" question-and-answer opportunities within the typical school setting.

Our team recognized that novice teachers, especially those with provisional licensure, are often in college programs to gain licensure and are often in their first "real job," leaving them juggling time and responsibilities. Therefore, it was important to know if the intervention was having unforeseen or potentially negative consequences on our teachers. Overburdening them would "undo" the positive outcomes we hoped to achieve. Regular "check-ins" were critical and helped the team pivot when necessary to ensure that participants were able to stay on the path to successful completion of their first year with the division.

CYCLES OF IMPROVEMENT

The Plan-Do-Study-Act (PDSA) cycle is designed to use and answer improvement questions. Planning requires the team to ask questions, design a change, make a prediction about the change, design a measure, and determine if the change made a difference. For this study, we spent a lot of time in the "plan" stage. Our planning included the team asking the following questions:

- Why is special education teacher retention difficult?
- What factors influence special education teachers to leave the field?
- Are novice special educators prepared to enter the workforce?
- What do novice special educators need to be successful?
- Do novice special educators have knowledge of and the skills to implement the HLP?
- Do novice special educators understand their role, the practices, and procedures of the division, and how they connect to the HLP?
- What does quality professional learning look like?
- How can we provide the needed professional learning to support our novice special educators?
- Will quality professional learning improve our teacher's confidence (self-efficacy) in their ability to be successful in the field?
- How will we know if our novice teachers improve their knowledge and skills?
- How will we support our novice teachers throughout the first year in the division at the building and division levels?
- Will teachers who have knowledge and strong self-efficacy be more likely to remain in the profession?

During the "plan" phase of the cycle, the team hypothesized that improving novice teachers' knowledge of and ability to implement HLP will likely improve their self-efficacy. The team further proposed that when teachers have strong self-efficacy and can identify their knowledge and abilities, they are more likely to stay in the field and be successful. Our team believes that confidence built on knowledge and skill not only improves outcomes for the teacher, but the students they teach, and the division. Confident and skilled teachers are instructionally and procedurally sound in their content delivery and ability to remain in compliance with the complex regulations governing special education.

Based on these hypotheses, the team planned a change or intervention. The intervention was an extensive professional learning series for novice special education teachers grounded in the HLP. Specific learning modules included "High Leverage Practices," "Getting to Know Our Staff," "Getting to Know Your Students," "Getting to Know Your Resources," "Back to School Preparation," "Special Education Basics," "Legal Considerations," "IEP Writing," "Data Collection and Progress Monitoring," "Co-Teaching," "Specialty Programs and Services," "Student Behaviors and Support," and "End of School Year Responsibilities." The novice teachers engaged in both in-person and online learning modules that included learning tasks and/or activities to complete, an independent book study of HLP, and structured mentorship activities. Participants completed an online pre-intervention and a post-intervention survey to determine if the change improved their knowledge and self-efficacy. Additionally, participants completed two online professional learning validity surveys to inform the research team about the usefulness of the different learning activities for the next cycle of improvement.

During the "do" phase of the PDSA cycle, the team implemented the intervention, collected the survey data pre- and post-intervention, and monitored the participants throughout the professional learning. Monitoring occurred through the mentorship provided by a school-based special education coordinator and a division-level special education supervisor. The research team was mindful of potential problems or barriers for participants while they engaged in the professional learning series and worked to ensure that the professional learning was job-embedded, provided resources, offered practice opportunities, included mentorship, and developed a colleague network.

The "study" phase of the cycle included analyzing the collected data to determine if the intervention improved novice teacher's knowledge of and ability to implement HLP and their self-efficacy. Implementation challenges and unexpected consequences were reviewed. Data were compared with the predictions and desired outcomes (aim) and summarized.

The final PDSA cycle phase, "act," consisted of making decisions about the intervention or change for future implementations. After the participants completed the professional learning validity survey in October the research team was able to review the comments regarding the participant's perceptions of the effectiveness of the professional learning activities and mentoring. This feedback allowed the research team to make any needed adjustments for the second cycle—specifically the in-person sessions that occurred in January and March. After the study's completion, the findings were shared with the division. The totality of findings and reflections informed the team so that they could adapt, adopt, or abandon the professional learning modules for the next cohort of novice teachers.

FINDINGS

Novice special educators were defined as the newly hired, first-year, special educators in the school division. The cohort of novice teachers was comprised of both provisionally and fully licensed special educators. At the beginning of the study, the majority of the 34 provisionally licensed teachers who chose to participate reported zero years of public special education teaching experience, except for six participants who reported between one and three years of experience. The 19 fully licensed participants who chose to participate reported an average of 9.9 years (ranging from 0 to 30 years) of public special education teaching experience. From the results of this study, we quantified the average self-reported growth in both knowledge and success at the implementation of targeted areas by comparing individuals' pre- and post-intervention responses from their surveys. Additionally, the average rating (1–5) for each area was presented for both provisional and fully licensed participants both pre- and post-intervention. The study also provided data from an educational validity survey that was conducted mid- and post-intervention, which included average rankings of "helpfulness" of the intervention and responses to open-ended questions. All new hires were asked to participate in four in-person sessions and to complete 14 asynchronous lessons/units of study, regardless of participation in the study, as part of their new teacher onboarding.

Participants completed a pre-intervention survey on July 27, 2021, before engaging in any professional learning. This survey was intended to provide a baseline of the individual's self-reported knowledge and belief in their ability to implement the HLP. Each participant rated their knowledge of and success in each of the topic areas of the asynchronous units that they would engage with in the coming months. Participants completed the same survey post-intervention, using the same rating scale, on March 2, 2022. The intervention was comprised of engagement in professional learning, which included four in-person group sessions, 14 asynchronous units/modules of study, and on-demand site-based mentoring opportunities that were specific to being a special educator in our division and grounded in the HLP.

The pre- and post-intervention surveys allowed the team to compare responses of the same individuals by comparing their responses using their unique PIN. Unfortunately, many participants were not able to remember their PIN, or they created a new PIN on the second survey, which limited comparisons of all participants/respondents. The initial pre-intervention survey yielded 53 responses, and the post-intervention survey yielded 45 responses. By matching PINs, response comparisons of 11 provisionally licensed and eight fully licensed novice special education teachers could be made to inform growth between pre- and post-intervention. The average responses of all respondents pre- and post-intervention could be made and provided informative data to the team. When comparing the pre- and post-survey results, respondents were broken into provisionally licensed and fully licensed novice special education teachers. It was assumed by the team that the "learning curve" for the provisionally licensed teachers would be greater, as most entered their positions with zero years of experience and minimal course work in special education. The fully licensed teacher group averaged 9.9 years of experience teaching special education, before coming to our division. Survey results, utilizing the matching PINs, of the 11 provisional and eight fully licensed respondents yielded gains on each question in the post-survey compared to the pre-survey. Average growth per question can be found in Figure 5.4. Average growth was calculated by comparing the difference of comparable individuals' (those who used the same PIN pre- and post-) rating, per question, pre-intervention, to the

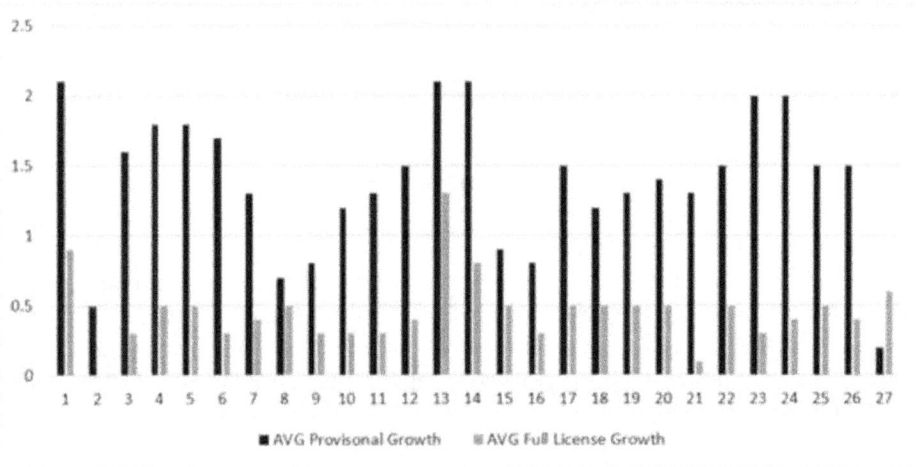

Figure 5.4. Average Growth per Question on a 1–5 Scale Pre- and Post-Survey

rating, per question, post-intervention, and calculating an average change rate of the collective participants, per question. The change rate demonstrated average growth in each question for both provisional and fully licensed participants.

Additionally, improved ratings were noted when analyzing the total average responses of all participants. While all participants could not be "matched" utilizing a PIN for growth, and the number of respondents varied pre- and post-survey, the data were informative to the team. There were 34 provisionally licensed respondents to the pre-survey and 30 to the post-survey and there were 19 fully licensed respondents to the pre-survey and 15 to the post-survey. These numbers varied due to absences on March 2, 2022, or nonparticipation in post-survey by participants. The average 1 to 5 rating for each question increased from the pre-intervention survey to the post-intervention survey for both provisional and fully licensed teachers. The average pre- and post-rating for each group of teachers, per question, can be found in Figure 5.4 for provisionally and fully licensed teachers. As desired by the team, provisionally licensed teachers (the "most novice" of the participants) averaged significantly higher levels of self-efficacy post-intervention than before the intervention. Thus, the aim of the study was achieved. Of note, the fully licensed special education teachers also reported higher levels of self-efficacy post-intervention, but their growth was smaller, as expected, due to their higher levels of experience and education before the provided intervention.

In addition to the pre- and post-intervention surveys, a midpoint and post-learning validity survey was offered to participants. The purpose of these surveys was to inform the team as part of the PDSA cycles. The midpoint learning validity survey was offered to participants on October 27, 2021, and the post-survey was given on March 2, 2022. For the midpoint survey, the participants were asked to rate the helpfulness of the asynchronous units of 1 through 7 and unit 11 (which were expected to be completed by the in-person session on October 27, 2022), how helpful the support was from their building level mentor, and to respond to the open-ended questions

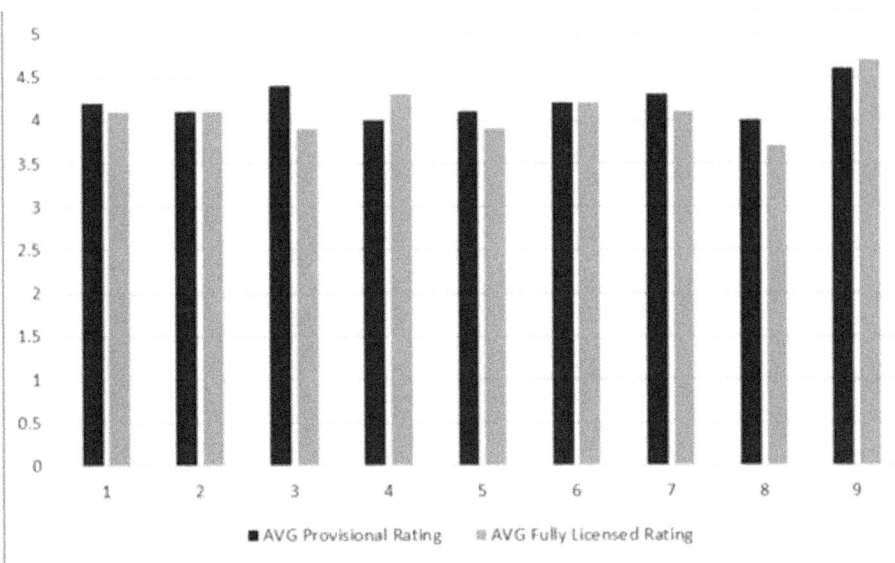

Figure 5.5. Midpoint Learning Validity Response Rating 1–5 of Helpfulness of Units and Mentor

of "What additional support could we provide to you, a first-year teacher within the division?" and "What additional topics of professional learning would you like for us to provide first-year special education teachers, in the future?" The participants' responses allowed the team to craft the upcoming in-person learning sessions that were scheduled for January 12, 2022, and March 2, 2022, more thoughtfully.

Responses to questions 1 through 9, from both the provisional and fully licensed teachers, demonstrated that they found the completed asynchronous units and support from their mentor to be helpful. Respondents were asked to rate from 1 to 5 with a 1 indicating "not helpful at all" to a 5 indicating "extremely helpful." Figure 5.5 provides the average rating for each question (1 to 9) on the midpoint validity survey by both provisional and fully licensed teachers. Thirty-one provisional and 15 fully licensed teachers participated in the midpoint learning validity survey.

While most respondents to the midpoint learning validity survey indicated positive responses to the support given, there were several who requested additional support with IEP writing. This specific request became the focus for the in-person learning on March 2, 2022, and for mentor-provided support between November 2021 and March 2022.

A post-learning validity survey was given on March 2, 2022. Twenty-nine provisional and 11 fully licensed novice special education teachers chose to participate in the post-learning validity survey. The post-learning validity survey was comprised of 14 ratable questions and two open-ended questions. Like the midpoint validity survey, the rating questions required the respondents to rate the helpfulness (using the same 1–5 rating as on the midpoint survey) of all the asynchronous units and their building level mentor and to answer the same open-ended questions as the midpoint survey. The responses to the post-learning validity survey provided the team with valuable

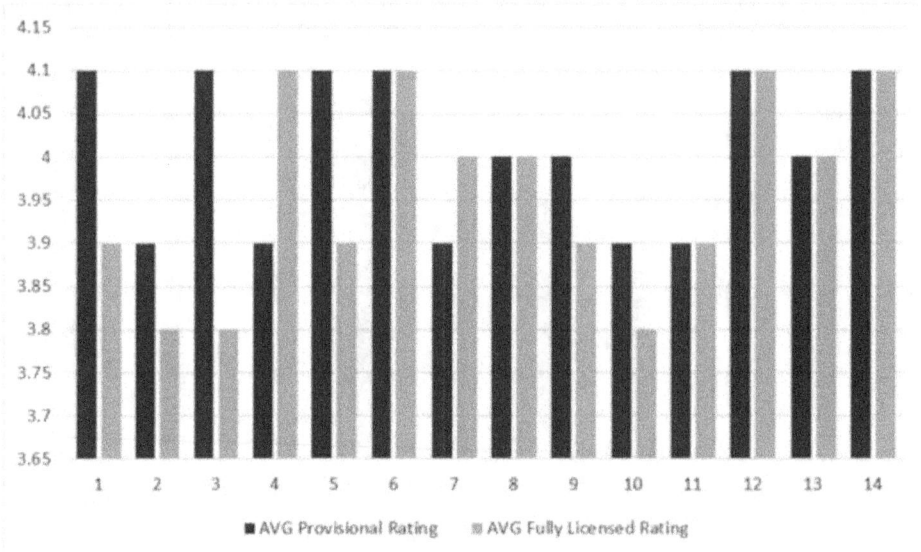

Figure 5.6. Post-Learning Validity Survey Results

information for further implementation of the intervention, beyond this study. The results informed the team regarding the helpfulness of the asynchronous units, additional desired topics, and timeline adjustments for future cohorts of novice special education teachers within the division. The average helpfulness ratings (1 to 5) of the asynchronous units and mentors for both the provisional and fully licensed novice special education teachers are found in Figure 5.6.

In summary, data collected through the course of this study with pre- and post-intervention surveys revealed that, when comparing individual responses pre- and post-intervention, growth was demonstrated in all categories surveyed. Additionally, the total response average for each question yielded improved ratings post-intervention from both provisional and fully licensed respondents. Thus, the team could surmise that the targeted aim was met because data indicates improved teachers' perception of working knowledge of and ability to implement the HLP and increases in self-efficacy related to targeted skills.

Additionally, the participants responded favorably to the learning validity surveys. Both provisional and fully licensed respondents rated above average, or greater, levels of helpfulness of the intervention provided. Narrative responses informed the team for planning future professional learning for novice special education teachers within the division. As noted, the growth rate was higher for provisionally licensed participants when compared to fully licensed participants, which was anticipated by the team based on the assumption that fully licensed teachers would have a stronger foundation entering their employment. Provisionally licensed teachers appeared to develop knowledge and skills at the foundational level while also learning about the practices and procedures within the division. It can be surmised that the fully licensed teachers had more foundational knowledge and skills upon entry but benefited from learning division-specific practices and procedures. This assumption was validated by the fully licensed teachers' rating of the "Getting to Know Division Resources" at a higher rate of helpfulness than the provisionally licensed teachers. Anecdotally, one of the more experienced fully licensed teachers reported to the team during the last in-person session that "this was the best training experience I have ever had, and I have been in several school districts, in several states."

Based on the feedback from the participants, the intervention from this study will not be abandoned. The driver measures of the online modules and mentorship will be tweaked, as appropriate, annually and before the start of the next cohort of novice special education teachers. While the online modules must remain current to federal, state, and division practices, procedures, and policies, the team will also look to improve the learning modules that had lower post-intervention ratings such as the co-teaching module, which averaged a 3.9 for provisional and a 3.8 for fully licensed teachers. The team will find additional ways to support novice teachers in this area going forward.

The process measures from this study included the pre- and post-intervention surveys and the learning validity surveys. These tools helped measure the reported growth of perceived self-efficacy by individual participants. The measures also provided an opportunity for the team to analyze which asynchronous units were rated higher or lower than others and to review the narrative feedback provided by participants. The data will aid in future planning. For example, the order in which future structured mentorship activities and in-person learning opportunities may be adjusted based on the responses provided by the participants in the learning validity surveys. Of note, many respondents reported that they would like more support in writing IEPs earlier in the school year. During the last in-person session, participants did a deep dive into reviewing an IEP written by someone else using a provided checklist which they reported was a very helpful lesson. They also enjoyed watching and evaluating the simulation IEP meeting that the team presented during the same in-person session. Based on the provided feedback, these two activities will be moved to earlier in future school years.

Narrative feedback provided by participants served as both balancing and process measures in this study. While novice teachers frequently feel overwhelmed as they learn their role, the mentor support designed to help ease these feelings will need to be improved, to afford more balance for the participants. Participants did report that they wished for more structured and scheduled time with their building-level mentor (school coordinator). While the building mentors could provide on-demand support as requested by the participant or when determined necessary by the mentor, the participants reported that when the research team provided structured time (the second in-person session) it was very helpful. Both novice teachers and mentors reported that carving out time to work together, while in the school with the inherent distractions, is difficult. This balancing measure deserves attention and further planning of structured, distraction-free, time for mentor-mentee support during future cycles of this work.

LESSONS LEARNED

The intervention used in this study will be continued within our division's special education department. The intervention, robust professional learning provided to the novice teachers, provided quality, engaging learning that was relevant, job-embedded, and grounded in the framework of the HLP. The asynchronous modules used in this intervention took approximately six to eight months for the team to develop as they simultaneously continued with their daily work responsibilities. Painstaking efforts were taken by the team during creation to be mindful of the design, functionality, and usefulness of the created modules because the vision was for these units to be sustainable and hold value over time. Each unit was designed to be topic-focused, but also aligned with the HLP. In addition to our novice special education teachers, all division employees had and will continue to have access to the asynchronous units, which will allow veteran special education teachers, administrators, and general education teachers to learn from or utilize the units as a resource. This open platform will require annual maintenance to ensure that the content, resources, links, and activities are current, relevant, and support the needs of the division. In addition, the in-person professional learning sessions will need to be planned annually to support the needs of the current cohort of novice teachers.

The Virginia Department of Education and Virginia's Training and Technical Assistance Centers (T/TAC) have begun to strongly emphasize the HLP within their communications and professional learning opportunities. This message both reinforces and emphasizes to our participants the importance of being knowledgeable of and successful at implementing the HLP. It further supports that the provided intervention is in alignment with best practices. Our team has been in discussions with several employees of T/TACs regarding this study and our intervention as a model for other school divisions within the state. Our division could become a "model site" for new teacher onboarding; however, our team would caution that our intervention should not be directly replicated, as it is division-specific, which is what makes it unique and personalized to our division employees. We feel that this element was what made our intervention "special" and most effective.

The model of professional learning for novice teachers used in this study will be an example within our school division. The yearlong approach to supporting first-year teachers with asynchronous content, in-person learning opportunities, structured and on-demand mentorship, with accountability measures for both participant and facilitator, can be used for all novice teachers, not just special educators. Other departments, English, for example, would need to create content that is specific and unique to their practices and procedures while aligning with our division's literacy plan and the state's Standards of Learning as a framework, like the HLP in Special Education.

Improvement science guides a researcher through analyzing a problem, hypothesizing, and planning and implementing a change idea, to improve the practice of an organization. A key takeaway from improvement science is that it is cyclical, ongoing, and evolving. In the case of this study, the PDSA model was used. This phased approach guided the team to ask questions, design a change, make a prediction about the change, design a measure of the change, and determine if the change made a difference.

Our team, faced with the same "teacher turnover" issue as many divisions, decided that we needed to change our teacher onboarding process to meet the needs of our new hires. Historically, our division has always been fortunate to fill our vacancies and to fill them with relatively qualified candidates. We decided to be proactive as we saw the special education teacher shortage slowly beginning to impact our division. Thankfully, our planning began pre-pandemic, which allowed us to be in a better position post-pandemic. During our "plan" phase, after reviewing internal data, asking many questions, and utilizing causal analysis tools the team hypothesized that improving novice special educators' knowledge and ability would improve their self-efficacy. Based on the hypothesis, multiple measures were designed, and an intervention was planned. The intervention or driver measures were carefully designed to include the professional learning and mentorship opportunities created for novice special education teachers.

In the "do" phase of the PDSA cycle, the intervention was implemented, and process measures were introduced. Pre- and post-intervention and mid- and post-learning validity surveys were completed as process measures to investigate how changes were occurring.

Studying the midpoint learning validity survey allowed for action changes during the intervention cycle. Changes or actions could be taken to improve the learner's experience in upcoming in-person learning. Final review of all assessment measures (surveys) drove the actions taken in the future. Balancing measures were considered during the "study" phase in preparation for the "act" phase. In this study, reviewing the balance measures of mentor feedback and participant feedback on the open-ended questions of the validity surveys was crucial to ensuring that the progress made with participants did not create an adverse impact in an unpredicted way.

In many organizations, particularly education, practitioners are often very solution-minded. They jump quickly to implementing a change, hoping for the desired outcome, without patience and willingness to first develop a deep understanding of the problem or plans to test changes allowing for course change, often without comprehensive data to make decisions. To further exemplify this point, by example, in education, students are "constant" for a limited amount of time, ideally only in an instructional grade for one year. This makes it challenging to implement some changes with fidelity because the topography is always changing. There are different students in the grade each year; therefore, if the intervention is grade-specific, you are not measuring the same students, over time. Alternatively, if you are measuring the same students over the years, the instructional content is different each school year. These challenges may appear as barriers to implementing change, but instead can be seen as an opportunity to utilize the formality and guidance of improvement science to systematically move from problem to desired outcome.

Our team has learned that complex problems, like ill-prepared teachers in a low recruitment and retention field, can be broken down into manageable issues utilizing the tools and processes of improvement science. Going forward, this team will utilize tools like fishbone diagrams and system improvement mapping before "jumping into" a change idea or intervention. In our department, we will utilize improvement science tools to assist in tackling other concern areas such as improving secondary student's transition plans and experiences.

As a division leader, I have grown as a practitioner of improvement science. In leadership roles, we are charged to "come up with a solution" for complex and multi-layered problems. These "problems" or areas of needed improvement typically have many stakeholders and complex cause-and-effect relationships. Division leaders often must face political challenges, financial constraints, resource limitations, and more when attempting to make changes that demonstrate measurable positive outcomes. I believe that utilizing a systematic approach like improvement science can provide transparency, data, and, ultimately, buy-in and sustainability to change ideas.

Implementing improvement science has taught this team to be more patient and to not put the solution before asking the questions. Means and Harris (2013) stated that researchers should become smarter about how to identify issues that matter to educators and about how to conduct quality research within the limitations of practicing education systems. Moving forward, my team will ask more questions while looking for solutions. Tichnor-Wagner and coauthors (2017) believe that to produce effective change, we must ensure that our PDSA cycle builds on practitioners' prior knowledge and current practices. This team also learned that building interventions on existing practices and procedures within an established framework, such as the HLP, creates more "buy-in" from all members of the team and the participants within the intervention. Tyack and Cuban (1995) reported that when comparing the implementation of radical change to incremental change, incremental change has been found to generate less resistance among implementers (as cited in Reese, 1996). Utilizing the HLP framework in a variety of ways within our division over the three years before this study provided an incremental introduction and ultimate expectation to utilize the HLP as our foundation for providing quality, job-embedded professional learning. Our mentors were able to build on existing practices and procedures and HLP knowledge to effectively support and guide the novice teachers, which further provided for successful onboarding and achieving the study's aim. In summary, the tools and processes of improvement science support a systematic approach to problem-solving in educational settings that benefits all stakeholders.

Chapter 6

Leading Change to Improve Academic Outcomes for Traditionally Marginalized Students

Jamie Soltis, EdD

CONTEXT

Archer Lane Middle School (ALMS) is located in a small city and is the school district's only middle school. The Silver Creek School (SCS) District is comprised of four elementary schools, one middle school (ALMS), and one high school. SCS serves approximately 3,700 students annually, approximately 900 of whom attend ALMS (Silver Creek Schools Data, 2023). The overall school district student demographic, including that of ALMS, is diversifying at a much more rapid rate than the city in which it resides.

Silver Creek City is a small city that geographically covers just over 14 square miles. According to the US Census Bureau website, Silver Creek City had a 2019 estimated population of 25,317 of which 87.4% were estimated to be white, 6.7% Black, 3.3% Hispanic, 1.7% Asian, and 3% estimated to consist of individuals identifying as two or more races (US Census Bureau Silver Creek, n.d.). As depicted in Figure 6.1, although the population has remained predominantly white from 2010 through 2019, the overall racial population demographics for Silver Creek City have shown a slow, steady increase in the percentage of minorities making up the overall population (US Census Bureau Silver Creek, n.d.). The city's governing body, the city council, is composed of four white men and one white woman, all of whom are 48 years or older. The white woman serves as the city's first female mayor. The five-member school board is appointed by the city council and is composed of three white men, one white woman, and one Black woman. Although Silver Creek is only 14 square miles, most of the economically disadvantaged Black families live in two subsidized housing projects. Many economically disadvantaged white students and Hispanic students live in one of four trailer parks on the outskirts of Silver Creek. Many of our white school staff members as well as our white community members have never set foot in these communities.

School district data show that ALMS's student population has become more ethnically diverse over the past 10 years. Since 2011, the percentage of Black students has risen from 10.7% to 16.9% in 2021 (Virginia Department of Education, n.d.). According to data from the Virginia Department of Education (VDOE) Fall Membership

Figure 6.1. Longitudinal Racial Demographics 2010–2021

Build-a-Table website and the utilization of the growth trend feature in Microsoft Excel, as seen in Figures 6.2 and 6.3, the student racial composition of ALMS will continue to become more diverse over the next 10 years (Virginia Department of Education, n.d.). As the ALMS student population has become more diverse, the ALMS teaching staff has remained primarily white. Although Black students make up 16.9%

Fall Membership	Total # of Students Enrolled in AMS	# of White Students	% White	# of Black Students	% Black	# of Asian Students	% Asian	# of Hispanic Students	% Hispanic	# of "2 or more race" Students	% 2 or More Race Students
2011	908	788	81.3	97	10.7	25	2.8	26	2.9	20	2.2
2012	883	712	80.6	100	11.3	21	2.4	22	2.5	26	2.9
2013	917	749	81.7	89	9.7	14	1.5	20	2.2	45	4.9
2014	931	749	80.5	96	10.3	17	1.8	17	1.8	51	5.5
2015	909	718	79.0	89	9.8	19	2.1	31	3.4	51	5.6
2016	907	705	77.7	105	11.6	19	2.1	37	4.1	40	4.4
2017	901	697	77.4	105	11.7	18	2.0	46	5.1	35	3.9
2018	924	709	76.7	110	11.9	12	1.3	48	5.2	45	4.9
2019	942	693	73.6	123	13.1	21	2.2	52	5.5	52	5.5
2020	916	680	71.0	146	15.9	24	2.6	44	4.8	51	5.6
2021	927	635	68.5	157	16.9	24	2.6	57	6.1	48	5.2
2022	930	651	69.9	145	15.6	20	2.1	65	7.0	59	6.3
2023	933	642	68.8	153	16.4	20	2.1	73	7.8	63	6.7
2024	936	634	67.7	160	17.1	20	2.2	81	8.7	67	7.1
2025	938	625	66.7	168	17.9	20	2.2	90	9.6	71	7.6
2026	941	617	65.6	177	18.8	20	2.2	101	10.7	76	8.1
2027	943	609	64.6	185	19.6	21	2.2	112	11.9	81	8.6
2028	946	601	63.5	195	20.6	21	2.2	126	13.3	86	9.1
2029	949	583	61.5	204	21.5	21	2.2	140	14.7	91	9.6
2030	951	585	61.5	214	22.5	21	2.2	156	16.4	97	10.2
2031	954	578	60.5	225	23.6	21	2.2	174	18.2	104	10.9
2032	957	570	59.6	236	24.7	21	2.2	194	20.3	110	11.5

Figure 6.2. ALMS: Longitudinal Racial Demographics 2010–2021 and Demographic Projections from 2021–2032 Based on Data from the VDOE

Leading Change to Improve Academic Outcomes for Traditionally Marginalized Students 133

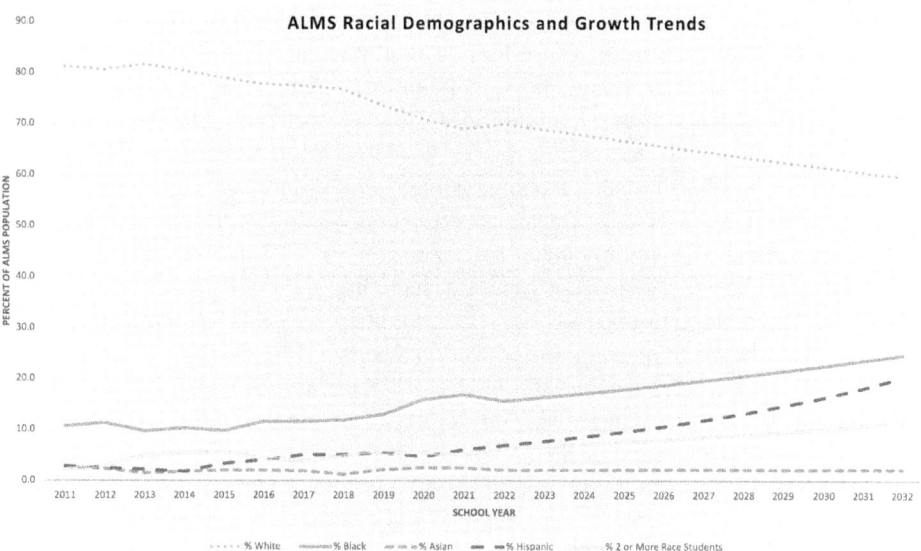

Figure 6.3. Longitudinal Racial Demographics 2010–2021

of the student population (Virginia Department of Education, n.d.) at ALMS, Black teachers make up only 7.4% of the teaching staff (Silver Creek Schools Data, 2021a).

Since the inception of Virginia's Standards of Learning (SOL) Assessment System, Black students have traditionally scored below their white peers on the SOL end-of-course (EOC) reading assessment. The increasing number of Black students makes the racial disparities in reading outcomes an even bigger issue to address due to its affecting more students and school accreditation.

THE PROBLEM

As a white male assistant superintendent with 26 years of public school experience in Virginia, I have witnessed both positive and negative impacts the public school system and educational staff members can have on children from various racial and ethnic backgrounds, including Black students. However, as a white student who attended both SCS and Rivercrest Community Schools, I never realized the lack of cultural responsiveness in staff members or the lack of curricular material culturally relevant to Black students. Having always been taught to be "colorblind" and to treat everyone equally, I was blind to the struggles of some of my Black friends to engage and be successful in school. In particular, I never recognized the racial disparities in the reading outcomes gap that existed. This gap was only magnified by the lack of diversity in my high school, where only 4 of the 375 students were students of color.

All this began to change during my college years when I became a roommate with three Black men. My roommates were from Hampton, Virginia; Washington, D.C.; and New Orleans, Louisiana. These friends attempted to open my eyes to the racism that still existed in the world and how my being colorblind perpetuated the systematic structures of oppression that continue to exist. They pointed to the lack of African American history and literature in their history and English classes, along with the lack of Black teachers at the university, as just a few examples. When we went shopping, they told me to observe how the workers watched them as they looked around the store. They challenged my belief that racism was an act and wanted me to realize that long-standing racist structures existed, including the public schools and universities that functioned to oppress non-white cultures. As I spent more time with my roommates, I began to question the education system.

During my time as a teacher and later as a secondary principal, I truly began to change my beliefs and realize what my college roommates had attempted to teach me was, in fact, true. As a teacher, I witnessed our school district become more and more racially diverse. As the years progressed, my role changed from being a teacher to becoming a middle school and a high school principal, before eventually becoming director of instruction, and finally an assistant superintendent. It was during these times that my jobs afforded me the ability to visit a multitude of classrooms. During these visits, I began to question both the cultural awareness and the responsiveness of the mainly white staff, as well as the curriculum itself. As a result, I began to take to heart the lessons from my college roommates.

Historically, the federal government has attempted to close the racial disparities in reading outcomes by enacting legislation such as the Elementary and Secondary Education Act, No Child Left Behind Act, and the Every Student Succeeds Act. Unfortunately, despite the efforts of lawmakers and educators, racial disparities in reading outcomes persist.

Researchers have been studying the racial disparities in reading outcomes for many years (Morris & Perry, 2016). The difference in academic achievement between Black students and their white peers has a long history in the United States and continues to exist today: "Nationally, a persistent 'Black-White Test Score Gap'" (Jencks & Phillips, 1998; as cited in Craig, 2016, p. 1), "has existed between African American and mainstream students for most of the last century" (Fishback & Baskin, 1991; as cited in Craig, 2016, p. 1). According to Potter and Morris (2017), "African American children tend to perform below their [W]hite counterparts at school entry (Lee & Burkham, 2002; Yeung & Pfeiffer, 2009), and the gap usually widens over time (Entwisle et al., 2005; Fryer & Levitt, 2004)" (as cited in Potter & Morris, 2017, p. 132). The National Assessment of Educational Progress (NAEP) is designed to assess student performance in a variety of subjects, including reading, using a random sample of fourth, eighth, and 12th grade students across the country (de Brey et al., 2019). The average reading scores on the NAEP assessment for white fourth, eighth, and 12th grade students were higher than those of their Black peers at the same grade levels each time the assessment was given from 1992 to 2017 (de Brey et al., 2019).

Failure to address the racial disparities in reading outcomes could have long-term impacts on the lives of African Americans: "Racial inequalities in adulthood in areas as diverse as employment, incarceration, and health can be traced to unequal academic outcomes in childhood and adolescence" (Belfield & Levin, 2007; as cited in Morris & Perry, 2016, p. 68). Determining the factors that contribute to the racial disparities in reading outcomes as well as implementing strategies designed to eliminate them is the moral responsibility of all educators, and a failure to do so jeopardizes the success of our nation.

As in many districts and middle schools across the country, Black students who attend the SCS District and its only middle school achieve a lower success rate on Virginia's EOC English Reading assessments as compared to their white peers. According to English Reading SOL Data (2012–2019), SCS's Black students are less likely to pass advanced and more likely to fail the English Reading EOC assessment as compared to their peers in the school district (Silver Creek City Schools Data, 2021b). Figure 6.4 shows the SOL pass rate of white students in grades six, seven, and eight at ALMS on the 2017, 2018, and 2019 Virginia Reading SOL assessment as compared to white students across SCS and Virginia (Virginia Department of Education, 2021a).

Figure 6.5 shows the pass rate of Black students in grades six, seven, and eight at ALMS on the same 2017, 2018, and 2019 Virginia Reading SOL assessments as compared to the overall school district as well as the state (Virginia Department of Education, 2021b).

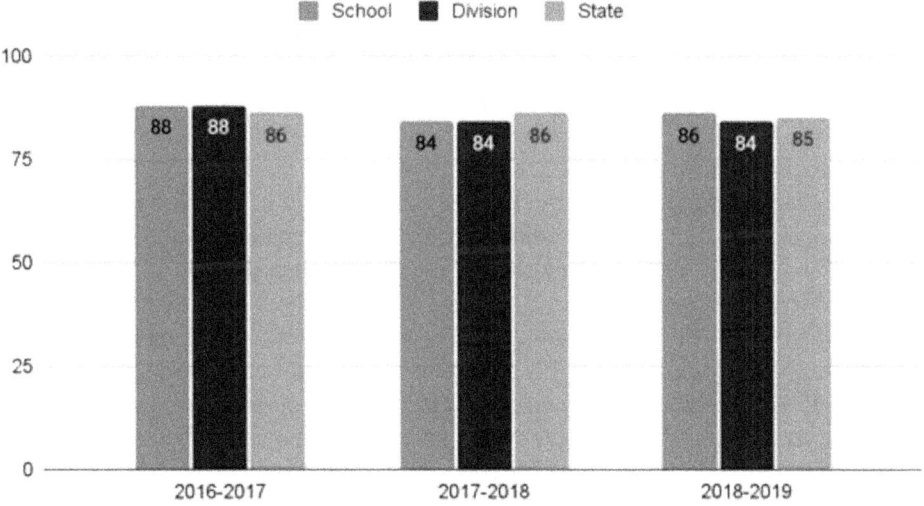

Figure 6.4. White Students' Reading Performance on the SOL (2016–2019)

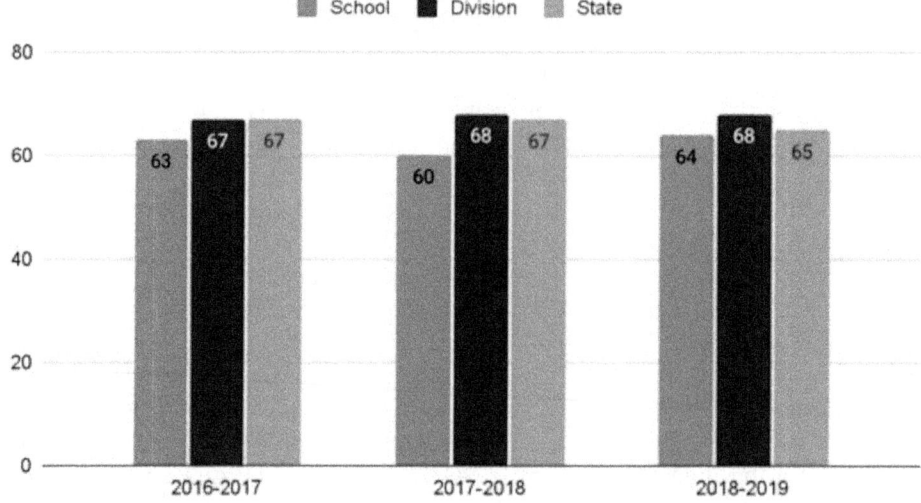

Figure 6.5. Black Students' Reading Performance on the SOL (2016–2019)

Comparing the data from Figure 6.4 and Figure 6.5, Black students passed the English Reading EOC SOL assessment at an average rate of 62.3%, whereas their white peers passed at an average rate of 86% (Virginia Department of Education, 2021a; 2021b). This data demonstrates the significant racial disparity (23.7%) that existed between Black students and their white peers over these three years. Further analysis of this data highlights the fact that Black students across Virginia, the SCS, and at ALMS consistently pass at a rate much lower than their white peers on the state reading assessments. Although Virginia's 19.4% average racial disparity in reading outcomes on the EOC Reading assessment over these 3 years is substantial, as is the average 17.6% Black reading disparity for the SCS, the Black reading disparity is even more pronounced at ALMS (23.7%).

I performed a quantitative data analysis using data from the ALMS grades six, seven, and eight EOC English Reading SOL data for the school years 2018–2019 and 2020–2021 to verify that a correlation existed that supported my belief that a racial reading disparity existed between Black and white students. I chose to include two years' worth of data so that the sample size was larger, thereby making the data more reliable. I did not include the 2019–2020 data because not all students tested due to the COVID-19 pandemic. A disproportionate number of Black and economically disadvantaged students did not test during that school year. I combined all the EOC English Reading SOL scores for all ALMS Black students and all ALMS white students into one spreadsheet. As seen in Figure 6.6, the mean score on the EOC English Reading SOL for Black students was 409 compared to 439 for white students (Silver Creek Schools Data, 2021b). On the EOC English Reading SOL, a score of 400 is considered a pass. This data indicates the average Black student is in danger of not passing the assessment. The median and mode scores for Black students were 413 and

Mean Black Score	Mean White Score
409.2319392	439.3256151
Median Black Score	Median White Score
413	443
Mode Black Score	Mode White Score
404	449

Figure 6.6. Comparison of Black and White Students on the Reading SOL (2019 and 2021)

404 respectively, whereas for white students, the median and mode scores were 443 and 449 (Silver Creek Schools Data, 2021c). The result of the quantitative analysis proved the existence of a correlation between the students' race and the outcome of the reading assessment.

Additionally, I used the data to develop a box and whisker plot. The box and whisker plot in Figure 6.7 showed the comparison of ALMS Black and white students in grades six, seven, and eight on the EOC English Reading SOL scores for the school years 2018–2019 and 2020–2021 (Silver Creek Schools Data, 2021b). The box and whisker plot demonstrated the racial disparity that existed showing the reading racial disparity at ALMS.

THE TEAM

To address the racial disparities in reading outcomes, I quickly realized the need to assemble a team comprised of a variety of stakeholders. After meeting with the school principal, we began to develop a list of key stakeholder groups and potential representatives who we believed needed to be involved in the process. These stakeholder groups were chosen due to their ability to impact or because they were impacted by the racial disparities in reading outcomes. In addition to building and district-level administrators, we wanted to make sure to include stakeholders from traditionally marginalized groups that are often left out of the school improvement process including Black teachers, Black students, and Black parents.

To ensure that I was able to find at least one representative from each identified stakeholder group, I brainstormed with potential team members to help identify other potential individuals they felt needed to be part of the team. As much as possible, I set up meetings to personally recruit the potential team members. During these meetings, I stressed the importance of each team member and the valuable perspectives and experiences they brought to the group. I also stressed the need for everyone to be

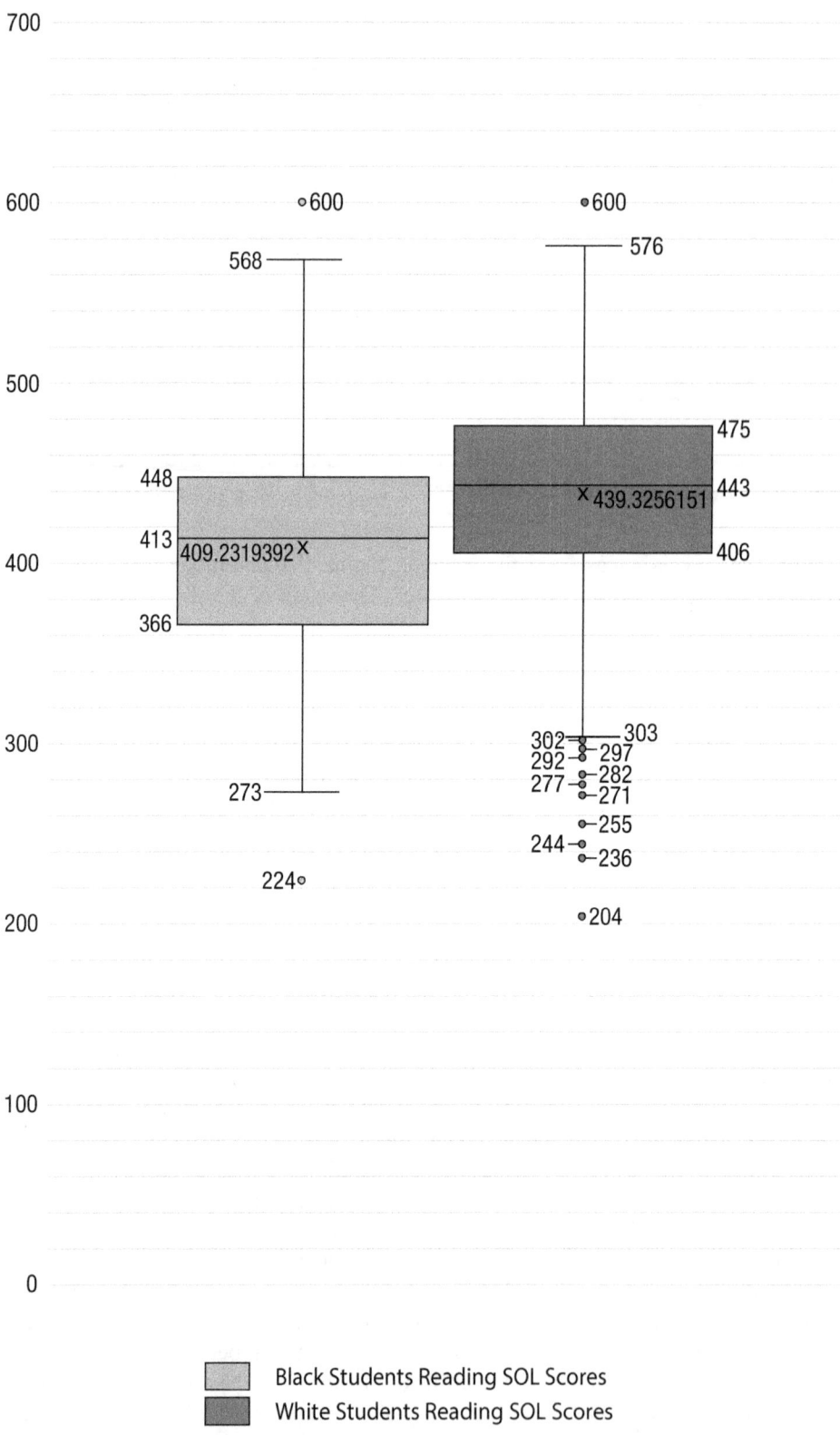

Figure 6.7. Comparison of Black and White Students on the English Reading SOL (2019 and 2021)

active participants throughout the process and that without learning together and gathering input from each of them, the likelihood of our successfully addressing the Black reading opportunity would be extremely low. The final team we assembled comprised the 11 members listed in Table 6.1 and me.

Table 6.1. Research Team

Stakeholder Group	Race
AMS English Teacher/Former AMS Student	White
SCS Secondary English Instructional Coach	White
AMS Instructional Coach/AMS History Teacher/Longtime community member	Black
AMS Reading Specialist	White
AMS Principal	White
AMS Parent	Black
AMS Student	Black
Elementary Assistant Superintendent of Instruction	White
Director of Special Education and Student Services	White
Superintendent	White
Director of Administrative Services/Former AMS Principal/Former AMS Teacher/Former AMS Student	Black

RESEARCH TEAM

Once the final team was assembled, I used Doodle Polls to schedule the initial and subsequent meetings (https://doodle.com/). One of the challenges was finding a time that worked for everyone when scheduling the team meetings. Unfortunately, not all stakeholders were able to attend every meeting. To address this challenge, I emailed the meeting agenda and research articles a week before every team meeting; and, after each meeting, I emailed the meeting notes and the PowerPoint I used to guide the meetings. During the first meeting, we completed an icebreaker activity, which included providing time for people to talk and establishing group norms. During the first research team meeting, I shared national, state, and local data to establish the racial disparities in reading outcomes as a problem that we have the moral imperative to address. I reiterated the importance of each research team member being actively engaged in the process if we were to successfully address the racial disparities in reading outcomes.

Before we began to address the racial disparities in reading outcomes, I provided the team with an overview of the improvement science process. During this overview, the goal was to ensure that each team member understood the basics of improvement science and what their responsibilities were as we moved through the process. We referred back to where we were in terms of the improvement science process at each meeting. As we began to address the racial disparities in reading outcomes, the first step was to understand the problem by using improvement science tools to perform a causal analysis.

The team began exploring the potential root causes of the racial disparities in reading outcomes at ALMS by participating in a Post-it note brainstorming activity.

140   Chapter 6

Each member wrote potential causes for the presence of racial disparities in reading outcomes at ALMS on separate Post-it notes. The team then collaborated to group these potential causes by themes. See Figure 6.8 for the resulting Post-it note sort. The team utilized the five whys questioning technique "developed by Sakichi Toyoda" (Hinnant-Crawford, 2020, p. 50) to drill down to determine potential root causes of the racial disparities in reading outcomes at ALMS.

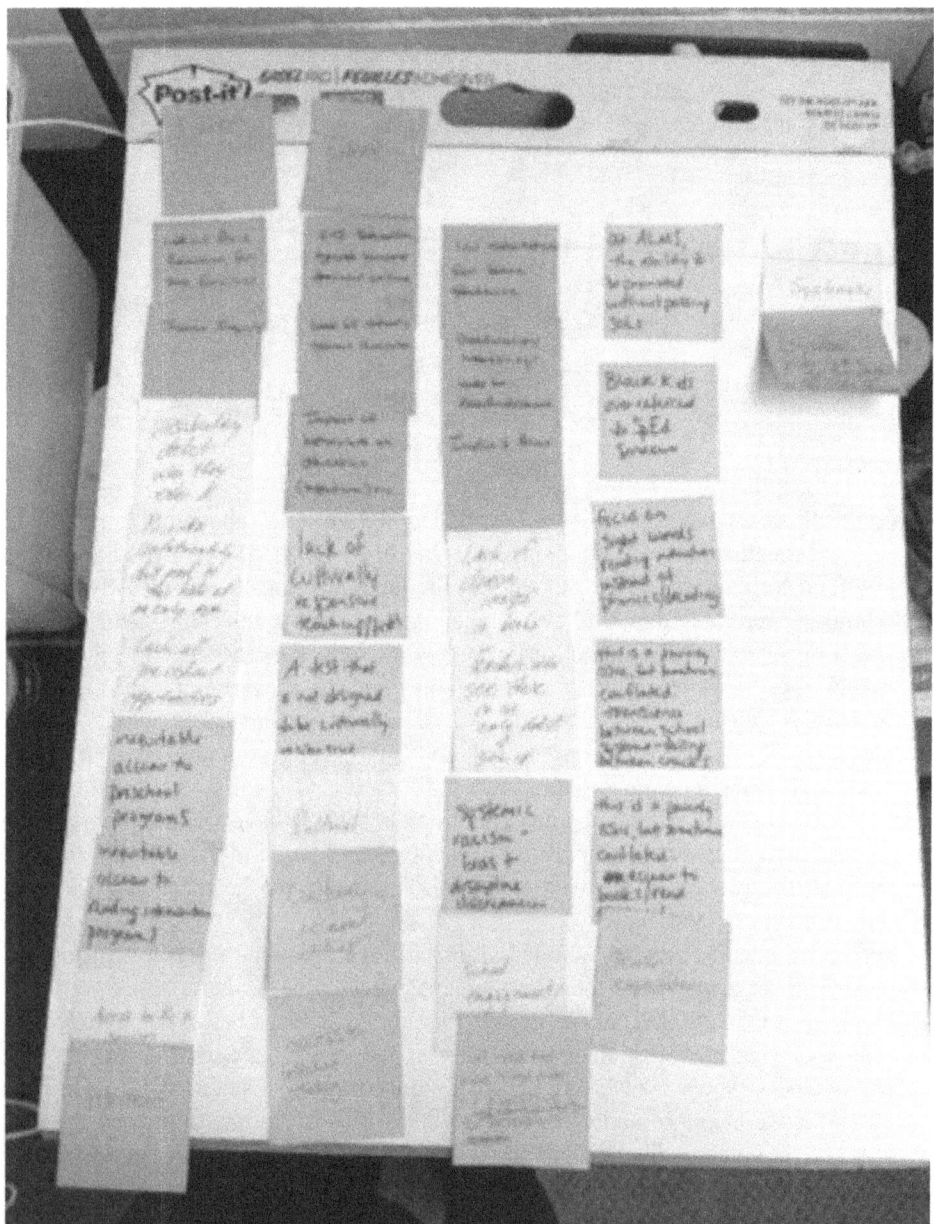

Figure 6.8.   Post-It Notes Brainstorm

Leading Change to Improve Academic Outcomes for Traditionally Marginalized Students   141

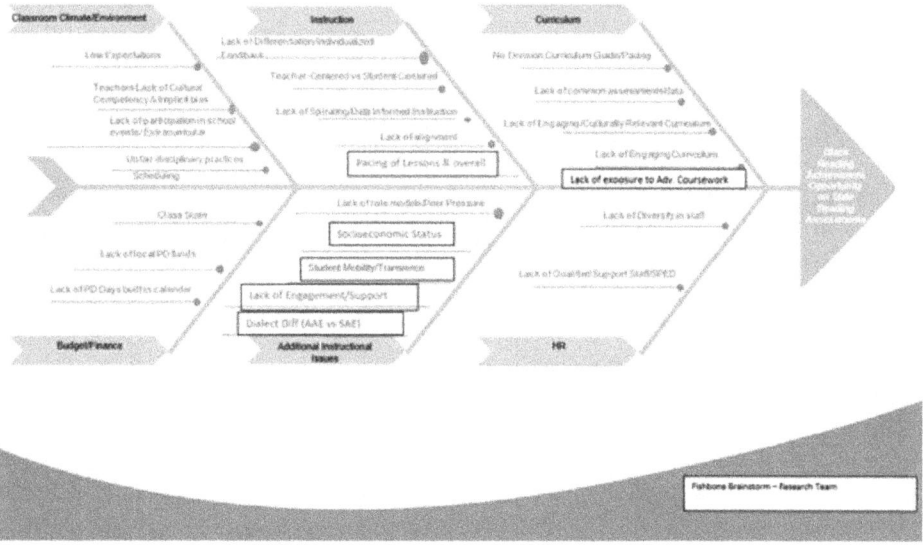

Figure 6.9.   Fishbone Diagram

In addition, the team completed a situational analysis to identify the systems and individuals involved in the racial disparities in reading outcomes. Finally, the research team created a fishbone diagram using the results of the Post-it notes activity, five whys activity, and situational analysis. The resulting fishbone diagram is in Figure 6.9.

To continue to gain an understanding of the problem, I conducted empathy interviews with Black students, parents, and teachers these students identified as being their "favorite teachers." I strongly believe that too often, educators leave Black stakeholders out of the process of both understanding and developing solutions to challenges that directly affect them. The team also read and discussed articles from the formal research base as well as the mainstream educational literature to gain a deeper understanding of the problem as well as how to potentially address the racial reading disparity at ALMS. I assessed the reading materials available in the bookroom and the novels being used by sixth, seventh, and eighth grade English teachers. There was a significant number of culturally diverse reading materials available; however, few of these materials were being utilized in classrooms according to the English instructional coach. In addition, I conducted classroom observations of the identified "favorite." I shared the qualitative data with the research team to facilitate a deeper understanding of the differences between teachers who are successful at engaging Black students and those who are not. Based on the data gathered and analyzed, we concluded that highly engaging teaching strategies, culturally relevant teaching material, and positive teacher-student relationships are necessary to address the racial disparities in reading outcomes.

The research team met regularly to discuss the findings of the empathy interviews, class observations, our lived experiences, research articles, and mainstream literature. As we began to determine how we would address the racial reading disparity at ALMS, we developed our working theory of improvement by creating a driver diagram. To begin this process, the team first identified primary and secondary drivers and began to develop initial change ideas the team felt would lead to achieving the aim of reducing the racial disparities in reading outcomes at ALMS by 5% annually based on Virginia's English Reading SOL assessment.

Understanding that every system is perfectly designed to get the results it gets and that the racial reading disparity is a complex problem, the research team identified the following primary drivers involved in the racial disparities in reading outcomes at ALMS: curriculum, instruction, climate, and human resources. Stakeholder feedback and the mainstream and formal research base identified each of these primary drivers as potential components of a complex system that could be contributing to the racial reading disparity at ALMS. All of the literature aligned with the stakeholder feedback indicated the need for culturally relevant pedagogy (CRP) at ALMS if we hoped to close the racial reading disparity.

Research from the literature indicated that for a curriculum to be culturally relevant to students of color, the curriculum needed to include materials that represented these students. Also, the stakeholder feedback indicated that when the curriculum included materials that were reflective of the students' lived experiences, the students were much more likely to engage and achieve at a higher level.

In addition, the research team identified instruction as a primary driver. From our work, the team determined that to engage students of color and, in fact, all students, teachers needed to implement instructional strategies that were highly engaging and relevant to the students' lived experiences. The team also recognized the importance of maintaining high expectations for students of color as imperative to their academic achievement. The research and mainstream literature bases and data attained from the observations of the teachers identified as "favorite" teachers by the Black stakeholders, and who were successful at increasing Black student achievement, supported the need for teachers to implement CRP as a primary component of tier one instruction. Teachers who had a higher self-efficacy in their understanding and ability to implement CRP in their classrooms had much greater success with Black students in terms of academic success (Blazar, 2021).

Additionally, the team recognized that students must feel safe and develop a sense of belonging before they can achieve academic success. The team recognized that the school and classroom climate was a primary driver that could have serious implications on student academic achievement. The data we gathered from our aforementioned sources indicated that Black students were more likely to be successful at ALMS if the school staff understood them and their culture, purposefully built relationships with them, and maintained a culture of high expectations for all students.

Last, the research indicated that students of color benefited academically and socially from being taught by a teacher of color. However, the research also indicated that white teachers who utilized CRP were more successful at raising the academic achievement of Black students than their peers who did not (Blazar, 2021).

After identifying the primary drivers, the team then identified secondary drivers, where a resulting change idea could be implemented and, thereby, accomplish the research aim. The resulting driver diagram including primary and secondary drivers is in Figure 6.10.

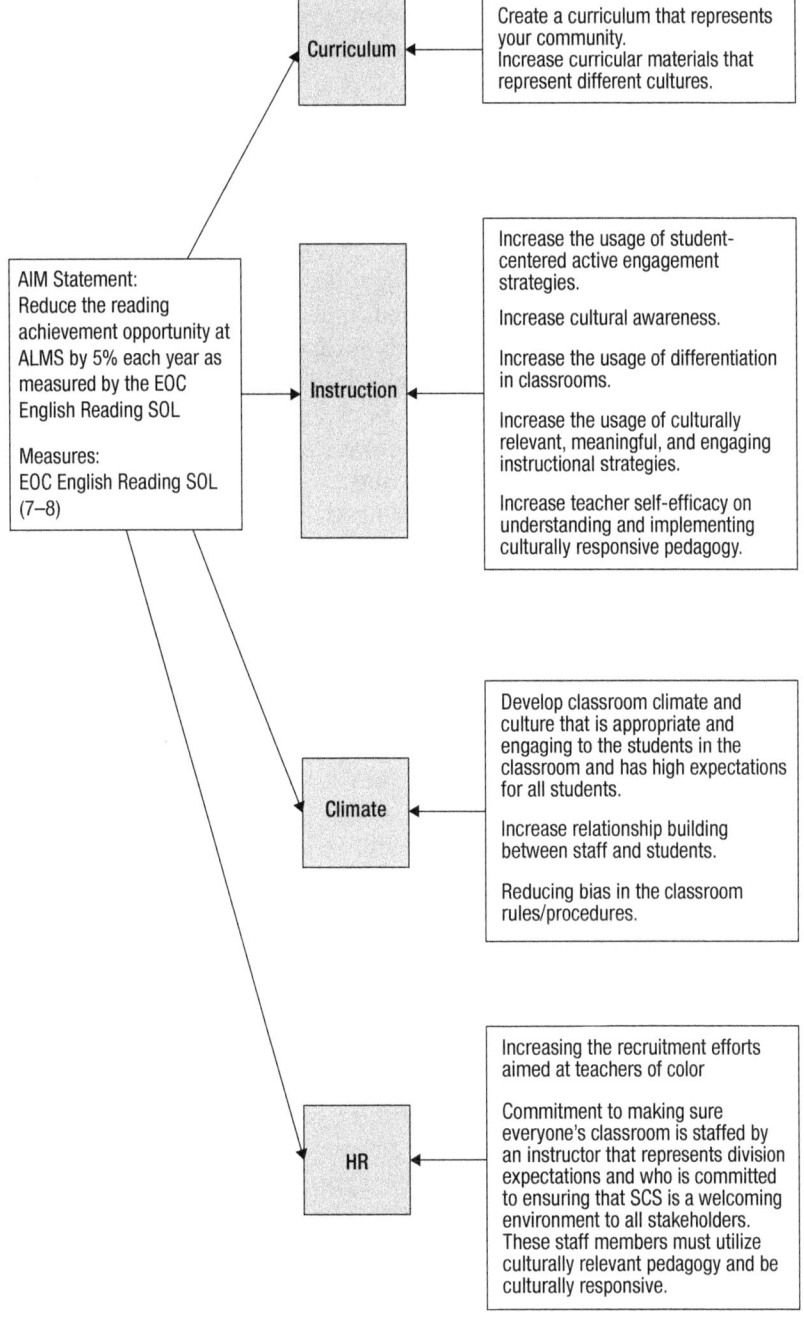

Figure 6.10. Primary and Secondary Drivers

Following the identification of the primary and secondary drivers involved in the racial disparities in reading outcomes at ALMS, the research team collaborated to develop potential change ideas. The team focused on developing change ideas that would result in fundamental change at the system level. Collectively, the team read and discussed research articles and discussed their personal experiences and beliefs to develop the following change ideas to address the identified secondary drivers associated with curriculum: develop and implement a defined, systematic process for curriculum mapping and material selection that ensures materials represent different cultures, develop and implement a systematic process (rubric) for determining the appropriateness of content selection (equity lens), develop and implement a systematic process for stakeholder review and participation in curricular material selection (parents/teachers), and integrate engaging materials, including student voice, into the curriculum.

The team identified the following change ideas to address the secondary drivers associated with instruction: develop and implement a district-wide professional development (PD) designed to add student engagement strategies into classrooms, design and implement a PD for administrators, utilize place-based instructional strategies designed to engage students, create rubrics for teachers and administrators that reflect the implementation of culturally relevant/responsive/sustaining pedagogy, and provide PD on CRP to ALMS English teachers.

The research team identified the following change idea designed to address the secondary drivers associated with climate: design and implement ongoing CRP PD to include components to address implicit bias and how it can affect student discipline, cultural competence, and awareness.

Last, the team identified the following change ideas designed to address the secondary drivers associated with human resources: partner with local colleges and universities to engage with Black teacher candidates and other prospective teachers of color (develop a pipeline), develop and implement a teacher and staff evaluation tool that includes the usage and implementation of CRP and the demonstration of cultural responsiveness, add questions into interviews that ask teaching candidates to display their beliefs regarding cultural responsiveness and CRP, develop a mentorship program whereby every new teacher of color is paired with a teacher of color to support their transition to SCS, and create a grow-our-own program that recruits interested students of color into education prep courses. The resulting driver diagram can be seen in Figure 6.11.

After determining the potential change ideas designed to fundamentally change the system, the research team worked to determine which change idea to implement based on the potential impact it may have on the racial disparities in reading outcomes at ALMS and the perceived ease of implementation. To accomplish this, the team plotted each change idea on a simple scatter plot diagram. The ease of implementation was placed on the horizontal axis, and the impact of change was placed on the vertical axis. Each change idea was assigned a number (see Figure 6.11) and plotted on the scatter plot diagram (see Figure 6.12).

Primary	Secondary	Change Ideas	Change Idea #
Curriculum	Create a curriculum that represents your community.	Develop and implement a defined, systematic process for curriculum mapping and material selection that ensures materials represent different cultures.	1
	Increase curricular materials that represent different cultures.	Develop and implement a systematic process (rubric) for determining the appropriateness of content selection (equity lens).	2
		Develop and implement a systematic process for stakeholder review and participation in curricular material selection (parents/teaching).	3
		Integrate engaging materials; including student voice into the curriculum.	4
Instruction	Increase the usage of student-centered active engagement strategies.	Develop and implement a district-wide professional development (PD) designed to add student engagement strategies into classrooms.	5
	Increase cultural awareness.	Design and implement a PD for administrators centered around the following - what do you look for when they come into your classroom? WHY - Admin needs to be well-versed in these things before teachers can be ?	6
	Increase the usage of differentiation in classrooms.	Utilize place-based instructional strategies designed to engage students.	7
	Increase the usage of culturally relevant, meaningful, and engaging instructional strategies.	Create rubrics that reflect what we want to see in the classroom and measure the criteria we want to see.	8
	Increase teacher self-efficacy on understanding and implementing culturally responsive pedagogy.	Professional development on cultural competency/awareness.	9
Climate	Develop classroom climate and culture that is appropriate and engaging to the students in the classroom and has high expectations for all students.	Design and implement culturally relevant PD for all teachers and staff. This PD must be on-going. Bring teacher leaders into PD circle & decision making.	10
	Increase relationship building between staff and students.	Design and implement a professional development program designed to help staff recognize their implicit bias and how they may have an impact on student discipline.	11
	Reducing bias in the classroom rules/procedures.	Design and implement a Professional Development on cultural competence/awareness.	12
HR	Increasing the recruitment efforts aimed at teachers of color.	Partner with local colleges and universities to engage with Black teaching candidates and other perspective teachers of color (develop a pipeline)	13
	Commitment to making sure everyone's classroom is staffed by an instructor that represents division expectations and who is committed to ensuring that SCS is a welcoming environment to all stakeholders. These staff members must utilize culturally relevant pedagogy and be culturally responsive.	Develop and implement a teacher/staff evaluation tool that includes the usage and implementation of culturally relevant pedagogy and the demonstration of cultural responsiveness. Develop indicators for administrators.	14
		Add questions into interviews that ask teaching candidates to display their beliefs regarding cultural responsiveness and culturally relevant pedagogy.	15
		Develop a mentorship program whereby every new teacher of color is paired with a teacher of color to support transition to SCS.	16
		Create a grow-our-own program that recruits interested students of color into education prep courses (Job Shadows/Senior Pathway Projects, etc.)	17

AIM Statement: Reduce the reading achievement opportunity at ALMS by 5% each year as measured by the EOC English Reading SOL

Measures: EOC English Reading SOL (7–8)

Figure 6.11. Driver Diagram with Change Ideas

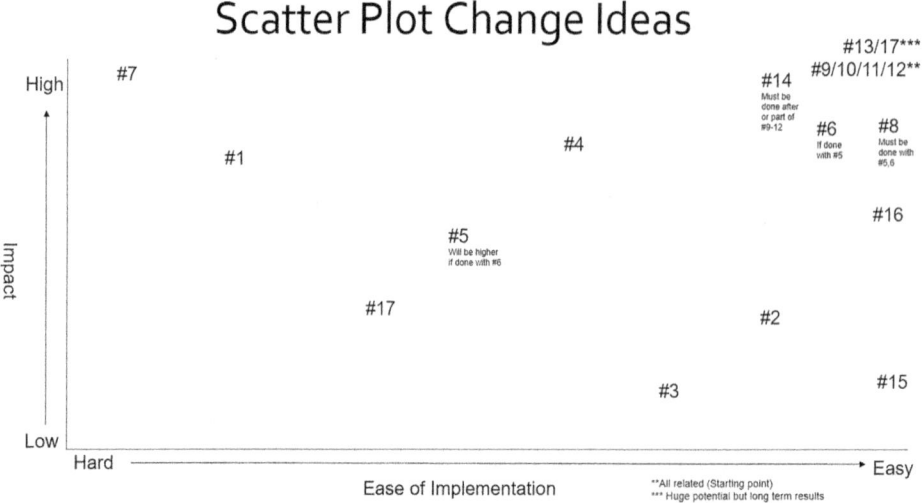

Figure 6.12. Scatter Plot of Change Ideas

Based on the resulting ease of implementation and potential impact, the team decided to design and implement a CRP PD program for ALMS English teachers. The team determined that the PD needed to be ongoing, personalized, and designed to increase the teachers' self-efficacy concerning understanding and implementing CRP. Moving from a working theory of improvement to a final theory of improvement requires that the change ideas identified be supported by evidence.

THEORY OF IMPROVEMENT

As the research team worked to move from a working theory of improvement to the final theory of improvement, the team consulted the scholarly research base. Too often this important step is not included as part of the traditional school improvement process. Frequently, educators fall victim to relying solely on their personal experiences rather than combining these experiences with stakeholder feedback and the information found in scholarly research before jumping to a solution. By consulting the scholarly research base, the team was able to deepen our understanding of culture and its impact on student achievement, develop a stronger research-based understanding of CRP and how it can be implemented to successfully increase Black student achievement and to determine and strengthen the components of our CRP PD.

By reviewing the scholarly research base and mainstream literature, the team gained a much deeper understanding of what is meant by culture and how cultural disconnects can have a major impact on educational outcomes for students of color. We learned that culture is a powerful concept that allows us to make sense of the world around us (Gay, 2013; 2018; Howard, 2019; Milner, 2015; Tatum, 2005). We learned that although educators must be careful not to stereotype individuals and must recognize that everyone is different based on their lived experiences, we must also recognize that "culture is at the heart of all we do in education, whether that is curriculum, instruction, administration, or performance assessment" (Gay, 2018, p. 8). Also, the scholarly research base supported our belief that if educators cannot recognize the importance of and need to utilize culture as a conduit to teaching all of our students, our educational system will continue to fail those whose cultures do not match the culture of the teachers leading their classrooms.

As we deepened our understanding of the term "culture," something we had inherently understood was an important factor in the educational outcomes of our Black students, the scholarly research base supported our understanding and helped us gain a deeper understanding of why this is true and how we could successfully address this challenge. Karatas and Oral (2015) purported, we cannot escape the fact that "education is a socio-cultural process" (p. 47). The fact that a white female teacher leads every English classroom at ALMS increases the chance that a cultural incongruence exists between these teachers and their Black students. Our next challenge was to determine the best method for addressing this cultural disconnect. Fortunately, as seen in Gloria Ladson-Billings's (2009) book *The Dreamkeepers: Successful Teachers of African American Children*, white teachers who implement CRP can have positive impacts on Black student achievement.

The formal research base and the mainstream educational literature are rife with articles and books that support the use of CRP as a method for improving outcomes for Black students (Alim & Paris, 2017; Aronson & Laughter, 2016; Blazar, 2021; Emdin, 2016; Gay, 2002; 2013; 2018; Hammond, 2015; Howard, 2019; Karatas, 2020; Ladson-Billings, 1992; 1995a; 1995b; 2009' 2014; Milner, 2010; 2012; 2015; Paris, 2012; Paris & Alim, 2014; Tatum, 2005). From the research base, we know that CRP is a strength-based theory that was constructed in response to the predominant "cultural deprivation" theory of this time, which argued that Black and low-income students performed at lower levels compared to their white peers due to the lack of cultural capital within their homes and communities (Gay, 2018).

> The theory [of CRP] postulates that the discontinuities between the school culture and the home and community cultures of low-income and students of color are an important factor in their low academic achievement. Consequently, the academic achievement of these students will increase if schools and teachers reflect and draw on their cultural and language strengths. (Gay, 2018, p. xii)

As the movement to meet the needs of an ever-diversifying student demographic has advanced, the terminology surrounding CRP has continued to evolve while maintaining its conceptual foundational roots grounded in the research of Gay and Ladson-Billings. Gay (2018) defined CRP as "using the cultural knowledge, prior experiences, frames of reference, and performance styles of ethnically diverse students to make learning encounters more relevant and effective for them. It teaches to and through the strengths of these students" (p. 36). Ladson-Billings (1995a) defined CRP

> as a pedagogy of opposition not unlike critical pedagogy but specifically committed to collective, not merely individual, empowerment. Culturally relevant pedagogy rests on three criteria or propositions: (a) Students must experience academic success; (b) stu-

dents must develop and/or maintain cultural competence; and (c) students must develop a critical consciousness through which they challenge the status quo of the current social order. (p. 160)

Throughout the research base and mainstream educational literature, the term CRP is often used synonymously with the term culturally relevant teaching (CRT) and now encompasses terms such as culturally sustaining pedagogy (Paris, 2012, p. 95) and the umbrella term culturally responsive education (Dover, 2013, p. 5).

Gay (2018) wrote,

Although called by many different names, including *culturally relevant, sensitive, centered, congruent, reflective, mediated, contextualized, synchronized,* and *responsive,* the ideas about why it is important to make classroom instruction more consistent with cultural orientations of ethnically diverse students, and how this can be done, are virtually identical. (p. 36)

Although as a research team we use the term CRP, we agree with Gay and use this term to encompass all the versions listed earlier that demonstrate the importance of understanding, valuing, and integrating strategies and mindsets that are aligned with the diverse student cultures that comprise classrooms at ALMS.

According to Gay (2018), "Teachers must learn to how to recognize, honor, and incorporate the personal abilities of students into their teaching strategies. If this is done, then school achievement will improve" (p. 1). In their synthesis of the research base, Aronson and Laughter (2016) provided numerous examples of research studies across the content areas, including English language arts that support the effectiveness of CRP as a method for increasing academic outcomes for minority students. Within these studies, numerous CRP strategies are highlighted and shown to be effective strategies for implementing CRP. As we read these studies, we collaborated to determine which strategies we would emphasize as part of the CRP PD program. Whereas the research base has long been flush with studies that use qualitative methods to demonstrate CRP as the likely mechanism (Blazar, 2021) for raising Black student achievement, Blazar's study demonstrated a causal link between the implementation of CRP and increased academic success for both Black students and white students. It is clear from the research base and mainstream educational literature that implementing CRP is a pathway to increasing achievement outcomes for Black students. As ALMS English teachers increase their understanding of the importance of implementing CRP to support the academic achievement of Black students, as well as the need to increase their self-efficacy in their knowledge, understanding, and ability to implement CRP, they are more likely to implement CRP in their daily practice and, thereby, make a difference in the reading achievement of Black students at ALMS. The research team predicted that ALMS English teachers who participate in the CRP PD program would demonstrate substantial growth in their self-efficacy to understand and gain the ability to implement CRP in their classrooms.

Our theory of improvement was that as ALMS English teachers increase their self-efficacy in their knowledge, understanding, and ability to implement CRP, they are more likely to implement CRP in their daily practice and, thereby, make a difference in the reading achievement of Black students at ALMS. The specific change idea was to provide an ongoing, personalized professional development program (CRP PD) designed to improve teacher self-efficacy in their knowledge, understanding, and ability to implement CRP. The CRP PD consisted of an initial PD session followed by the development of an ongoing, personalized CRP PD plan based on an initial planning meeting that would include a coaching cycle consisting of five sessions over six weeks.

A significant challenge the team had to overcome was determining who would implement the change idea. After many lengthy discussions and looking at a variety of options including outside organizations, the research team determined the best person to implement the CRP PD program was the ALMS English instructional coach. The ALMS English instructional coach was not only part of the research team, but she also provided job-embedded PD to the ALMS English teachers as part of her job responsibilities. The ALMS English instructional coach was knowledgeable of both CRP and instructional coaching and had previously provided CRP PD to teachers across the state as part of a state organization. Last, and perhaps most importantly, the ALMS English instructional coach was respected by all the ALMS English teachers and did not have a supervisory role.

PDSA CYCLES

The research team used the Plan-Do-Study-Act (PDSA) model of continuous improvement as the methodological process (Hinnant-Crawford, 2020) for gathering data to build a deeper understanding of the effectiveness of the implementation of the ongoing, personalized culturally responsive pedagogy PD designed to increase teacher self-efficacy in their ability to both understand and implement culturally responsive teaching. Two PDSA cycles were used to test the theory of improvement on a small scale before potential implementation across the system. To make changes necessary to make the CRP PD program effective, we developed process, driver, and balancing measures. We administered these measures at various times during the iterative PDSA cycles.

Although the team easily identified the outcome measure we would use to determine the effectiveness of the CRP PD, we found developing or identifying appropriate process, driver, and balancing measures used to collect data needed to make adjustments both during and after the PDSA cycles very challenging. Although no one on the research team was an expert in building surveys, the team developed both the process survey used after the initial PD and the process survey administered at the midpoint of the coaching cycles for both PDSA cycles. After reviewing the research base, the team was able to find and modify an observation protocol that we determined could be used to collect process data as well as a survey regarding culturally responsive teacher self-efficacy that could be used as a driver measure. A brief description of the types of measures, purpose of each measure, and specific instruments that were used during the PDSA process is next.

Outcome Measures

Outcome measures are used to determine if the PD was successful (Hinnant-Crawford, 2020). The research team analyzed the results of the Virginia Reading SOL to determine if ALMS was successful in reducing the racial disparities in reading outcomes by 5%. Due to the limited scope (three teachers) of the initial PDSA cycle, and the second PDSA cycle (three additional teachers), we did not anticipate the aim would be met in this first year, but, if successful and expanded to include all English teachers, achieving the aim is expected in the second year.

Driver Measures

Driver measures are used to determine if the change idea is "working" (Hinnant-Crawford, 2020, p. 140). The data we collected from these measures were analyzed to determine if the CRP PD program was effectively increasing the teachers' self-efficacy in understanding and implementing culturally responsive pedagogy. The research team used a modified version of the Culturally Responsive Teaching Self-Efficacy Survey (CRTSE) developed by Siwatu (2007) as a driver measure. The survey was administered after the PDSA cycles to determine teacher self-efficacy.

Process Measures

According to Hinnant-Crawford (2020), "Process measures are collected frequently, so you can detect variation and deviation in the process from what is desired" (p. 141). To determine if the PD was being implemented effectively, a short survey was provided to participating teachers following the initial PD sessions. The purpose of this survey was to collect data as to the effectiveness of the initial PD in serving as an introduction to various components of CRP, including self-awareness, instructional strategies, learning environments, and community engagement. We used the data collected from this survey to modify the components of the initial PD session for future iterations. Additionally, the survey was designed to collect feedback from the participating teachers on challenges that might hinder their ability to implement this work. The participating teachers were administered a separate process survey at the midpoint of each coaching PD cycle. The team designed the process measure survey to determine the effectiveness of the CRP PD program in increasing teacher self-efficacy in understanding and implementing CRP in their classrooms. The team analyzed the data collected from these surveys, consequently modified the components and structure of the overall CRP PD program for subsequent PDSA cycles, and personalized the second half of the CRP PD program for each participating teacher. Also, the ALMS English instructional coach used the ALMS Culturally Responsive Instructional Observation Protocol (CRIOP) tool (Powel et al., 2017) to observe participating teachers' classrooms as part of the coaching cycle to determine if culturally responsive teaching was being implemented in classrooms.

Balancing Measure

Balancing measures are used to ensure that the change idea is working as intended (Hinnant-Crawford, 2020). For this study, I must assess if implementing CRP PD had any unintended consequences. To check for potential unintended consequences, the following open-ended questions were added to the process survey: (1) What challenges do you see keeping you from implementing this work? (2) Have things gone as expected? Explain.

PDSA CYCLE RESULTS

PDSA Cycle 1: Initial PD Results and Analysis

Three ALMS English teachers volunteered to participate in the first PDSA cycle. The three teachers included two eighth grade teachers and one seventh grade teacher. The three teachers participated in an initial CRP PD session designed to serve as an introduction to various components of culturally relevant/responsive/sustaining pedagogy, including self-awareness, instructional strategies, learning environments, and community engagement. The CRP PD was designed by the ALMS English instructional coach and reviewed by me before implementation. Following the initial CRP PD, the three ALMS English teachers were invited to participate in an anonymous online survey. The survey was designed to gather teacher feedback on the effectiveness of the initial CRP PD in introducing the aforementioned components of CRP. Although only three teachers participated in the PD and completed the survey, the data was valuable for addressing the teachers' experiences and for planning the next PDSA cycle.

The data collected from the initial CRP PD process survey indicated that the initial PD session was successful in addressing the topic of self-awareness. A teacher indicated that they felt all teachers needed to be reminded of CRP concepts regularly. The teachers indicated that the CRP PD addressed both culturally responsive classroom learning environments and community engagement. One teacher indicated the need to clarify what the term *community* means in CRP PD.

Based on the results of the initial CRP PD process survey, the initial CRP PD was successful in addressing the self-awareness, instructional strategies, learning environments, and community engagement components of CRP. The ALMS English instructional coach and I collaborated and analyzed the survey data to plan adjustments to the initial CRP PD for the second PDSA cycle as well as to determine important components of CRP that needed to be targeted in subsequent ongoing personalized CRP PD sessions. The need to emphasize the definition of community to include both the classroom and the surrounding community beyond the school walls was one of the main topics identified in the survey data as an important component to be included in both the ongoing PD sessions and the initial CRP PD session in PDSA Cycle 2.

PDSA Cycle 1: Ongoing Personalized PD Results and Analysis

After the initial CRP PD, each of the three teachers met independently with the ALMS English instructional coach to develop personalized CRP PD or coaching goals. Before meeting with each teacher individually, the ALMS English instructional coach shared the results of the ALMS Student Measure of Culturally Responsive Teaching (SMCRT) survey with each of the three participating teachers. The ALMS SMCRT survey had been previously administered to all Black students at ALMS by the school's principal. The ALMS SMCRT survey was a modified version of the SMCRT survey designed by Dickson, Chun, and Fernandez (2016). The survey was administered to Black ALMS English students by the ALMS principal to gather data on students' perceptions of culturally relevant classroom practices in English classrooms at ALMS. The teachers were asked to review the student responses before their initial personalized PD planning session with the ALMS English instructional coach. Also, the ALMS English instructional coach shared with the teachers the modified ALMS Culturally Responsive Instruction Observation Protocol (CRIOP) tool (Powell et al., 2017). During the initial personalized PD planning meeting with each teacher, the ALMS English instructional coach reviewed the components of the initial CRP PD as well as the participant feedback from the initial CRP PD survey, the student results of the ALMS (SMCRT) survey, and the components of the CRIOP tool. After reviewing this information collaboratively, individual teachers chose personalized CRP PD goals. Following the goal-setting meeting, each teacher participated in a coaching cycle that included co-planning lessons, modeling/co-teaching, observation, feedback, and self-reflection.

The ALMS English instructional coach developed a personalized CRP PD plan based on the initial planning meeting with each of the three participating ALMS English teachers. Each coaching cycle consisted of five sessions over six weeks. One teacher (Teacher A) set a goal in the instructional component of CRP. The teacher's goal was to scaffold instruction and increase student engagement using CRP. Teacher B set a goal within the discourse component of CRP. The teacher's goal was to increase student voice and student-led discussion in the classroom. Last, Teacher C set a goal in the instructional component of CRP to implement student-centered instructional approaches in the classroom. The ALMS English instructional coach used the modified ALMS CRIOP tool to conduct a classroom observation of each teacher during a mutually agreed upon class period and date.

The data from the classroom observations indicated the need to continue to reaffirm what CRP is and what it is not. The data indicated that due to classroom management challenges, Teacher A was struggling to scaffold and engage students in instruction. Last, the results from the data collected using the modified ALMS CRIOP tool indicated a need for the CRP PD to include specific, actionable strategies designed to increase student engagement and student voice.

At the midpoint of each teacher's personalized PD coaching cycle, the three participants were administered an online anonymous process survey designed to collect feedback on the effectiveness of the ongoing CRP PD in increasing the teachers' understanding of and ability to implement CRP. Each of the three teachers completed the survey.

The data from the ongoing personalized PD process survey indicated that the ongoing personalized CRP PD was effective at increasing the teachers' understanding of the need for CRP in their classrooms. The data also indicated that the ALMS English instructional coach met with each teacher to develop a personalized PD plan and that each plan involved planning, modeling, observing, and providing feedback before the administration of the midpoint process survey.

The data from the midpoint survey indicated that the implementation of each teacher's personalized CRP PD plan increased their ability to implement CRP with their students. The data from the midpoint process survey also indicated that the teachers believed they were successful in incorporating CRP in their classrooms as a result of the CRP PD program. One teacher stated,

> I enjoyed the opportunity to incorporate new pedagogy into my existing teaching strategies that was intentionally designed to engage my students and gives them the opportunity to share their lived experiences and see themselves represented in the content and curriculum. The PD has been incredibly successful.

Based on the data collected from the midpoint ongoing CRP PD process survey as well as the observations collected by the ALMS English instructional coach using the ALMS modified CRIOP observational tool, we made several minor adjustments to the second half of the coaching cycle. To address the challenges identified in PDSA Cycle 1 using data gathered from various sources, the ALMS English instructional coach continued to reaffirm what CRP is and what it is not, increased verbal feedback about specific elements of CRP seen in the classroom, emphasized strategies to increase student engagement and to increase the ratio of student voice to teacher voice, and continued to emphasize how CRP establishes high expectations for all students and how CRP instruction can make information relatable to students and, therefore, lead to better outcomes.

Overall PDSA Cycle 1 Results and Analysis

After the teachers completed the entire CRP PD program, they were administered the modified ALMS CRTSE survey designed to measure the overall effectiveness of the CRP PD program at increasing the teachers' understanding of and ability to implement CRP. Overall, the three teachers responded very positively to the CRP PD and its impact on their self-efficacy in understanding and being able to implement CRP.

In response to a question that asked teachers to determine the extent to which they felt they had grown in their knowledge and ability to implement CRP, one teacher responded tremendously, and two teachers responded somewhat. When asked at the end of the survey for additional comments, one respondent stated,

> I'm very grateful to have participated in this opportunity, but realize this is a drop in the bucket. As a reflective practitioner, I always have so much to learn. The coaching has been the most valuable asset of this program for me.

These responses as well as the data collected throughout the first PDSA cycle indicated the program was effective at substantially growing the participating teachers' self-efficacy to understand and to have the ability to implement CRP in their classrooms. The data also indicated the need for the PD program to be continuous and not a one-time PD program. To integrate CRP into daily classroom practice will require additional ongoing support.

After further analyzing the ALMS CRTSE survey results as well as qualitative data collected from conversations between the ALMS English instructional coach and participating teachers, the ALMS English instructional coach and I identified several concepts that needed to be addressed/implemented in the second PDSA cycle. Teachers seemed uncomfortable with bridging the gap between community, home, and school. Also, teachers lacked a deep understanding of Black culture. Furthermore, additional staff need to be trained in both improvement science and how to lead CRP PD to meet the ultimate goal of providing personalized CRP PD to all ALMS' and SCS's teachers.

Changes for PDSA Cycle 2

To address the overall concepts identified earlier, the ALMS English instructional coach and I collaborated and adjusted the CRP PD before beginning PDSA Cycle 2. Specifically, the CRP PD program was modified to include additional specific strategies and PD components to support the teachers' ability to learn more about other cultures. An additional PD session was designed to support teachers' understanding of Black culture(s). The additional PD session was embedded as a component of the ongoing personalized component of the CRP PD.

Additionally, the ALMS English instructional coach and I triangulated the data attained from the teacher responses from the initial CRP PD survey, the ongoing PD midpoint process survey, the modified ALMS CRIOP observation tool data, and the ALMS CRTSE survey. Several adjustments were then made to the initial CRP PD session before beginning PDSA Cycle 2. ALMS's changing demographic data was shared with teachers to help lay the foundational "why" teachers need to increase their understanding of and ability to implement CRP. Increased time was provided during the initial PD to allow more time for teacher reflection and discussion on their current practices and how they could implement more CRP practices in teaching once the tenets of CRP were reviewed. The ALMS English instructional coach emphasized strategies for learning more about student cultures. The ALMS English instructional coach purposefully reiterated the definition meant by *community* (not classroom community). Also, the coach introduced community engagement strategies as a component of CRP designed to engage students and build a bridge between the school and the students' communities. Last, recognizing that more stakeholders needed to be trained in CRP to address the district's diversifying student population, the English language learner (ELL) coordinator and elementary literacy coach were invited to participate in the initial and ongoing CRP PD program to begin exploring how to expand this work to K–5 as well as to meet the needs of the growing ELL student population.

In addition to changes made to the initial CRP PD session, the ALMS English instructional coach and I collaborated to make changes to the ongoing CRP PD sessions for PDSA Cycle 2 based on the data collected from the initial CRP PD survey, the ongoing PD midpoint process survey, the modified ALMS CRIOP observation data, and the ALMS CRTSE survey. We implemented an additional planning session before beginning the coaching cycle. This session was designed to help teachers gain a better understanding of student culture and to identify the teachers' areas of lesser strength associated with CRP. Additionally, the instructional coach purposefully included a greater emphasis on student voice and choice when planning instructional activities with the teachers. Furthermore, the coach reinforced and built upon community engagement strategies (such as building relationships with families and place-based education) much earlier and continuously throughout the ongoing CRP PD sessions.

PDSA Cycle 2: Initial PD Results and Analysis

A recruitment email was sent to the remaining seventh and eighth grade ALMS English teachers inviting them to participate in the CRP PD. Three teachers, two from the seventh grade and one from the eighth grade chose to participate in the PD. Before expressing their willingness to participate, each of these teachers had had conversations with the teachers who had previously participated in PDSA Cycle 1. It is important to note that none of the three teachers had expressed a desire to participate in the first PDSA cycle. Based on this fact, we recognized the need to stress the rapidly changing student demographic to these teachers. We determined the need to emphasize how CRP is essential to meeting the needs of our increasingly diverse students. Most importantly, we emphasized the importance of teachers changing their pedagogical approach to teaching to include CRP as a method of engaging all students. This approach was grounded in the research-based evidence and shared with teachers. The teachers participated in an initial PD session. The initial CRP PD implemented for PDSA Cycle 2 was the modified version of the initial CRP PD provided to teachers in PDSA Cycle 1. Following the initial PD session, the teachers were administered an anonymous online. The survey was designed to gather teacher feedback on the effectiveness of the initial CRP PD in introducing the aforementioned components of CRP. All three teachers completed the survey.

The data derived from the process survey from the initial CRP PD PDSA Cycle 2 session indicated that the initial PD was successful in addressing the topic of self-awareness. Each of the three teachers responded they strongly agreed that the initial CRP PD session addressed the self-awareness component of CRP. When asked to provide additional comments, one teacher replied, "It was a good discussion of our current school population in regards to both students and teachers," and another teacher replied, "I appreciated knowing/learning the demographics in our won [sic] school system as compared to others around us and how these demographics are changing." These statements indicated the impact of using demographic data to establish the "why" for understanding and implementing CRP is imperative. Establishing the "why" was extremely important with this group of teachers who were not early adopters of CRP.

In response to the question of the initial CRP PD session's effectiveness at addressing how to create a culturally responsive classroom environment, one teacher stated, "There were lots of suggestions and ideas presented"; a second teacher added that it was a

> good start but we didn't get to all the strategies in the slides. I did go through the slides to see what we ran out of time for. Reflection in the beginning was good but maybe went too long because I would have liked time to get to more of the strategies.

Based on these comments as well as follow-up discussions with the ALMS instructional coach, future initial CRP PD sessions will be lengthened to a half-day or a whole-day PD due to the time constraints when offering this as an after-school PD. Also, teachers will be provided substitutes to allow them to attend the initial PD during the school day if the PD cannot be scheduled on a district PD Day. Furthermore, the ALMS English instructional coach will continue to emphasize strategies the teachers can implement to create a culturally responsive classroom climate during the ongoing CRP PD sessions.

The teachers agreed that the CRP PD was successful in addressing the topic of community engagement. One teacher stated, "This is a tough area to think about the best way to improve." This aligned with the findings of PDSA Cycle 1 which also indicated the difficulty and apprehension teachers had at addressing community engagement. Based on this consistent finding, this area will require additional time and continued sustained PD to be addressed successfully and ingrained in teacher practice.

Last, when asked what challenges teachers thought might hinder their ability to implement CRP, one teacher stated, "I think some students may not feel as comfortable sharing about their culture and /or background." This statement served as a reminder to the research team that all students, regardless of race and culture, bring individual-lived experiences and personalities to the classroom. Strategies to address these students were included in the ongoing PD sessions. A second teacher stated, "I feel overwhelmed by all the things I am juggling at the moment. Looking forward to implementing these strategies and becoming more self-aware, but I am nervous about meetings and coaching and it's 'one more thing' on my plate." Feeling overwhelmed by new initiatives and feeling as if they do not have time are common reactions many teachers express when provided PD or new pedagogical strategies. To support the successful implementation of CRP in the classroom, the PD team must keep in mind that when providing ongoing personalized PD to teachers, they need to keep a pulse on the teachers' states of mind and adjust and modify as necessary. It is important to start small and celebrate successes as the teachers progress through the coaching cycle.

PDSA Cycle 2: Ongoing Personalized PD Results and Analysis

The process followed for PDSA Cycle 2 mirrored the process followed in PDSA Cycle 1 with only slight modifications based on teacher feedback. Based on the feedback, the ALMS instructional coach followed the initial planning meeting with a second meeting with each teacher to provide an additional PD designed to help each teacher gain a better understanding of student culture and to identify their area of lesser strength associated with CRP. During this second meeting, the ALMS English instructional coach collaborated with each teacher to develop a personalized CRP PD plan. The teacher's individual plan included a coaching cycle comprised of co-planning lessons, modeling/co-teaching, observation, feedback, and self-reflection. As in PDSA Cycle 1, the coaching cycle for PDSA Cycle 2 consisted of five sessions over six weeks. One teacher (Teacher D) set a goal in the instructional practices component of CRP. The teacher's goal was to increase the implementation of student-centered instruction and to release control to students. Teacher E set a goal within the discourse component of CRP. The teacher's goal was to increase student voice and student choice in the classroom. Last, Teacher F set a goal in the instructional practices component of CRP to implement strategies designed to increase community engagement and student voice in the classroom. The ALMS English instructional coach used the modified ALMS CRIOP tool to conduct a classroom observation of each teacher during a mutually agreed upon class period and date.

The data from the classroom observations indicated the need to continue to support teachers on their journeys in implementing CRP even when it was uncomfortable for them. Teacher D demonstrated strength in the purposeful planning of a CRP lesson; however, the teacher still struggled with classroom management in a culturally diverse class and with the ability to recognize that noise does not necessarily equate to a lack of engagement. Teacher D also acknowledged that they struggled with relationship-building with students. The ALMS English instructional coach emphasized the following with Teacher D during the second half of the ongoing CRP PD: informed the teacher about cultural norms, pushed the teacher out of their comfort zone by continuing to relinquish control and focused on strategies that allow students to express who they are as individuals.

Based on the CRIOP tool and follow-up conversation with the ALMS English instructional coach, Teacher E demonstrated strength in the area of relationship-building with students. Teacher E also demonstrated the ability to plan CRP lessons. The observation data indicated that Teacher E was still struggling with implementing daily strategies to provide student choice. The ALMS English instructional coach continued to provide personalized support to Teacher E during the second half of the ongoing personalized CRP PD. Teacher F demonstrated great strength in the area of relationship-building with students. However, the CRIOP tool data indicated that Teacher F still struggled with maintaining high academic expectations for students. The ALMS English instructional coach continued to provide Teacher F with personalized support on strategies they could use to ensure high academic expectations were maintained for students while implementing CRP.

In addition to the individualized supports identified for each teacher, general observation data indicated the need to continue to provide all the teachers with classroom management strategies that deemphasized compliance and prioritized authentic student engagement and strategies to include specific, actionable strategies designed to increase student engagement and student voice.

Just as in PDSA Cycle 1, an anonymous process survey was emailed to each of the participating teachers at the midpoint of the coaching cycle. The data from the ongoing personalized PD process survey indicated that the ongoing personalized CRP PD was effective at increasing the teachers' understanding of the need for CRP in their classrooms. All three teachers responded they strongly agreed that CRP was needed. One teacher provided the following additional comment: "Just having more conversations about all aspects of CRP has helped make me more aware of many things to think about while planning and teaching." The data also indicated that the ALMS English instructional coach had met with each teacher to develop a personalized PD plan and that each plan involved planning, modeling, observing, and providing feedback before the administration of the midpoint process survey. Additionally, one teacher stated, "The suggestions in planning and modeling were very helpful." This supported the coaching model as a vital component of the CRP PD.

All three teachers responded they strongly agreed that the CRP PD had increased their ability to implement CRP with their students. This midpoint data indicated that the CRP PD had been successful in increasing the teachers' self-efficacy in implementing CRP into their classrooms. The data from the midpoint process survey also indicated that the teachers believed they were successful in incorporating CRP in their classrooms as a result of the CRP PD program. However, two teachers indicated they were somewhat successful at implementing CRP into their teaching at the midpoint of the ongoing PD. One teacher stated, "It's always a work in progress, but this has been helpful and widened my perspective on things to be mindful of when planning and teaching." This data indicated the need for ongoing support. In response to the survey question about what challenges the teachers felt could hinder their ability to implement CRP, one teacher stated,

> The class that we are focusing on is just a tough class. Many many low needy students with big personalities and attention-seeking behaviors. It's easier when the instructional coach is with me, simply because two adults in the room go further than me being by myself with so many needs. I like trying new things and this training has increased my awareness but implementing while also having successful class management has been just as tough as before this training.

Another teacher stated, "Keeping all the balls in the air and meeting all goals" was hindering their ability to implement CRP. This data indicated the need to continue to support teachers in releasing responsibility to students while maintaining high expectations for all students and the need for additional classroom management strategies. When asked if things had gone as expected, one teacher stated,

> Things have gone better than expected with students reading their choice novels! The choice party has been great! Managing the voice part has been tricky for me with so many big personalities but I do feel like it's getting better.

A second teacher responded, "I expected to learn and have help with new ideas and that has been the case."

Based on the data collected from the midpoint ongoing CRP PD process survey as well as the observations collected by the ALMS English instructional coach using the ALMS modified CRIOP observational tool, the ALMS English instructional coach made minor adjustments during the second half of the coaching cycles. The coach continued to reaffirm the need to maintain high academic expectations for all students. The ALMS English instructional coach observed each teacher twice a week instead of once a week and provided personalized feedback based on the individual teacher's goals and other aspects of CRP. These frequent observations were imperative to support these teachers and provided face-to-face time to celebrate small victories for our more reluctant teachers whose stamina to continue this work was by nature not as strong as other teachers who embraced CRP from the outset.

Additionally, the ALMS English instructional coach emphasized classroom management strategies that deemphasized compliance and normalized authentic student engagement. The coach also stressed the need to implement student choice as a component of CRP. Furthermore, the coach facilitated intentional conversations and planning regarding community and family involvement during observation reflection conversations. Lastly, the EL coordinator was invited to participate in a coaching session to begin expanding CRP to meet the needs of our EL students.

After PDSA Cycle 2, the teachers were administered the modified ALMS CRTSE survey designed to measure the overall effectiveness of the CRP PD program in increasing the teachers' understanding of and ability to implement CRP. Overall, the teachers responded very positively to the CRP PD and its impact on their self-efficacy in understanding and being able to implement CRP.

In response to a question that asked teachers to determine the extent to which they felt they had grown in their knowledge and ability to implement CRP, two teachers responded tremendously, and one teacher responded somewhat. When asked at the end of the survey for additional comments, one respondent stated,

> Doing this coaching cycle has made me more aware of approaching classroom procedures with more awareness for the students in my classroom from different cultures. I have focused on being more flexible (choice and voice) and operating a different noise level as I try to include more students' voices and less of my voice all the time!

A second respondent stated,

> [The instructional coach] and another member of my group have helped me see additional ways to allow students to work together to help each other learn in small group settings. Being more hands-off has helped my students take a more active role in their learning. It has been great to see.

Before beginning the CRP PD, all three of the teachers involved in PDSA Cycle 2 were hesitant to participate and expressed the concern that this PD would be "one more thing"; however, after completing the CRP PD, each of the three teachers expressed a desire to continue working with the ALMS instructional coach to add additional CRP tools into their respective educational toolboxes. One teacher stated, "After I saw the response of the students when they were taught this way and seeing the increased level of engagement as well as the decrease in classroom discipline, I recognize the importance of implementing CRP in my classroom." The same teacher shared with the ALMS instructional coach that one of her Black female students approached her after a class and said, "We have been talking and you've been a really good teacher this month. Thank you!" The teacher indicated that this was "the ultimate aha moment" for her and that this was necessary and meaningful work. These responses as well as the data collected throughout the first and second PDSA cycles indicated the ongoing personalized CRP PD program was effective at substantially growing the participating teachers' self-efficacy in understanding and the ability to implement CRP in their classrooms.

Although the data indicated the effectiveness at increasing the participating teachers' self-efficacy in their ability to understand, the participating teachers' desire to continue working with the ALMS instructional coach as well as the number of responses to the questions on the CRTSE survey indicated the need for the PD to be ongoing and continuous for CRP to become ingrained into the teachers' instructional practice. According to the ALMS English instructional coach, "the teachers' metacognitive growth was evidenced during the reflection parts of the coaching cycle and they could realize/articulate student growth/benefits in ways they could not/did not during class or right after class." This and other feedback from the teachers to the ALMS English instructional coach indicated that the reflection/debriefing portion of the coaching cycle was a critical component of the CRP PD program. Last, the data collected from the PDSA cycles indicated the need for the initial CRP PD session to be implemented during a half-day or full-day PD session.

SPREADING CHANGES

It is clear from the research base and mainstream educational literature that implementing CRP is a pathway to increasing achievement outcomes for Black students. As ALMS English teachers increase their understanding of the importance of implementing CRP to support the academic achievement of Black students, as well as the need to increase their self-efficacy in their knowledge, understanding, and ability to implement CRP, they are more likely to implement CRP in their daily practice and, thereby, make a difference in the reading achievement of Black students at ALMS. The data collected supported the implementation of ongoing personalized CRP PD as an effective change idea to address the racial disparities in reading outcomes at ALMS due to its success at increasing teacher self-efficacy in their knowledge, understanding, and ability to implement CRP in their classroom. By providing teachers with ongoing personalized PD in CRP, the data indicated that they increased their self-efficacy; and, as a result, they are more likely to implement CRP in their classrooms and, thereby, their Black students should achieve at higher levels on the EOC reading SOL.

As a central office instructional leader in the SCS District, I will collaborate with the ALMS English instructional coach, other central office staff, and building-level administrators to incorporate the CRP PD program as part of our district-wide PD structures. Currently, our district has a structured PD program in which new teachers to SCS participate for their first three years. The CRP PD will be implemented as a foundational component of our PD program. Also, the district will offer the CRP PD program to teachers whom administrators determine need to participate in the CRP PD as a result of the culturally responsive component of the teacher evaluation process. Last, the district will offer the CRP PD program to all interested staff.

To expand the implementation of the CRP PD program in a meaningful and effective manner across our school district, we must heed the following structural key learnings. The CRP PD must be ongoing. Educators across the country can attest to the ineffectiveness of one-time PD sessions. The CRP PD must be personalized to meet the individual needs of teachers. The personalization component of the PD program is imperative to engage the teacher in meaningful participation. PD offerings are rarely personalized and instead are presented in a cookie-cutter manner that leads to dissatisfaction among teachers and contributes to the "this too shall pass" mentality that many educators bring to PD. We must continue to set an expectation that all teachers will implement CRP in their classrooms and make the PD program job-embedded and supported through continual instructional coaching. Recognizing that the role of the instructional coach is pivotal to the success of the CRP PD program, I plan to work with the ALMS English instructional coach to train additional instructional coaches, the elementary English instructional coach, the ELL coordinator, and department chairs in both CRP and instructional coaching so that they can provide the CRP PD to others in the district. We will provide training to administrators in CRP so they have the foundational understanding necessary to identify teachers who may need additional support implementing CRP in their classrooms. District leadership and school administrators will regularly meet with the instructional coach and provide additional support as needed.

In addition to the key structural components, SCS District will have to navigate many of the current divisive political challenges that we are likely to encounter as we grow the CRP PD program to scale. As the assistant superintendent, it will be imperative that I continue to bring key stakeholders including teachers, students, parents, administrators, school board members, and members of the city council together. During these meetings, I will need to utilize both demographic and student achievement data to explain why the implementation of culturally responsive pedagogy is imperative to the success of our rapidly diversifying student population. As the assistant superintendent who oversees the district's comprehensive planning process, I will continue to collaborate with stakeholders and provide research articles and the data gained from our pilot CRP PD program to demonstrate how the implementation of CRP aligns with our district's vision and mission. Integrating CRP as part of our comprehensive plan will facilitate the expectation that all teachers demonstrate cultural competency and reinforce the district's belief that teachers must implement CRP to provide a loving and engaging environment that inspires children to reach their full potential.

LESSONS LEARNED

As I reflect on my use of the improvement science process to address the reading racial disparity at ALMS, many of my personal beliefs regarding the best way to address a complex problem were affirmed. As a long-time building and central office administrator, I have embraced the use of data to establish whether a problem exists as well as to support "why" addressing a problem is important. Early on in my career, I recognized the need to involve a diverse group of stakeholders including those who were impacted by the problem, as well as those who could address the problem as key stakeholders in the school improvement process.

Although I have long recognized the importance of engaging stakeholders in the improvement process, logistically this is very difficult to put into practice. This challenge began to manifest itself as members of our research team had competing life priorities and were unable to attend various meetings. To overcome this challenge, I created and emailed agendas before meetings, provided virtual options, shared meeting notes, and had follow-up conversations with stakeholders who were unable to attend in-person or virtually to ensure they were able to continue to feel part of the team and were able to continue to make meaningful contributions.

An additional challenge that frequently occurred is the inability to assemble a diverse stakeholder team. As we began to assemble the team, we utilized several strategies designed to ensure we assembled a diverse team. First, I leveraged my current relationships with stakeholders by making personal contact. During these conversations, I focused on being authentic and using data to explain why addressing the racial reading disparity was imperative. I provided an overview of the process we would undertake and why we needed the stakeholder's participation.

In addition to the earlier affirmations, I learned many valuable lessons throughout my journey using the improvement science process. Too often in education, we fall victim to addressing problems we identify by simply using our experiences as a guide. Rather than jumping straight to implementing a solution, for complex problems, we should assemble a team and acquire a deep understanding of the problem by exploring the research base, as well as the mainstream educational literature. Furthermore, if we hope to address complex problems, stakeholders must identify and examine all the complex systems involved and gain an understanding of how these systems are related, as well as identify which of these components we can influence.

Furthermore, throughout this process, I have been able to add many tools and understandings of improvement science to my leadership toolbox. These tools and understandings will enhance my ability to address complex problems as I move forward in my career. The fishbone diagram and the five whys activity will help me collaborate with stakeholders to gain a deeper understanding of the problem through a root cause analysis. By using driver diagrams to identify primary drivers, secondary drivers, and ultimately change ideas based on a theory of improvement, our chance of addressing complex problems effectively will greatly increase.

Perhaps the most valuable lesson I learned from using improvement science was the need to develop PDSA cycles that include process measures, balancing measures, and driver measures. The PDSA cycles and important measures enable educators to collect data along the way and make necessary modifications instead of waiting until it is too late based on the outcome measure. Testing change ideas on a small scale before spreading the change is much more likely to lead to systemic change than the traditional method in education of globally implementing a solution. Globally implementing untested change ideas before ensuring the change will make a positive difference reinforces the current resistance to change many of us see in our schools.

Chapter 7

Editors' Commentary

Edwin Nii Bonney, Sarah A. Capello,
and Maxwell M. Yurkofsky

We asked each practitioner in part 1 of this book to share the lessons they learned from their improvement journey at the end of their chapter. One common thread throughout the cases was the need for improvers to operationalize and adapt improvement tools or processes depending on their setting and problem of practice. Not all practitioners, for example, started with an improvement team; however, they were each driven by problems of practice they had personally experienced or observed in their setting. Sometimes the improvement team was formed because of shared interests or because of the educational leader's invitation to other stakeholders. Operationalizing the tools and processes of improvement science ensures that they are relevant and meaningful to the practitioner and their team in addressing the problem in their context.

Another common thread across the lessons and improvement journey was the insistence on bringing diverse collaborators and communities as part of the improvement process. Although each chapter touched on how practitioners engaged with diverse collaborators, most practitioners wished they could have formally engaged more groups such as students in the improvement work. Many did not attempt to do so because they anticipated additional university Institutional Review Board (IRB) challenges to include students in the work since they were enrolled in doctoral programs when they undertook their improvement activities. This unfortunate reality is indicative of the complexity of undertaking improvement work as both a researcher and practitioner. Nonetheless, all the practitioners claimed that despite inviting and engaging only a few groups and individuals in their improvement journey, they still gained a more comprehensive understanding of the problem because of who was at the table. The few collaborators greatly contributed to shaping the discussions, conducting causal analysis work, and identifying ideas for change.

The challenge practitioners experienced in bringing and engaging diverse communities directly and indirectly impacted by the problem to the table is a noticeable gap in the improvement science field. Having diverse people at the table is great but it is not enough. There is also important work for the practitioners to do in creating an engaging and safe environment for everyone, especially marginalized groups, to share their perspectives and to participate in the improvement work. We encourage practitioners to consider modifications to engage all stakeholders including one-on-one conversations, separate affinity group discussions, and whole group discussions that promote active participation of the diverse collaborators at the table. We recognize that although practitioners may also desire to, they may not have the confidence or expertise to facilitate difficult and charged conversations with diverse groups. There is still work to be done in equipping and empowering practitioners, especially in leadership preparation programs, to facilitate discussions and engage in perspective-seeking after they have brought the different groups, at times with seemingly opposing interests, to the table in improvement efforts.

Furthermore, a common challenge in improvement science for practitioners is to overcome the tendency to rush into selecting a solution without fully understanding the problem. Engaging in reflective practice in a community of diverse collaborators would help practitioners and improvers refrain from making assumptions and jumping to solutions during the analysis of the problem. We encourage improvers to reflect on the data used in improvement efforts and to consider what other meaningful data could have been included or what data or perspective might be missing. This practice prompts a critical examination of the available information and encourages a more comprehensive and robust investigation by all those involved in or impacted by the problem. By expanding the scope of data collection and analysis, teams can gain deeper insights and uncover hidden factors that contribute to the problem at hand before considering change ideas. The practitioners in this section show us how.

An emerging question in the literature is whether and how improvement science can be used as a tool to address issues related to racial inequities and injustices. The chapters in this section provide some insight. Many of the practitioners sought to use improvement science to inquire into and address problems related to racial inequities and injustices—related to racial disparities in academic outcomes, student discipline, or access to advanced coursework. Improvement science offered many affordances for taking on this work. Practitioners described how it prompted them to involve community members who are directly impacted by these problems (particularly students), that it offered ways of having data and evidence-driven conversations about these problems with diverse stakeholder groups, and that, by emphasizing rapid, small-scale, tests of change, it helped teams build the confidence and skill so that they could carry out equity-focused change on a larger scale. At the same time, practitioners were also aware of aspects of the problem that were beyond their locus of control. In these cases, we hope that leaders think creatively about how they might address these challenges. For example, consider how Tracy and Kelly realized that their problem of practice was systemic across the Commonwealth. Rather than focus just on their school, Tracy and Kelly developed an online module that aimed to help other schools inquire into and address this problem of practice in their organizations.

Looking across these chapters, it is clear that practitioners used improvement science not only to address a specific problem of practice but also to enact wider and deeper cultural change in their organizations. Practitioners integrated improvement science into their approach to school and division-level leadership, which now involved: centering the perspectives of students, families, and other stakeholders they are trying to serve; moving beyond a one-size-fits-all approach to supporting teachers;

slowing down to deeply understand a problem before jumping to solutions; and relying on data and evidence, rather than intuitions.

An implication of the various work highlights across the chapters is that it is not enough for leaders who use improvement science to carry out an effective series of Plan-Do-Study-Act (PDSA) cycles. We believe Courtney said this best when she reflected on how "incidental change . . . is not enough. We need to continue to expand the work and spread change with purpose, or we will not see sustainable change over time." The task for those (like us) who support leaders in using improvement science is thus to focus on what it might look like for leaders to integrate the lessons of improvement science into their school systems. Courtney argues:

> We must find ways to operationalize improvement science in the authentic school context. This means that timeframes will be shorter, pressures will be multifaceted, and some aspects of the problem and resulting solution will be constrained by outside factors such as division or state initiatives and mandates.

Crucially, how we operationalize improvement science in the context of a three-year dissertation in practice will necessarily look different from how leaders might operationalize improvement science as part of their leadership, systems, professional learning structures, and collaborative processes. We believe that this is the next level of work for those who study and teach improvement science and school system leadership.

After reading the different improvement journeys in part 1, you should note that, for all the practitioners, completing a PDSA cycle or two was not the end of the problem they sought to address but rather the beginning of the change effort. It is evident that improvement work is an ongoing and iterative process and requires continuous learning and adaptation. As you read this book, many of the practitioner authors who contributed chapters are still actively engaged in further rounds of improvement or making efforts to spread the change beyond their immediate building or district. The initial success some achieved through the implementation of their change ideas fueled their determination to expand the impact and create sustainable improvements. These practitioners understand that true transformation is a long-term commitment and are dedicated to building upon their initial progress to achieve even greater outcomes. Their resilience and persistence serve as an inspiration and a reminder that improvement work is a journey, and the true measure of success lies in the sustained positive change brought about in the lives of those they serve.

Part II

CASE STUDIES FOR PRACTICE AND DISCUSSION

Megan Crew; Michelle Greene, EdD; Megan Hawley; Amy Johnson, EdD; Andrew Nester, EdD; Felicia Preston, EdD; and Kim Rygas

In part 1, you read comprehensive narratives of six leaders' improvement journeys. Although improvement work rarely "ends," these six chapters provided you with an account of each of the major stages of the improvement science process—collaboratively identifying a problem, seeing the system that contributes to that problem, developing a theory of improvement and measurement system, iteratively testing change ideas, and spreading and sustaining promising approaches.

Seeing how all of these phases of the improvement science process connect can be quite helpful, especially for leaders who are in the beginning stages of an improvement project. At the same time, we imagine that most readers of this book are engaging in, leading, coaching, or advising an improvement journey that is still unfolding—somewhere in between identifying a problem and spreading successful change ideas. These middle stages of the improvement journey are often rife with complexity and doubt. *Have you collected enough data? Involved the right stakeholders? Attended to all the important elements of the system contributing to the problem? Identified the most important drivers of change?*

Reasoning through these questions is no simple matter. For that reason, in this second section of the book, we delve into cases of educators who are in the midst of their improvement work and invite you to critically reflect on the choices these leaders made, and what they might do next. Each case study provides a comprehensive account of the early stages of an improvement process as leaders identify a problem of practice, draw on qualitative and quantitative data to understand the problem more deeply, and begin to identify causal factors contributing to that problem. Each case also provides necessary contextual information so that you can analyze the challenges they face, the complexities of their environments, and the strengths and limitations of their approaches. However, we have intentionally left each case without a resolution. Instead, we offer discussion questions to prompt you to reflect on the decisions the leaders made, what you might have done differently, and what you might advocate doing next. One of our goals for this section is to help readers build the skill of analyzing the complex and messy work of improvement. We hope that by practicing this skill, you will be better able to confront and productively make sense of the dilemmas you (or those you teach, advise, or coach) will inevitably encounter as part of improvement work.

We also hope that you will use these cases as jumping-off points for practicing discrete elements of the improvement science process. For each of the cases, we invite you to respond to the following prompts:

- What is the specific problem that the leader is seeking to address? What evidence informs their conclusion about this problem and its importance?
- What are the factors contributing to this problem? How might you visually represent this causal analysis of the problem? One effective technique for this analysis is the fishbone diagram, a powerful visual tool that helps uncover the root causes behind complex issues. It enables improvers to identify the underlying causes behind problems, leading to more informed decision-making and targeted problem-solving efforts (see Figure 8.1). You could also make your own visual map of the problem.

Figure 8.1. Fishbone Diagram Template

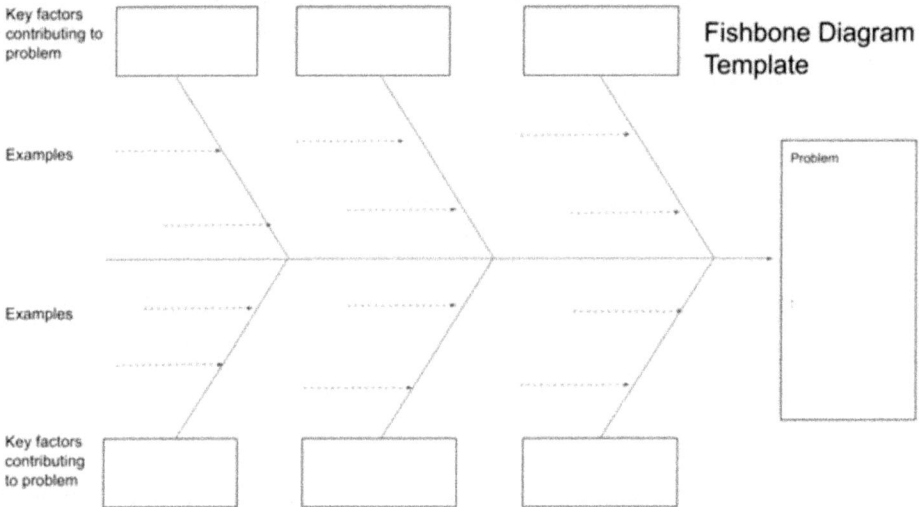

- Which of the contributing factors that you identified would you prioritize to address? Consider factors that are within the leader's sphere of control and that act as root causes, rather than symptoms of deeper causes. Consider engaging in a "Five Whys" protocol to identify root causes.
- What is an ambitious but feasible aim for improvement? What might the leader accomplish over the next one to two years?
- What might your theory of improvement be to address this problem of practice? When developing a theory of improvement, you may want to start by considering the contributing factors you chose to prioritize. What drivers of change and specific change ideas would address these contributing factors? We encourage you to represent your theory of improvement as a driver diagram. A driver diagram helps to create a shared understanding of the system and the critical factors that

must be addressed to achieve the desired outcome (see Figure 8.2). It facilitates the identification and alignment of improvement efforts by highlighting the areas that require attention and intervention. It also helps in identifying key drivers that have the potential to bring about substantial change.

Figure 8.2. Driver Diagram

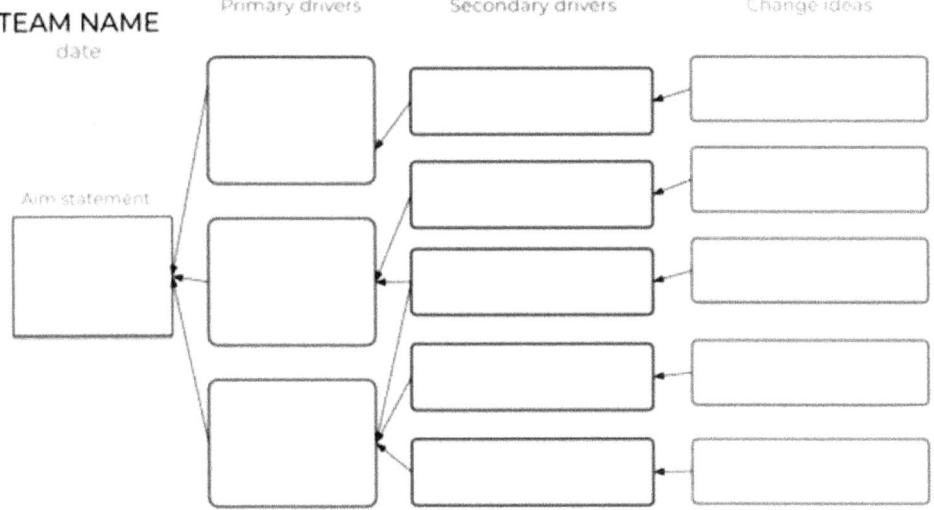

- From this theory of improvement, what specific change idea might you try out first? We encourage you to be specific here. For example, instead of saying "professional development" as a change idea, you might identify specific protocols, routines, or learning experiences that would be essential to this professional development. We also encourage you to bind the scope of your change. Who specifically would you want to involve in this change?
- What measures would you use to assess this change? Try identifying at least one process measure, driver measure, outcome measure, and balancing measure.
- Finally, and perhaps most importantly, who would you need to involve in decision-making at the different stages of this process, and why?

To get the most out of this section, we strongly recommend engaging in these prompts and the chapter-specific discussion questions in a group. We believe that the most powerful learning will come from discussing and working through these prompts as a group. In particular, it will be helpful to have each group member develop their responses to a set of prompts from each case, share their responses, and then engage in a critical and in-depth discussion of why they might have responded to the prompts in different ways.

Part 2 provides a variety of case studies, each representing a complex problem of practice. As you engage with these narratives, activities, and discussion questions, challenge yourself to explore the inquiry process, consider the strengths and gaps of each practitioner's inquiry process, and leverage improvement science tools to advance your understanding of what can be or should be done in each case. We invite you to embark on this journey—hopefully with some friends, peers, or colleagues—and actively build the skill of making sense of the complex work of using improvement science to address real-world educational problems.

Case 1

EL Family Engagement and Sense of Belonging

Jane Carter is the Division Coordinator of English learner (EL) programming in Lakeside City, a primarily blue-collar community nestled in the mountains of Virginia. Jane's position was created just two years ago when the school division recognized there was an increasing need for someone dedicated to working with EL and immigrant students and families. Her position was created in response to the growing need for dedicated support for EL and immigrant students in the school district. With a background of 18 years in education, including experience in religious and private schools, Jane brings a wealth of knowledge to her position. She has worked previously as a Director of Children and Youth Ministries at a local church in the area, as a director of a private preschool housed in another local church, and as a public school teacher within the school division where she now serves as an administrator.

Lakeside City's school district serves an increasingly diverse student body, with many students arriving from Central or South America. Lakeside City High School, with a population of 1,200 students, is a relatively small high school in a conservative suburban neighborhood boasting about 63 EL students. Although the EL student population is 5% of the high school, it is comprised of many native countries, dialects, and languages.

Determined to learn about the unique challenges faced by EL students and their families in Lakeside City, Jane began collaborating with EL teachers and central office personnel to initiate an inquiry into the needs of EL and immigrant students. Their approach involved multiple data collection methods, including discussions of student well-being, tracking of EL students' language proficiency over time, and conducting interviews with EL and immigrant families. By collecting diverse perspectives, Jane and her team aimed to shed light on the multifaceted challenges faced by this subgroup within the school system. To systematically analyze the problem, Jane created a fishbone diagram that represented various aspects of the EL program. From this diagram, her team identified two specific areas of focus: human resource data and behavior-related data.

First, Jane and her staff chose to consider Human Resource data, specifically the ratio of student to faculty within the division according to race and ethnicity. She and her staff noticed the underrepresentation of faculty members of color in the school division, particularly at the high school level. Analyzing the data revealed a significant disparity between the racial composition of students and the number of teachers and support staff from different racial backgrounds. This data suggested a potential lack of relatability and cultural understanding among the teaching staff, especially for minority and EL students. Jane and her team found the faculty and staff of color are sorely underrepresented when compared to students of color.

Table 8.1 is representative of this, according to the school division's Student Record Collection reported to the Virginia Department of Education on December 1, 2021. Considering Table 8.1, Hispanic students account for 8.3% of the Lakeside City Schools student population. Alternatively, the Hispanic faculty population for Lakeside City School as 1.2%. Asian students comprise 2.5% of the student population while 0.72% of Asian faculty comprise the total staff and faculty. White students comprise 70% of the student population while 91% of the staff and faculty are white. Note the disproportionality between races and the inverted statistic of adults versus students when it comes to the white population. In Lakeside City Schools, white is the only race where the percentage of staff and faculty exceeds the percentage of students. Jane's team considered: Could this be where EL students potentially feel underserved?

Table 8.1. Comparison of Self-Identified Student and Faculty and Staff Race in SY2021–2022

	Faculty and Staff	Students
Asian	5	96
Black	42	538
Hispanic	6	324
White	455	2,658
2 or More	7	179
Total	515	3,801

Jane and her team thought the disparity in the faculty/staff to student ratio could be a challenge especially for EL students to feel a sense of belonging in their school setting if they don't see teachers who look like them, speak their language, and understand their culture. Jane felt, at the very least, that as a school system, they need to ensure they are addressing this potential challenge this creates for students—to have teachers who are relatable to and understand their EL students.

Second, she and her team investigated behavior-related or "incident" data concerning EL students' discipline. They wondered whether EL students had a disproportionate amount of behavior referrals. If they did, how could this contribute to the treatment of EL students and families? The team determined that there is much to consider here. Considering behavior data for the current year at Lakeside City High School, 20% of office or behavior referrals involved EL students. Although there are only EL students make up only 5% of the population, Lakeside City High School recorded 140 incidents involving EL students, suggesting a disproportionality in EL students' behavior referrals. The team was left with larger questions about repeat offenders and repetition among specific faculty members. This disproportionality raised concerns about the underlying causes, potential biases, and the overall treatment of EL students within the disciplinary system.

Last, Jane and her team determined that conducting interviews directly with families would help confirm or deny these initial claims found in the data. As part of their inquiry into the needs of EL and immigrant students in Lakeside City Schools, Jane Carter and her team conducted interviews with EL and immigrant families to gather insights on their feelings of acceptance and sense of belonging within the school community. The Hernandez family immigrated from Guatemala two years ago. They have two children attending Lakeside City School. Mr. Hernandez shared during the interview that his children often feel excluded and isolated in the school environment. He mentioned that his children have faced difficulties in making friends and struggle with language barriers, which has affected their self-esteem. According to Mr. Hernandez, his children have not found many opportunities to connect with other students who share similar cultural backgrounds or speak their native language. He expressed a desire for more inclusive activities and support systems to help his children feel a sense of belonging. Mrs. Hernandez added that they have encountered limited cultural representation within the school curriculum, making it challenging for their children to see themselves reflected in the materials they study. She emphasized the importance of recognizing and appreciating diverse cultures within the school community. The Kidane family fled Eritrea four years ago as refugees. They have one child, Fitsum, who attends Lakeside City School. During the interview, Fitsum's mother shared her satisfaction with the school's commitment to fostering a sense of belonging for EL and immigrant students. She mentioned the various support programs that helped her child integrate into the school community smoothly. Fitsum's mother also appreciated the efforts made by one particular teacher to create an inclusive classroom environment where cultural diversity was celebrated and respected. She also had known another Eritrean parent who helped her answer her questions about school. She felt her child was accepted, valued, and supported by both peers and educators, enabling them to thrive academically and socially. Mr. Nguyen, on the other hand, who immigrated from Vietnam five years ago with his family, expressed concerns about his child feeling like an outsider in the school. He mentioned that his child had experienced bullying and discriminatory remarks that he felt were due to cultural differences.

As Jane Carter and her team concluded their interviews with EL and immigrant families, they were left with a wealth of insights and contrasting experiences. The interviews shed light on the complexities of creating a sense of acceptance and belonging for these students. Determined to create a more inclusive and supportive school environment, what initiatives would Jane and her team devise? How would they address the challenges and disparities uncovered by their inquiry?

DISCUSSION QUESTIONS

1. Do you think the data collected was comprehensive enough to address the challenges faced by this subgroup? What further data could have deepened Jane Carter's understanding of the needs and experiences of EL and immigrant students in Lakeside?

2. In the interviews conducted with EL and immigrant families, what were the common themes and concerns expressed by the Hernandez family, the Kidane family, and Mr. Nguyen? How do their experiences and perspectives shed light on the challenges faced by EL and immigrant students in Lakeside City School?
3. What actions would you recommend Jane Carter and her team take next to address the identified challenges and promote a greater sense of belonging for EL and immigrant students in Lakeside City School? How would you prioritize these actions and why?

Case 2

Discipline and In-School Suspensions

Spencer Shannon is a Black educator in the Hillsberry School Division (HSD). Having worked in the same division for the past 19 years, Mr. Shannon has held various positions, including school counselor, building-level administrator, and now a central office administrator. Recently, while reading yet another article from the front page of the local newspaper he noticed yet another tragic incident involving a former student of HSD. He realized that within the past year, he had seen at least 16 former students in the local newspaper reported dead, or involved in murders, gun violence, and other violent offenses. Most of these students were his Black male students who had received many discipline referrals, suspensions, and some alternative placements as early as elementary school. The stories of gun violence and crime had become disturbingly commonplace, prompting Mr. Shannon to question what could have been done differently to make a positive difference in the lives of these young men.

Reflecting on his time in the HSD, he realized tha the had counseled or suspended those same students he read about so many times in the newspaper. The families of these students were also families that he had all types of conversations with regarding concerns the school had about their children. Mr. Shannon knew the struggles that some of the students were facing outside of school that others in the school did not know. The relationships that he garnered with the students and families meant so much to the work he had committed to. After seeing his former students in the news time after time, Mr. Shannon began questioning his own decisions to suspend some of those same students when they presented in his office years before when he was a principal and the advice he had given to the parents for how to address these situations outside of school. He reasoned within himself what he could have done differently to change the trajectory of these students' lives and figured there must be a better way. In speaking with his colleagues, he realized they too had some of the same concerns.

HSD comprises less than 1,900 students with five schools—one of which houses only preschool programs, two elementary schools (K–5), one middle school (6–8), and one high school (9–12). The demographic composition of the school division is currently Black (58.3%), white (19.2%), Hispanic (14.9%), Mixed Race (6.2%), Asian (1.0%), and Native Hawaiian (0.2%). The four neighboring divisions all have at least one school with almost as many students as HSD's total population. The school division's service area covers a mere 11 square miles and on a normal day, any trip between schools can take a matter of minutes.

Mr. Shannon and his colleagues decided to delve into Hillsberry's discipline-related data to see if there were gaps in services, support, or resources for the students who were often referred for behavior infractions. The initial team included central office staff: the Coordinator of Alternative Programs, Director of Student Services, school psychologist, and Coordinator of Academic Supports, along with school-level personnel, including the middle school principal, the high school assistant principal, and the middle school dean of students. They first examined the short-term suspension data for the school division. Starting with the suspension data for three consecutive school years 2018–2019, 2019–2020, and 2020–2021 (Figures 9.1, 9.2, and 9.3), the team made a significant observation. The team discovered a disheartening trend within the suspension data. Similar to the stories on the front pages of the newspaper, the majority of suspensions involved Black students. This led the team to question whether these students were being disproportionately suspended compared to the size of their respective subgroups. They were aware that disproportionality in out-of-school suspensions (OSS) and exclusionary practices had been an ongoing issue in education.

Mr. Shannon had read research spanning back to the start of desegregation indicating that schools had historically used suspension and expulsion as a means to "get rid" of students of color, perpetuating racial disparities in disciplinary practices (Nielsen, 1979). Three months after Mr. Shannon and his team's inquiry, the state's Department of Education also sent out the quarterly bulletin highlighting the increasing rates of suspensions across the state as a problem. The state emphasized that research does not support the pattern that students of color are more likely to engage in problem behavior than white students yet students of color are suspended at a higher rate than their

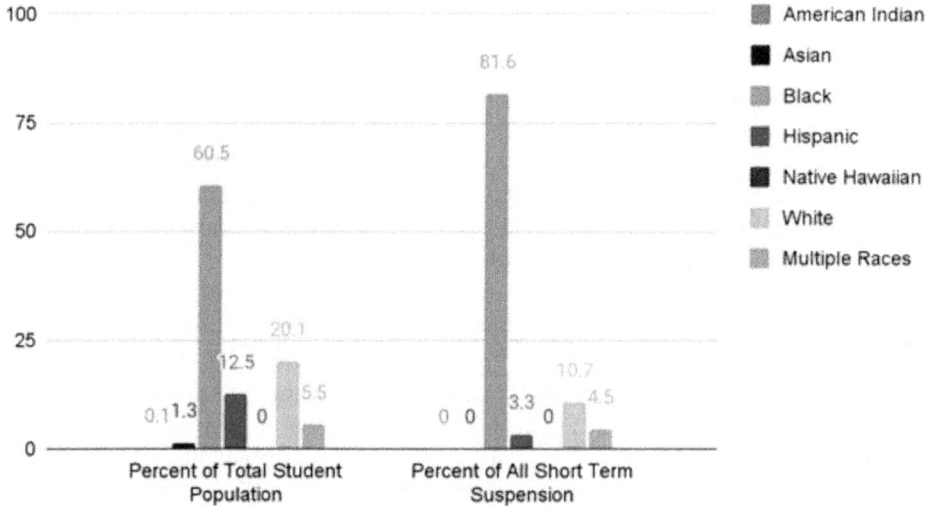

Figure 9.1. Short Term Suspensions (2018–2019)

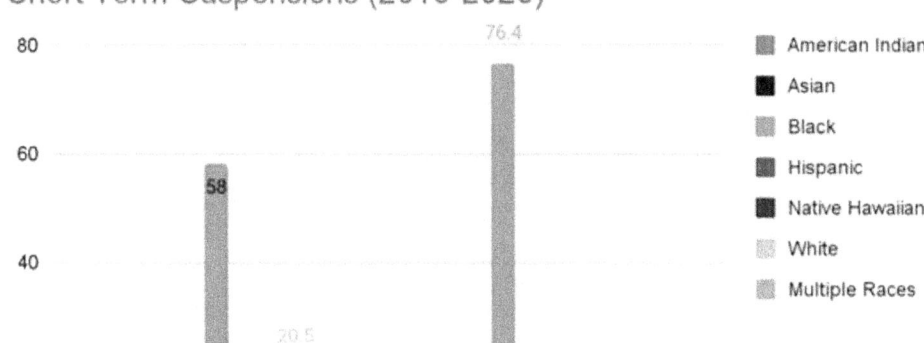

Figure 9.2. Short Term Suspensions (2019–2020)

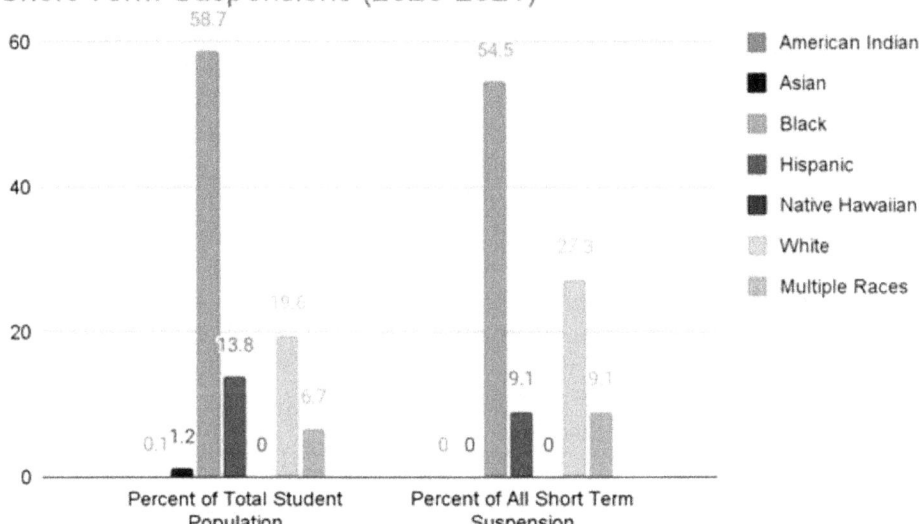

Figure 9.3. Short Term Suspensions (2020–2021)

white counterparts. Across the state, while Black students made up 22% of the total population; they represent 54% of all students suspended echoing what Mr. Shannon had read (Bloomberg, 2003), that Black males receive the most OSS. These exclusionary practices were contributing to the achievement gaps experienced by students from diverse backgrounds. With this information, the state asked that school divisions like

HSD should not only review their discipline procedures and how they disproportionately discipline students of color, but they should also find ways to effectively keep students in the educational environment.

Knowing the information regarding disproportionality and looking more deeply into the data of Hillsberry's schools, Mr. Shannon knew he had to have a mindset shift. Before he thought there was no relationship between the students who had been suspended and the students who were in the newspaper, but now he was thinking differently. Could there be something the school division was missing that could have helped these students moving forward, are there changes that could be made that could aid in the outcomes for students currently in the division?

Suspensions and overall discipline practices in the division have been a concerning topic for many years, however, in the school year 2017–2018, chronic absenteeism was added to the state's accreditation system and the discussions about the rates of suspension became more prominent. Because chronic absence was defined as missing school for any reason, suspensions would impact that data negatively thus risking being accredited. When students are suspended, they are absent from school, which not only adversely impacts their academic achievement but also places a school at risk of not being accredited. Mr. Shannon noticed that because the state wanted to drastically reduce OSS, HSD shifted primarily from tackling why students were being suspended to finding ways to keep students in school but not necessarily in the classroom. Administrators had complained to Mr. Shannon that they felt their hands were tied with the new accountability measure of chronic absenteeism and the shift from suspending students to intervening and providing support in the building. Teachers had also told Mr. Shannon that behavior disruptions were frustrating and time-consuming and that they affected learning for other students.

Mr. Shannon and his team examined the OSS data for six consecutive years and found there were fluctuations with huge gaps in the number of suspensions between years (see Table 9.1). Infractions recorded included behaviors of a safety concern, physical aggression against others, and behavior in general. The team recognized that students were often suspended with no interventions to assist with correcting the negative behaviors. Mr. Shannon also realized, that most sanctions were reactive and, although school counselors were often called in to speak with students, there were no long-term solutions to support students.

Table 9.1. Number of OSS by School Year

School Year	Total Number of OSS
2016–2017	421
2017–2018	331
2018–2019	268
2019–2020*	165
2020–2021*	11
2021–2022	326

*Indicates COVID year; all students were not in school for the entire year.

A principal at the high school acknowledged during an empathy interview with Mr. Shannon the overrepresentation of certain student groups, particularly Black students, in OSS, and expressed concern about the potential long-term consequences on their educational outcomes. Another principal also highlighted the need for alternative approaches to discipline, emphasizing the importance of addressing root causes and providing necessary support to students. Both leaders, Mr. Shannon noticed, expressed challenges trying to balance disciplinary measures, keep students in the school environment safe, and the academic success of all students, acknowledging the limited resources available to address behavioral issues effectively. Two former students of HSD (and close connections of a team member) who had been suspended more than once while they were students shared that repeated suspensions made it difficult to maintain focus and motivation in school. One felt the cycles of suspensions led to a disconnection from the learning environment. The other students mentioned feeling misunderstood by teachers and then alienated because they fell behind when they returned to the classroom.

Mr. Shannon and his team felt from looking at the data that exclusionary practices are at times a knee-jerk reaction to an inconvenience to a teacher or administrator. In trying to respond to building-level administrators' and teachers' concerns of accreditation or disruption, in addition to the state requirement to keep students in the building, Mr. Shannon, in collaboration with his colleagues, spearheaded the creation of an in-school suspension (ISS) option for students who were suspended for a range of 1 to 10 days. Traditionally, alternative programs and ISS have been used for students with extreme behavior difficulties or those who pose a safety risk to the general school environment. However, this new approach aimed to ensure that students would not miss crucial instructional time, while also addressing their social-emotional needs. The team wanted this newly established ISS program to go beyond mere supervision and idle time. They wanted to provide a structured and supportive environment where students would receive direct instruction from teachers, engage in meaningful academic activities, and have access to counseling and social-emotional support services. The program's focus extended beyond punitive measures to encompass restorative practices, helping students understand the impact of their actions, make amends, and develop skills for positive behavior and conflict resolution. By offering these resources and interventions within the school setting, Mr. Shannon and his team hoped this would somewhat disrupt the cycle of exclusionary practices that had perpetuated inequities within HSD. They understood that providing a supportive and inclusive learning environment was essential for all students, regardless of their disciplinary history. Mr. Shannon still felt that this ISS approach did not fully address why Black students were disproportionately suspended in HSD but within his sphere of control, he could at least ensure students were engaged in learning and not out of school. More work would perhaps be needed to address those who were responsible for suspending students.

DISCUSSION QUESTIONS

1. Was the data Mr. Shannon and his team collected sufficient to inform their inquiry? What further steps could Mr. Shannon and his team take to gather additional data and gain a deeper understanding of the issue?
2. What do you see as the strengths and limitations of Mr. Shannon's decision to prioritize developing an ISS option for students who were suspended for 1 to 10 days?
3. Who else might Mr. Shannon consider including on the team to inquire into and address this problem of practice?
4. Reflecting on Mr. Shannon's position and his commitment to fostering equitable learning environments, what would you have done in his position? How would you have approached the inquiry and subsequent actions differently?

Case 3

Transitioning from Middle School to High School

County High School is a large, rural, comprehensive high school with approximately 2,000 students and 190 instructional staff members. Each year enrollment fluctuates by plus or minus 100 students. The average graduation rate is 92%. Approximately, 7–9% of students each year do not finish high school with their cohort. In addition, approximately 7–9% of first-time ninth graders are not promoted to the tenth grade. Discipline and attendance are significant factors impacting ninth graders' academic performance. Ninth graders make up almost 40% of the overall discipline referrals. On average, the number of ninth grade students with five or more discipline referrals in a given year is approximately 9%. Amanda and Fred are two administrators in County High School who have noticed and discussed informally the challenges and trends they have observed in the data and with students in ninth grade. Although they do not have any evidence of any direct correlation between ninth grade discipline referrals and dropout rates, because the percentage of students not completing high school is at a similar rate, they cannot help but wonder if there are interconnecting, contributing factors. They are convinced that "dropping out is more of a process than an event" (Rumberger & Rotermund, 2012) and so they set out to identify and recognize students early on who may be at risk for not completing high school.

Amanda is a veteran educator with 22 years of experience, including five years as an elementary teacher, three years as an instructional coach, and 14 years as a high school administrator. Amanda grew up in a lower-middle-class household with parents who did not complete high school. She experienced academic struggles and knows firsthand the importance of teacher relationships and support in her high school completion. As an administrator, she is familiar with expectations, rules, policies, and procedures for students and teachers, but she acknowledges the need to further examine teacher and student perspectives to understand their points of view. Additionally, she is aware that her position as an evaluator and the authority she carries may influence her teachers' responses and students' reactions as she inquires more into this problem.

Fred has been an educator for 16 years in County Public Schools. He initially taught Algebra I to grades 9–12 while coaching football for nine and a half years. He then became the dean of students at the County Middle School for one and a half years before returning to County High School as a building assistant principal for the past five years, primarily dealing with discipline and campus operations. In his current role, Fred is the primary disciplinarian at County High School, and he is seen by many students as one of the main enforcers of discipline throughout the campus. Fred knows that his imposing physical presence, characterized by his significant stature, can be intimidating to students, which may contribute to their apprehension or unease. He knows something needs to be done to improve discipline as he continues to process referrals using the campus discipline matrix. He ensures that students who make poor decisions resulting in referrals will be treated fairly and consistently regardless of their previous referral history. Fred would like a reduction in disciplinary incidents, but not by disregarding or failing to document referrals to manipulate improvement data. Disciplinary referrals are issued for student actions and behaviors on campus, in the classroom, or on the bus. Fred handles the majority of referrals within the school building and more than 50% of bus-related referrals.

Because Amanda and Fred are both building-level administrators working together in the same building on campus, they often collaborate on projects and have been doing so for the past 14 years, with the last six years spent as part of the same administrative team. In their roles, they evaluate various departments, handle disciplinary matters, and engage with the school community across the campus.

From their experience over many years, they have observed that at-risk ninth grade students do not always transition well to high school. For Amanda and Fred, an at-risk student struggles with one or more of the following: academics, behaviors, or chronic absenteeism (when a student misses 10% or more of the school year). In previous years, Amanda and Fred have had conversations with students about how overwhelming their campus is to navigate and how hard it may be for students to find their "place." They have learned that from two former students who were seniors at the time. The two students, Maddie and Abigail, shared with Amanda in informal conversations how difficult it felt during their freshman year because they all came in from different middle schools in the county and everything felt new.

To gain further insight, Fred and Amanda decided to conduct a focus group interview with a small group of students who were part of a credit recovery program designed for at-risk students, to discuss their transition from middle school to high school. Although the students were either in their third or fourth year in County High School, they ranged from 9th–12th grade. Students were asked if they felt they had support and knew who to get support from when they entered high school for the first time. Students responded with a positive perception of knowing whom to go to when they needed support but there was some indication that students did not feel supported by their teachers or administration to help them be more successful in their first year. During the interview, several students mentioned that they felt if they had "teachers that helped me more" or "cared about me" then they would have been more successful in their ninth grade year. Students overwhelmingly indicated that they would have preferred more help and a caring relationship with their teachers. Students shared that they felt confident while in middle school before moving to the high school, but when they arrived they did not feel that they had the support of both teachers and administrators compared to when they were in middle school. Overall, the two administrators learned that the transition from middle school to high school can be overwhelming for many students. The increased workload, different teaching styles, and larger school environment may contribute to feelings of being lost or disconnected, leading to academic struggles.

The discussion with students confirmed what Amanda and Fred felt—that ninth grade is a pivotal make-or-break year for a student's on-time graduation and the place to begin to examine why students are not successful throughout high school. They shared what they learned with various school personnel. A group of educators and resource faculty met to determine how they can better serve at-risk ninth graders. They wanted to examine if there were any other contributing factors to why ninth grade students are retained or not promoted to the tenth grade. From their discussions, they identified the following:

- *Academic Preparation*: Some students may lack the necessary academic skills or foundational knowledge required to succeed in high school. This could include gaps in reading, writing, mathematics, or other subjects, making it challenging for them to keep up with the curriculum.
- *Attendance and Punctuality*: Students who frequently miss school or arrive late may fall behind in their coursework, struggle to catch up, and consequently face the risk of retention.
- *Lack of Support Systems*: Students from at-risk backgrounds may lack adequate support systems at home or in their communities. Limited access to resources such as tutoring, mentorship, or parental involvement can hinder their academic progress and contribute to retention.
- *Socioeconomic Factors*: Economic disadvantages can impact students' ability to focus on their studies. Financial instability, the need to work part-time jobs, or responsibilities to support their families may distract students from their academic responsibilities.
- *Behavioral Issues*: Persistent behavioral issues, such as frequent disruptions, aggression, or noncompliance with school rules, can lead to disciplinary actions that may result in retention.
- *Social and Emotional Factors*: Emotional well-being, mental health concerns, or challenges with peer relationships can impact students' ability to engage in their academics effectively. Unaddressed social or emotional issues may contribute to retention.
- *Limited Access to Resources*: Some students from underserved communities have limited access to quality educational resources, including textbooks, technology, or extracurricular activities. The lack of necessary resources can hinder their overall academic performance.

After multiple discussions, the group determined the best way to improve ninth grade retention was to focus on supporting students through the transition from middle school (eighth grade) to high school (ninth grade). After reviewing and reflecting on the preliminary data that they had collected, the team decided to pair students who were identified as at-risk with mentors (building-level administrators). These mentors would volunteer to meet with and check in on their assigned ninth grader periodically throughout the year. Mentors would also monitor students' progress to ensure they felt supported in the new high school environment, knew how to access needed resources, and began to build positive relationships with school administrators.

During one of the discussions, a team member observed unforeseen challenges that would need to be addressed before moving forward with the mentorship program. Firstly, it was recognized that mentors should receive appropriate training to ensure they understood expectations, including meeting frequently with the student and consistent documentation of the student's progress. Additionally, the team acknowledged that mentors would be better equipped to support their mentees if they had prior knowledge of the student beyond disciplinary records. One potential solution proposed was the implementation of an end-of-year survey in middle school to gather information about students' interests, which could then be used to pair mentors and mentees. To further enhance the effectiveness of the mentorship program, the team explored the idea of involving student leaders as mentors. Fred suggested that having older students mentor younger ones could foster a stronger sense of connectedness and potentially contribute to the success of struggling students. Additionally, it was acknowledged that students labeled as at-risk may not necessarily have a high number of discipline referrals. To ensure equal opportunities for support, the team proposed considering secondary data, such as attendance, academics, and staff recommendations, when selecting mentees.

As these challenges and potential solutions were brought to light, Amanda, Fred, and the team contemplated the path forward. How could they address the need for mentor training and a deeper understanding of the mentees? Would involving student leaders prove to be a valuable addition? And how could they create a fair selection process for all students in need of support? Would the mentorship program be enough to improve students' transitions from middle to high school and their sense of belonging in County High School?

DISCUSSION QUESTIONS

1. To what extent do you think the mentorship program is likely to address the factors the team identified as contributing to the problem of practice? What other initiatives or programs could Amanda and Fred have considered to improve the transition and support for ninth grade students?
2. Amanda was concerned that "her position as an evaluator and the authority she carries may influence her teachers' responses and the students' reactions as she inquires more into this problem." How might her role have influenced what she learned from her inquiry? What might she do to proactively address these concerns?
3. How might you address the scenario posed at the end of this case—that students labeled as at-risk may not have a high number of discipline referrals? What other criteria could be used to select mentees and ensure equal opportunities for support?

Case 4

Reading Achievement

Elm Elementary School is part of Riverside City Schools in a southern state, serving preschool through second grade students, ages three to eight. There are approximately 400 students who attend. For the 2021–2022 school year, there were 22 classrooms, which are broken down as follows: preschool (n = 4), kindergarten (n = 6), first grade (n = 6), second grade (n = 6). The 2020 fall membership by subgroup data was broken down as follows: white, 64.1%; Black, 15.2%; Hispanic, 9.6%; multiple races, 8.5%; Asian, 1.5%; and Native Hawaiian, 1.1%. Elm has a total of 8.1% of students with disabilities. There was also a 55.9% subgroup of economically disadvantaged students, meaning that Elm qualified as a Title I school. There was a 0.5% population of English learners. Elm Elementary has had different administrators for three consecutive years. Jennifer Blue was hired as the new principal of the school effective July 1, 2021. Before being hired as principal at Elm, she served as a first grade teacher for nine years, a reading specialist for three years, an instructional specialist for one year, and an assistant principal for two years in Piney County, a neighboring school division.

Elm Elementary is confronted with the continual change in its student demographics. Between the 2012–2013 and 2021–2022 school years, Elm has witnessed a significant shift in its socioeconomic landscape. The economically disadvantaged subgroup, which accounted for 40% of the student population in 2012–2013, surged to 55% in 2021–2022. Additionally, a striking 70% of students enrolled after the beginning of the school year were economically disadvantaged. Consequently, this demographic change has led to an influx of new students living in poverty. Concurrently, the neighboring Bill Martin University experienced a decline in student enrollment, prompting the utilization of university student housing for low-income housing.

Jennifer believes that one of the most critical skills a child must acquire is how to read, and that by learning how to read each child is empowered to learn and gain access to the world around them (Morrow & Gambrell, 2019). In her professional experience, Jennifer has observed firsthand the implications of students who do not meet reading benchmarks and how it affects their learning for years to come. For Jennifer, students should begin learning to read the day they begin school as kindergarteners, for some as preschoolers. Unfortunately, in her experience, students do not always obtain the necessary knowledge and skills they need to be successful as early readers.

She sees too many gaps in learning and, without intervention, the gap widens, making it seemingly impossible for students to catch up (Stanovich, 1986).

Jennifer completed an analysis of school-wide data to determine the current reality of reading achievement at Elm Elementary School. She first focused on Phonological Awareness Literacy Screening (PALS) data. A state assessment, called Phonological Awareness Literacy Screening (PALS) assessment, is used to measure primary grades to measure students' knowledge of several important literacy fundamentals: phonological awareness, alphabet recognition, knowledge of letter sounds, spelling, oral reading in context, and comprehension. At least 25% of students in grades K–2 scored below expected reading benchmarks on the PALS assessment in Spring 2021. By analyzing results over time, Jennifer also found that there has been a significant increase in students scoring below the PALS benchmark after the COVID-19 pandemic (see Figure 11.1, which shows the change from over four consecutive school years; in Spring 2020, no data were collected due to the COVID-19 school closure). She also noticed that second grade students have historically not performed as well on PALS assessments compared to kindergarten and first grade students. Pre-pandemic, some issues needed to be addressed about reading achievement. These problems have gotten much worse since the pandemic. Jennifer was convinced that an intervention must be put in place to address the learning loss of students at Elm.

At the kindergarten level, the data showed a significant increase in students not meeting the PALS benchmark after returning to school after the COVID-19 school closure in 2020. When breaking down data from the 2020–2021 school year even further, data were collected from students attending both fall and spring at Elm Elementary. Figure 11.1 data indicate that while 26% of kindergarten students scored below the Fall 2020 PALS benchmark, the number of students below the benchmark

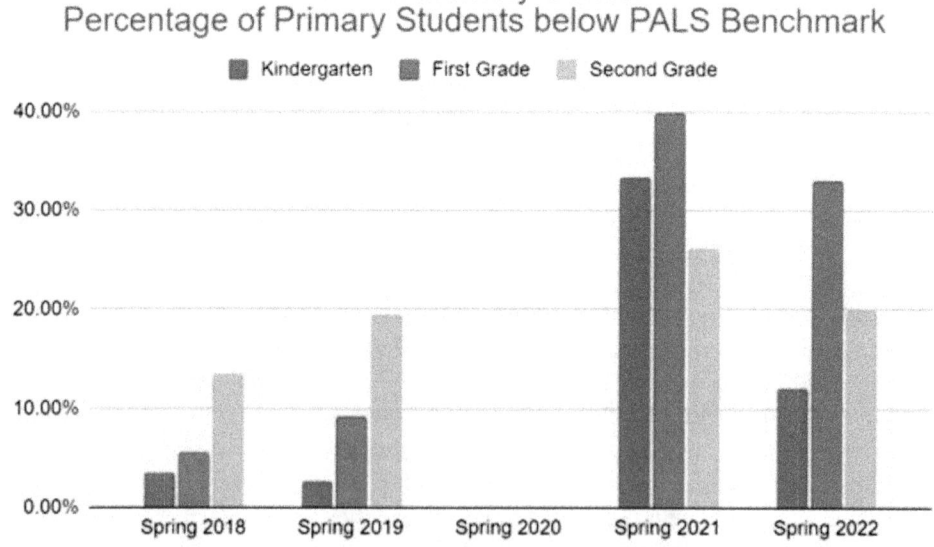

Figure 11.1. Percentage of Primary Students Below PALS Benchmark

in the spring was 33%, resulting in a seven-percentage-point increase in students not meeting the benchmark.

For students in first grade, data from students attending both fall and spring indicated that in Fall 2020, 34% of first grade students did not meet the PALS benchmark. In Spring 2021, 40% of students did not meet the expected PALS benchmark, resulting in a six-percentage-point increase in students not meeting the benchmark.

For students in second grade, data collected from students who attended both Fall 2020 and Spring 2021 indicated that in Fall 2020, 42% of second grade students did not meet the PALS benchmark. In Spring 2021, there were 23% of students that also did not meet the PALS benchmark. The result was a decrease in the failure rate by 19 percentage points. Figure 11.1 shows that in Fall 2020, 108 second grade students were assessed. Forty percent of students fell below the benchmark. In Fall 2021, 115 students were assessed, and 37% of students were below the benchmark.

Jennifer was alarmed in looking at the PALS data because of the rate of students scoring below reading benchmarks, even more so after students returned to school for the 2021–2022 school year from the COVID-19 pandemic. Looking at the data, she felt there were gaps in reading instruction in all grades before COVID-19, but to address the additional learning loss from the COVID-19 pandemic, instruction had to be more intentional than ever before (Blevins, 2017). She therefore wanted to examine what instructional practices were in place, how new teachers were equipped in literacy instruction, and what assessments were used to measure learning.

Jennifer wanted to probe deeper into these challenges and understand the factors contributing to reading achievement at Elm Elementary. She spoke with Sheila, the literacy coach for the Riverside City Public Schools District. Sheila is a former first grade teacher and reading specialist who is also new to the role. Jennifer asked the literacy coach a series of questions about Elm and her overall impression of reading instruction at Elm. Sheila was also concerned that the first grade PALS scores for this year were the lowest that they have ever been. She also expressed concerns about the grade level having many teachers with less than five years of teaching experience. She acknowledged that instructional time was lost due to the COVID closure as well, including other factors nationwide that impacted students' overall well-being. The literacy coach also shared strengths she saw with reading instruction. She shared that Elm has an aligned phonics curriculum, which is Orton-Gillingham based. Orton-Gillingham is an instructional approach and multi-sensory teaching method designed to support individuals with dyslexia and other learning difficulties. She felt that although the approach has been beneficial to the school, she was concerned that teachers may not be implementing it with fidelity and will sometimes utilize activities that are "cute" versus those that target students' instructional needs. Sheila told Jennifer that she feels the school is behind in using assessments to inform reading instruction.

Sheila had also recently completed Language Essentials for Teachers of Reading and Spelling (LETRS) training and as part of a division initiative, she revealed to Jennifer that she was planning to train 14 teachers at Elm Elementary. She feels this training will be key to future reading success. Sheila said that in her training in LETRS, the current Fountas and Pinnell assessment that Elms uses for reading records is very time-consuming for teachers and does not give teachers an overall depiction of their students as readers. Sheila believed LETRS would be beneficial to teachers at a tier 1 level because it would provide knowledge about the science of reading. Sheila perceived this knowledge base would provide a stronger tier 1 (80–85% of students) approach to instruction. Sheila told Jennifer that other areas that need to be improved are the amount of time devoted to reading, phonics, and writing instruction. She shared that many teachers have a 90-minute literacy block and have the flexibility to create their schedules. From her LETRS training, she would like to see classrooms utilize 40% of their time focused on phonics instruction. She thinks moving forward, establishing a schedule to define the literacy block would address some of the concerns she has.

For the upcoming LETRS training, Sheila disclosed to Jennifer that teachers will receive six hours of face-to-face training along with modules teachers will complete. She shared that LETRS (units 1–4) covers the theoretical model from reading science; phonology, basic and advanced phonics; and screening and educational diagnostic assessment. She plans to work on ways to facilitate their learning when they look for transfer opportunities in classrooms. She also planned to show teachers how to utilize the different assessments they conduct like DIBELS (Dynamic Indicators of Basic Early Literacy Skills, is an assessment system used to measure and monitor the development of early literacy skills in students. It is primarily designed for students in grades K–6.), PALS, and Heggerty (an educational program designed to support the development of early literacy and language skills in young children; it provides a structured and systematic approach to teaching phonemic awareness skills through daily lessons), which will better drive their instruction to target students' needs.

After talking with Sheila, as the new principal at Elm Elementary Jennifer felt this was an opportunity to also hear from and work closely with her new staff on this problem. She created a team that included a teacher from each grade level, a reading specialist, a literacy coach, and an assistant principal. She and the team looked at the PALS data and they shared what they were observing. Jennifer led the team to create a fishbone diagram to identify what may be causing low reading achievement for students (see Figure 11.2). Jennifer asked team members to write on sticky notes any factors they believed contributed to low reading achievement in primary grades. The team came up with an extensive list of potential contributing factors that included: COVID-19 pandemic and the loss of instructional time, renovations at Elm, behavioral challenges, ineffective instructional practices, teachers with limited experience, teacher preparation, lack of mentorships, lack of training, classroom environment, lack of resources, lack of equity, lack of feedback, and trauma experienced after the COVID-19 pandemic. After completing the brainstorming activity, Jennifer asked the team if they could find any themes to categorize contributing factors. The improvement team identified students' backgrounds, teacher knowledge, and learning environment as main themes. From the themes that emerged, the team wanted to focus on increasing teacher's instructional knowledge as the primary change factor to increase student achievement.

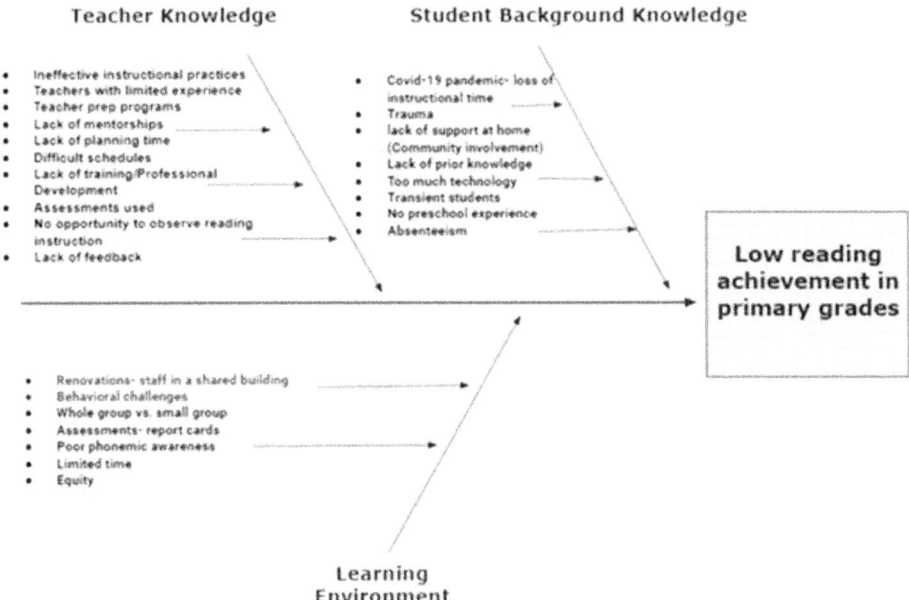

Figure 11.2. Fishbone Diagram

As Jennifer and her team stood before the fishbone diagram, filled with an extensive list of potential contributing factors to low reading achievement, the room was abuzz with anticipation. The identified themes of students' backgrounds, teacher knowledge, and learning environment resonated deeply. While Sheila was eager to jump into the LETRS training, a point of tension arose. Some team members questioned whether immediate training was the best course of action, emphasizing the need for further exploration and data analysis to prioritize interventions effectively. As they paused, uncertainty hung in the air, leaving everyone wondering which path they would choose and what transformative steps lay ahead on their journey to improve reading outcomes at Elm Elementary School.

DISCUSSION QUESTIONS

1. Do you believe that Jennifer's team is ready to jump into LETRS training, given their inquiry up to this point? Why or why not? Are there other forms of data you might recommend her team collect?
2. To what extent, or in what ways, do you believe LETRS training will address the factors Jennifer's team identified as contributing to the problem of practice? Do you recommend her team consider other changes in addition to, or instead of, LETRS training?
3. As a new principal, Jennifer turned to Sheila, the reading specialist, as a key data source for understanding the problem of practice. What do you think of as the strengths or limitations of this approach?

4. How do you think Jennifer's role as a new principal might have influenced what she learned from the staff at Elm Elementary School? Do you have recommendations for how she might have navigated this dual role as a principal and scholar-practitioner?

Case 5

Teacher Burnout

Mrs. Walker and Mrs. Cooper have been educators for 15 years in the Riverside School Division (RSD). Before serving the district as educators, they were both students in the school district. Mrs. Walker attended a large urban school and Mrs. Cooper attended a small rural school. As high school students, they were both active in student clubs and sports, while maintaining scholastic honors. They also attended the same local university. Mrs. Walker majored in early childhood education and Mrs. Cooper majored in elementary education. After graduation, they stayed in the RSD.

Mrs. Walker taught first and third grade in an affluent elementary school for nine years. During her time as a teacher, she served the school community in multiple capacities. She served on the leadership team and in her last year she was a teacher and the principal designee. Mrs. Walker then became an assistant principal at Magnolia Elementary School (MES), and two years later she was named the principal at MES.

Mrs. Cooper, a former teacher in the same school district, taught second, third, and fourth grades in a Title I elementary school. She also served the school community by participating in multiple leadership teams and academic teams and mentoring new teachers. Mrs. Cooper joined the MES administrative team after 11 years as a classroom teacher.

Mrs. Walker and Mrs. Cooper began their leadership journey pre-pandemic as administrators of a rural Title I school. They are currently the longest-standing principal team in the district, whereas many schools see turnover in administrative teams. The RSD is comprised of many distinct communities, from urban to rural. The district educates approximately 10,000 students and employs about 2,000 individuals among 11 elementary schools, four middle schools, four high schools, one alternative education school, and the central office.

MES is a Title I, fully inclusive, accredited school with preschool through fifth grades spread among 30 classrooms. There are 600 students and 94 staff members (teachers, support staff, and facilities). Sixty-three percent of the teaching staff have only worked for RSD. Ten percent of teachers at MES have taught for three years or fewer, whereas 63% of teachers at MES have taught for more than 10 years. Twenty-one instructional staff members are new to MES within the last five years. The student population is made up of 91% white students, 5% are two or more races, 2% are

Hispanic or Latino, and less than 1% are Black or Asian. MES has approximately 50% of the students receive free or reduced lunch. MES has about 10% of students requiring specially designed instruction serviced through individualized education plans.

During their first year as an administrative team, schools had to adjust to virtual learning due to the COVID-19 pandemic. MES had to find ways to reach all students while students learned remotely. Teachers made weekly packets that were mailed to students' homes and they created plans that were posted in Google Classroom. Teachers worked incredibly hard to meet the ever-changing demands. Mrs. Walker and Mrs. Cooper would also visit students' homes to check in, since many homes in the rural community did not have access to internet services. Many school teams rode on school buses to deliver meals to students and constantly looked for ways to engage and connect with students and families. During school closure, teachers had Wednesdays as a planning day and they were able to work from home.

As former teachers, Mrs. Walker and Mrs. Cooper became acutely aware of the struggles teachers faced when they returned to the classroom post-pandemic. Upon returning to MES after school closure due to COVID-19, Mrs. Walker and Mrs. Cooper noticed increased stress among their teachers. They believed teachers were mostly stressed about safety, low salaries, and lack of resources. It was difficult to pinpoint the exact need because everything felt overwhelming. They learned about struggles through listening to teachers in their building and across the district, and reading national headlines. However, when Mrs. Walker and Mrs. Cooper spoke with their teachers, many expressed frustrations with various tasks, such as lesson planning and data documentation. It was difficult for teachers to take days off for mental well-being and take care of their appointments because there appeared to be a substitute shortage as well. Some teachers expressed the need to have Wednesdays as a teacher workday to complete their daunting task lists. Wednesday teacher workdays were a result of the pandemic and a support that many teachers valued. Mrs. Walker and Mrs. Cooper knew they would have to learn to navigate the many concerns that teachers had that were only exacerbated due to the pandemic.

As former teachers and now leaders of a large Title I elementary school, they were aware of the additional responsibilities, tasks, documents, and regulations that must be followed and documented to meet local, state, and federal policies. Mrs. Walker and Mrs. Cooper knew they had to find the real causes rather than continue to make assumptions about why staff morale was low. One task that consumes teacher time is progress monitoring student interventions and data, specifically if students are in identified gap groups. Also, as part of a Title I school plan, there are additional evening events to engage with families. Teachers also shared their frustrations with the lack of flexibility during instructional times. For example, using specified curriculum resources, following a tight schedule, and finding ways for intervention and extension groups. Mrs. Walker and Mrs. Cooper also reviewed preexisting school survey data, started to collect data through empathy interviews, conducted informal observations, created new survey information, reviewed team planning notes, and documented conversations and personal reflections as field notes. These data points provided additional insight into other factors that created stress for teachers. Mrs. Walker and Mrs.

Cooper hoped collecting a variety of data points would answer the many questions they had surrounding teacher burnout and morale.

Mrs. Walker and Mrs. Cooper also began analyzing the school district's anonymous survey that was completed by staff at the beginning of the year. The open-response questionnaire asked for district staff to, "Provide your suggestion for areas of collaboration to provide support and alleviate some of the workload for this school year." The only identifying factor in the survey was the participants selected the specific school where they work. Mrs. Walker and Mrs. Cooper began sorting through the 149 responses. They filtered the responses to show the 94 elementary staff responses and sorted the responses by each school (the only identifying factor) and into Title I and non-title schools. Some of the responses from their staff left them feeling defeated and worried. They were defeated because they had worked hard to increase staff morale and worried that teachers were struggling. While they read each response, they inductively coded themes present in the data and disaggregated data into district, title, and non-title schools.

After they read through and coded each response, they calculated the frequency of each response and created a Pareto chart to get a better understanding of the key issues contributing to increased teacher stress. Mrs. Walker and Mrs. Cooper noticed the most common themes creating additional stress for teachers were lesson planning expectations, time (lack of planning time and time worked beyond the contractual day), and the number of meetings. The two school leaders were shocked at the results as they expected to see low compensation and student discipline at the top of the list. After analyzing the survey data completed by 16% of the district's certified teachers, they discovered that the most common stressor among their teachers was lesson planning: 43% of responses from their teachers mentioned lesson planning. The second most common concern was time (planning time and time outside of contractual hours). Thirty-one percent of their teachers' responses mentioned time contributing to the increased workload this school year.

After reviewing the Pareto chart based on teacher survey data, Mrs. Walker and Mrs. Cooper knew they needed to talk with teachers to gain a better understanding of teacher burnout; specifically focusing on the areas of lesson planning, hours spent working beyond contractual hours, and the amount of meetings they are expected to attend. They began by conducting empathy interviews with two of their teachers with varying years of experience. Mrs. Walker and Mrs. Cooper developed interview questions to gather teacher perspectives on various parts of their day and what was causing them to burn out. One teacher worked for the district for many years and the other was a first-year teacher. The teacher with many years of experience reflected on the relationships she had with previous administrators and how the resources and expectations have changed over the years. The new teacher's responses focused more on how to complete the day-to-day demands, meet students' needs, and find a work-life balance. Both teachers shared insightful information.

Mrs. Walker and Mrs. Cooper also reached out to a colleague in another district to conduct additional empathy interviews to determine if the teacher concerns were school-district-specific or similar across districts. They individually interviewed six teachers in a school with similar student populations and demographics. Since they

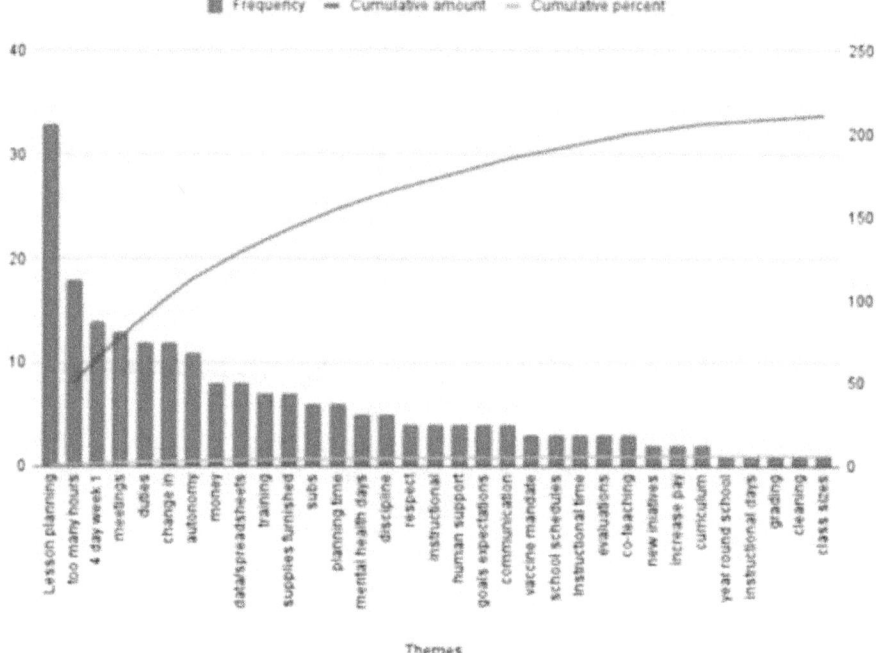

Figure 12.1. Division Survey: Teacher Suggestions for Support and Ways to Alleviate Workload

did not have a relationship with these teachers, they wanted the interviews to be more conversational. Common themes from these interviews included additional duties, lack of support from students' families, and student behaviors as sources of stress. Mrs. Walker and Mrs. Cooper's conversations with these six teachers indicated that the problem extended beyond their school district. One thing that surprised both Mrs. Walker and Mrs. Cooper was that teachers from another district did not mention lack of time as a stressor, even with only 30 minutes of planning and having additional duties.

After the interviews, they began to informally observe teachers' interactions and conversations, to continue gathering qualitative data and teachers' perspectives on some of the themes from the interviews. Mrs. Cooper kept notes in a field journal to document information, conversations, and observations. Based on conversations with teachers, writing lesson plans with specific expectations was not the biggest concern; instead it was the number of plans teachers were expected to write each day.

The administrative team had to find a way to organize themes they were learning about through the data they collected as well as the literature. They created a fishbone diagram to outline the concerns and information learned about teacher burnout, retention, and morale.

The fishbone diagram grew quickly as they organized teacher's concerns from survey and interview data, and literature. As leaders, Mrs. Walker and Mrs. Cooper wanted to find a way to create a change for teachers in the school district, so they reached out to the district to form an inquiry team to collaborate in furthering their understanding of teacher burnout. Their team consisted of representatives from the RSD's human resources department, another principal, a teacher, and a facilities manager to ensure they had multiple perspectives present on the team. They presented the data they had collected through empathy interviews, surveys, observations, and the fishbone diagram.

The inquiry team created an opportunity for Mrs. Walker and Mrs. Cooper to continue diving into the problem at the district level. As the inquiry team delved deeper into the data and engaged in discussions, the evidence they gathered painted a troubling picture of teacher burnout, with the overwhelming workload, lack of planning time, and excessive meetings emerging as the primary culprits. Could it be that this epidemic of teacher burnout was a systemic problem, deeply rooted in the fabric of the entire education system and not just a result of the COVID-19 pandemic?

DISCUSSION QUESTIONS

1. As an educational leader, what additional steps would you take to inquire into the problem of teacher burnout? How would you gather more data to understand the causes and impacts of burnout?
2. Based on the information provided in the case, what are the main concerns expressed by teachers at MES? Which concerns would you prioritize as you develop a theory of improvement?
3. How did Mrs. Walker and Mrs. Cooper navigate the challenge of inquiring into a problem that they were so directly involved in? What were the strengths and limitations of their approach, and what might they have done differently?
4. To what extent did Mrs. Walker and Mrs. Cooper take an asset-based lens in their inquiry?

Afterword

Wendy Durham, EdD; Sandy Strayer, EdD;
Elizabeth Motley, EdD; and Matthew Woods, EdD

WHAT IMPROVEMENT SCIENCE MEANS TO US

The four of us are division leaders from Henry County Public Schools (HCPS) who recently graduated from Radford University's (RU) EdD program, where we learned and applied the principles of improvement science to address problems of practice across HCPS. We experienced and continue to experience firsthand the positive impact improvement science has on addressing and solving problems of practice. We each recognize the tools and processes of improvement science are so powerful in leading transformational change, that we are sharing our learning with all leaders and practitioners in HCPS. We each wanted to conclude this book with our work and our reflection on how improvement science can transform the way we work in education to address inequities.

WENDY

I am Director of K–12 Instruction for HCPS. To improve student learning and achievement, HCPS is transitioning from traditional grading practices to standards-based learning in their elementary schools. Instead of a top-down approach where I tell faculty and division leaders what to do, my team and I devised a method inspired by improvement science for every teacher to have input on this transition and "test small changes" (Bryk et al., 2015). My instructional team and I decided to start small, working only with kindergarten teachers to design HCPS's approach to implementing standards-based learning. For a year, we met with groups of kindergarten teachers to create pieces of the HCPS standards-based learning model. After each meeting with my team, we gathered feedback and input from those closest to the problem using their responses to guide the next steps. Through multiple methods, such as surveys and focus groups, teachers involved in this change process shared with the team and me how they felt their ideas and input were heard. They shared that they could see how their ideas were truly influencing our work. Teachers appreciated they had a hand in designing the standards-based learning model they would implement. Using improvement science to implement this change by involving and collaborating with teachers and giving them a voice in how to make improvements created more support and buy-in from teachers. When the standards-based learning model is finally implemented, we will hold focus group meetings to gather feedback from teachers, continue to study the effects of the change idea implemented, and make adjustments based on what is learned from the first iteration.

SANDY

As superintendent I embedded the use of improvement science in my leadership team meetings, using the principles of improvement science to investigate and dig deeper into the issues and barriers to improving teaching and learning in HCPS. Instead of jumping to a solution the HCPS senior leadership team believes will solve the problem, we "examine the problem from the point of view of the user—the person who is experiencing it firsthand" (Bryk et al., 2015, p. 13). Senior leaders in Henry County are learning how imperative it is to hear and listen to various stakeholders' voices to get to the root of the problem. Instead of one administrative team solving issues, senior HCPS administrators are working with faculty and staff to gather input and feedback on problems facing the district. Additionally, I also draw from the process and tools of improvement science when working with principals in the district. Informed by improvement science I involve the principals in identifying the root causes of challenges facing the district and I also guide principals in identifying the root causes of challenges their schools encounter. As a result, principals use the tools and problem-solving methods of improvement science with their school improvement teams.

ELIZABETH

I am an elementary school principal at HCPS. Improvement science emphasizes that collaboratively engaging with stakeholders to both understand the problem and craft potential solutions is key to solving complex problems. When meeting with my school improvement team to analyze data and determine goals for our school improvement plan, I use improvement science to guide the team's work. My team and I use the five whys, fishbone diagram, and driver diagram to identify the root causes of gaps in student achievement and areas where change can occur. I also find that because of the various improvement science tools and problem-solving strategies, as a team, we have richer, more action-oriented, and meaningful conversations. Instead of arbitrarily selecting strategies we hope and think will improve student achievement, we are better informed by our learning of the problem through the improvement science process we conduct. Using the data we collect, we write more intentional and meaningful goals, objectives, and strategies for our school improvement plan.

MATTHEW

I serve as Director of Student Support Services in HCPS and I use the improvement science process and tools to assist school-based administrators as they make decisions about student discipline. Instead of immediately jumping to solutions, I work with principals to dig deep into the problem, identifying drivers of discipline, attendance, and social-emotional challenges facing HCPS students. Using the tools of improvement science, I encourage principals and their school-based tiered systems of support teams to examine the systems they have in place that hinder improvements in student behavior and attendance. I also collaborate with schools to identify possible solutions and change ideas that will improve the systems and procedures in place to better support students' academic, social, and emotional well-being. I also meet monthly, collaborating with the division student support team to examine the various change ideas the division can implement to provide the structural support schools need to implement the change ideas they are testing.

As HCPS leaders strive to solve problems that impact teaching and learning, they plan to continue using the principles of improvement science to include those closest to the problem in identifying the root of the problem, testing change ideas, and conducting Plan-Do-Study-Act cycles. The goal is to continue to model and use the principles of improvement science when tackling division-wide and school-wide problems of practice. It is the hope this intentional use of improvement science will expand its use and influence in all schools, making improvement science the HCPS problem-solving model. We continue to embrace the opportunity for continuous improvement and look forward to working with the education professionals in HCPS to improve the academic, social, and cultural learning environments in classrooms.

FOR PRACTITIONERS WHO ARE NEW TO IMPROVEMENT SCIENCE

In HCPS, during administrative meetings, the use of improvement science tools such as the fishbone and the five whys are used regularly when discussing problems. Wendy and Sandy communicated with division leaders about the importance of gathering input from those closest to the problem, stressing the significance of "starting small to learn fast" (Bryk et al., 2015, p. 121), as evidenced in work with standards-based learning. "Go slow to go fast" is now the guiding principle for the implementation of new initiatives and solving division-wide problems.

Matt feels improvement science is a way to dial down to the root of a systemic problem and make large-scale changes. Typically, as administrators, we are doing our best to keep our heads above water and are operating from a reactionary mindset most of the time. The role of an administrator has morphed so much in the last several years, especially due to the pandemic. Improvement science gives administrators applicable ways to apply theory in practical, everyday environments that we are accustomed to seeing.

As a school leader, Elizabeth has faced many situations where problems are presented and our teachers want immediate fixes for those problems. That's where improvement science comes into play. There have been many times that we put to use improvement science tools including a fishbone diagram or the five whys protocol to ensure that we understand the root cause of the problem and are not just trying to create a quick fix that temporarily addresses the problem. There are many uses for improvement science, even on a school level, to create sustainable systemic change that ultimately benefits our students.

In conclusion, the impact of improvement science in addressing problems in education cannot be overstated. Through our collective experiences as leaders in HCPS, we have witnessed firsthand the transformative power of embracing a collaborative continuous approach to improvement. Improvement science has provided us with a set of tools and processes that enable us to engage stakeholders, understand the root causes of problems, and develop effective solutions. By involving teachers, administrators, and other stakeholders in the improvement process, we have fostered a sense of ownership, collaboration, and buy-in that is leading to more sustainable and meaningful change. As we reflect on our respective roles within HCPS, we see the profound effects of improvement science in action. From the Director of K–12 Instruction engaging teachers in designing a standards-based learning model to the superintendent and principals using improvement science to delve deeper into the challenges facing the district and schools, improvement science has become an integral part of our problem-solving approach. It has guided our decision-making processes, enriched our conversations, and resulted in more intentional and impactful strategies for improvement.

Moreover, improvement science has provided us with a framework for addressing systemic issues comprehensively and systematically. It has allowed us to shift from reactive problem-solving to proactive problem identification to create intentional and long-lasting solutions, enabling us to identify and address the root causes of challenges faced by our students. By examining the systems and procedures in place and involving all relevant stakeholders, we have been able to implement changes that better support students' academic, social, and emotional well-being. For practitioners who are new to improvement science, we encourage you to embrace its principles and tools. Starting small, gathering input from those closest to the problem, and analyzing the root causes before implementing solutions are key tenets of improvement science that can lead to more effective and sustainable change. By going slow to go fast, you can ensure that your initiatives are grounded in a deep understanding of the problem and are more likely to yield positive outcomes.

As we look to the future, we are committed to continuing our journey with improvement science in HCPS. We aim to model and promote its use throughout the district, making improvement science the problem-solving model of choice for all educators. By embracing the principles of improvement science and fostering a culture of continuous improvement, we can create transformative change and provide our students with the best possible educational experiences. Together, we can build a brighter future for education.

References

FOREWORD

Bandura, A. (1999). Social cognitive theory: An agentic perspective. *Asian Journal of Social Psychology, 2*(1), 21–41.

Deming, W. E. (1942). On a classification of the problems of statistical inference. *Journal of the American Statistical Association, 37*(218), 173–185.

Langley, G. J., Moen, R. D., Nolan, K. M., Nolan, T. W., Norman, C. L., & Provost, L. P. (2009). *The improvement guide: A practical approach to enhancing organizational performance*. Wiley.

Sealey-Ruiz, Y. (2022). An archaeology of self for our times: Another talk to teachers. *English Journal, 111*(5), 21–26.

Usher, E. L., & Pajares, F. (2008). Sources of self-efficacy in school: Critical review of the literature and future directions. *Review of Educational Research, 78*(4), 751–796.

INTRODUCTION: THE PRACTITIONER VOICE IN IMPROVEMENT SCIENCE

Bonney, E. N., Yurkofsky, M. M., Capello, S. (forthcoming). EdD students' sensemaking of improvement science as a tool for change in education. *Journal of Research on Leadership Education*.

Bryk, A. S. (2021). *Improvement in action: Advancing quality in America's schools*. Harvard Education Press.

Bryk, A. S., Gomez, L. M., Grunow, A., & LeMahieu, P. G. (2015). *Learning to improve: How America's schools can get better at getting better*. Harvard Education Press.

Capello, S., Yurkofsky, M., & Bonney, E. N. (2023). The practitioner inquiry course sequence: Centering improvement science in the design of an EdD program. In C. Benedetti & A. Covarrubias (Ed.), *Teaching critical inquiry and applied research in Ed.D. programs: Moving beyond traditional methods*. Myers Education Press

Christie, C. A., Inkelas, M., & Lemire, S. (Eds.). (2017). *Improvement science in evaluation: Methods and uses: New directions for evaluation*. Wiley.

CPED [Carnegie Project on the Education Doctorate]. (2022). *#CPED22 Convening: Transforming the advanced preparation of educational professionals to lead through scholarly and equity-minded practice* (Call for Proposals). CPED.

Crow, R., Hinnant-Crawford, B. N., & Spaulding, D. T. (Eds.). (2019). *The educational leader's guide to improvement science: Data, design and cases for reflection.* Stylus Publishing.

Gomez, L. M., Biag, M., Imig, D. G., Hitz, R., & Tozer, S (Eds.). (2023). *Improving America's schools together: How district-university partnerships and continuous improvement can transform education.* Rowman & Littlefield.

Hinnant-Crawford, B. N. (2020). *Improvement science in education: A primer.* Stylus Publishing.

Lewis, C. (2015). What is improvement science? Do we need it in education? *Educational Researcher, 44*(1), 54–61.

Oswald, D. P., Coutinho, M. J., Best, A. M., & Singh, N. N. (1999). Ethnic representation in special education: The influence of school-related economic and demographic variables. *The Journal of Special Education, 32*(4), 194–206.

Perry, J. A., Zambo, D., & Crow, R. (2020). *The improvement science dissertation in practice: A guide for faculty, committee members, and their students.* Myers Education Press.

Peterson, D. S., & Carlile, S. P. (Eds.). (2021). *Improvement science: Promoting equity in schools.* Stylus Publishing.

Peurach, D. J., Russell, J. L., Cohen-Vogel, L. & Penuel, W. (2022). *The foundational handbook on improvement research in education.* Rowman & Littlefield.

Rohanna, K. L. (2021). *Leading change through evaluation: Improvement science in action.* Sage.

Spaulding, D. T., Crow, R., & Hinnant-Crawford, B. N. (Eds.). (2021). *Teaching improvement science in educational leadership: A pedagogical guide.* Stylus Publishing.

Yurkofsky, M., Bonney, E. N. & Capello, S. (2023). Navigating the challenges of re-imagining leadership preparation by incorporating improvement science as a signature pedagogy. In E. Anderson & S. D. Hayes (Eds.), *Continuous improvement: A leadership process for school improvement.* Information Age Publishing

CHAPTER 1: LEADING CHANGE IN RACIAL DISPARITIES IN DISCIPLINE

Amemiya, J., Mortenson, E., & Wang, M.-T. (2020). Minor infractions are not minor: School infractions for minor misconduct may increase adolescents' defiant behavior and contribute to racial disparities in school discipline. *American Psychologist, 75*(1), 23–36. https://doi.org/10.1037/amp0000475

Blake, J. J., Smith, D. M., Unni, A., Marchbanks, M. P., Wood, S. & Eason, J. M. (2020). Behind the eight ball: The effects of race and number of infractions on the severity of exclusionary discipline sanctions issued in secondary school. *Journal of Emotional and Behavioral Disorders, 28*(3), 131–143. https://doi.org/10.1177/1063426620937698

Chung, S. Y., Swanson, I., Roberts, K., & Hankinson, A.. (2018) Evidence-based survey design: The use of continuous rating scales in surveys. *Performance Improvement, 57*(5), 38–48.

Cruz R. A., Manchanda, S., Firestone, A. R., & Rodl, J. E. (2020). An examination of teachers' culturally responsive teaching self-efficacy. *Teacher Education and Special Education, 43*(3), 197–214.

Fenning, P., & Jenkins, K. (2018). Racial and ethnic disparities in exclusionary school discipline: Implications for administrators leading discipline reform efforts. *NASSP Bulletin, 102*(4), 291–302. https://doi.org/10.1177/0192636518812699

Gastic, B. (2017). Disproportionality in school discipline in Massachusetts. *Education and Urban Society, 49*(2), https://doi.org/10.1177/0013124516630594

Girvan, E. J., Gion, C., McIntosh, K., & Smolkowski, K. (2017). The relative contribution of subjective office referrals to racial disproportionality in school discipline. *School Psychology Quarterly, 32*(3), 392–404. https://doi.org/10.1037/spq0000178

Hammond, Z. (2015). *Culturally responsive teaching and the brain: Promoting authentic engagement and rigor among culturally and linguistically diverse students.* Sage.

Hassan, D., & Bengt, B. A. (2005). Validation and findings comparing VAS vs. Likert scales for psychosocial measurements. *International Electronic Journal of Health Education, 8*, 178–192. http://files.eric.ed.gov/fulltext/EJ794094.pdf

Heilbrun, A., Cornell, D., & Konold, T. (2017). Authoritative school climate and suspension rates in middle schools: Implications for reducing the racial disparity in school discipline. *Journal of School Violence, 17*(3), 324–338. https://doi.org/10.1080/15388220.2017.1368395

Losen, D. L. (2015). Introduction. In D. L. Losen (Ed.). Closing the school discipline gap: Equitable remedies for excessive exclusion. (pp. 1–14). Teacher College Press.

Monroe, C. R. (2005). Why are "bad boys" always black? Causes of disproportionality in school discipline and recommendations for change. *The Clearinghouse: A Journal of Educational Strategies, 79*(1) 45–50. http://doi.org.10.3200/TCHS.79.1.45-50

Okonofua, J. A., Paunesku, D., & Walton, G. M. (2016). Brief intervention to encourage empathic discipline cuts suspension rates in half among adolescents. *Proceedings of the National Academy of Sciences of the United States of America, 113*(19), 5221–5226. http://www.pnas.org/cgi/doi/10.1073/pnas.1523698113

Reporter, S. (2013, September 21). Four more schools lose full accreditation—The Suffolk news. *Herald.* Retrieved February 4, 2023, from https://www.suffolknewsherald.com/2013/09/20/four-more-schools-lose-full-accreditation/

Rocque, M. (2010). Office discipline and student behavior: Does race matter? *American Journal of Education, 116*(4), 557–581. http://doi.org:0195-6744/2010/11604-0004

Schiff, M. (2018). Can restorative justice disrupt the "school-to-prison" pipeline? *Contemporary Justice Review, 21*(2), 121–139. https://doi.org/10.1080/10282580.2018.1455509

School Division. (2020). *Trend and Enrollment Data.* Author.

School Division. (2023). *2019–2020 Free and Reduced School Level Data Report.* Author.

Skiba, R. J., Horner, R. H., Chung, C.-G., Rausch, M. K., May, S. L., & Tobin, T. (2019). Race is not neutral: A national investigation of African American and Latino disproportionality in school discipline. *School Psychology Review, 40*(1), 80–107. https://doi-org.lib-proxy.radford.edu/10.1080/02796015.2011.12087730

Skiba, R. J., Michael, R. S., Nardoc, A. C., & Peterson, R. L. (2002). The color of discipline: Sources of racial and gender disproportionality in school punishment. *The Urban Review, 34*(4), 317–342. https://doi.org/10.1023/A:1021320817372

State Department of Education. (2020). [State] Department of Education School Quality Profile [Slateville] County Elementary School. Author.

US Census Bureau. (n.d.). Quickfacts: [County Name] County, Virginia. (n.d.). Retrieved March 18, 2023, from https://www.census.gov/quickfacts/[county name] countyvirginia

CHAPTER 2: LEADING CHANGE IN ENROLLMENT OF BLACK AND BROWN STUDENTS IN GIFTED PROGRAMS

Bryk, A. S., Gomez, L. M., Grunow, A., & LeMahieu, P. G. (2015). *Learning to improve: How America's schools can get better at getting better*. Harvard Education Press.

Card, D., & Giuliano, L. (2016). Universal screening increases the representation of low-income and minority students in gifted education. *PNAS, 113*(48), 13678–13683.

Ford, D. Y. (2010). Underrepresentation of culturally different students in gifted education: Reflections about current problems and recommendations for the future. *Gifted Child Today, 33*(3), 31–35.

Harvard Civil Rights Project. (2000). *Opportunities Suspended: The Devastating Consequences of Zero Tolerance and School Discipline Policies*. Report from a National Summit on Zero Tolerance [Proceedings] (Washington, DC, June 15–16, 2000). Retrieved from https://eric.ed.gov/?id=ED454314

Hinnant-Crawford, B. N. (2020). *Improvement science in education: A primer*. Myers Education Press.

National Equity Project. (n.d.). *Introduction to liberatory design*. Medium. https://www.nationalequityproject.org/frameworks/liberatory-design

Mountain Vista Governor's School. (2020). *Mountain vista governor's school at-a-glance*. https://www.mvgshome.org/mvgs/docs/MVGS_three_year_program_2020-21.pdf

Polaris Charter Academy. (2023). *History*. https://www.pcachicago.org/about/history/

Robalewski, M. (2021). *Liberatory design*. https://www.liberatorydesign.com/

Stanford University. (2023). *Resources/liberatory design—overview*. https://dschool.stanford.edu/resources/liberatory-design-cards#:~:text=Liberatory%20Design%20is%20a%20process,and%20influenced%20by%20design%20work.

Theoharis, G. (2009). *The school leaders our children deserve: Seven keys to equity, social justice, and school reform*. Teachers College Press.

Transforming Education. (2020). *Self-efficacy toolkit*. https://transformingeducation.org/resources/self-efficacy-toolkit/#:~:text=High%20self%2Defficacy%20reflects%20confidence,their%20own%20needs%20and%20supports

Virginia Department of Education. (2023). *Governor's schools*. https://www.doe.virginia.gov/teaching-learning-assessment/specialized-instruction/governor-s-schools

Wells, A. S., Fox, L., & Cordova-Cobo, D. (2016). How racially diverse schools and classrooms can benefit all students. *The Century Foundation*. https://tcf.org/content/report/how-racially-diverse-schools-and-classrooms-can-benefit-all-students/

Woods, Julie. (2016). State and federal policy: Gifted and talented youth. *Education Commission of the States*. http://www.ecs.org/wp-content/uploads/State-and-Federal-Policy-for-Gifted-and-Talented-Youth.pdf

CHAPTER 3: LEADING CHANGE IN TEACHER STRESS AND MENTAL HEALTH

Alfuqaha, O., & Alshra'ah, H. (2018). Burnout among nurses and teachers in Jordan: A comparative study. *Archives of Psychiatry and Psychotherapy, 20*(2), 55–65.

Alisic, E. (2012). Teachers' perspectives on providing support to children after trauma: A qualitative study. *School Psychology Quarterly, 27*(1), 51–59.

American Psychiatric Association. (2013). *Posttraumatic Stress Disorder*, 1–2. https://www.psychiatry.org/File%20Library/Psychiatrists/Practice/DSM/APA_DSM-5-PTSD.pdf

Anama-Green, C. (2020). Intrapersonal mindfulness is associated with reduced risk of burnout among Central Appalachian educators. *Explore*, 1–6.

Bercier, M. L., & Maynard, B. R. (2015). Interventions for secondary traumatic stress with mental health workers: A systematic review. *Research on Social Work Practice, 25*(1), 81–89.

Berger, R., Abu-Raiya, H., & Benatov, J. (2016). Reducing primary and secondary traumatic stress symptoms among educators by training them to deliver a resiliency program (ERASE-Stress) following the Christchurch earthquake in New Zealand. *American Journal of Orthopsychiatry, 86*(2), 236–251.

Bober, T., & Regehr, C. (2006). Strategies for reducing secondary or vicarious trauma: Do they work? *Brief Treatment and Crisis Intervention, 6*(1).

Borntrager, C., Caringi, J. C., van den Pol, R., Crosby, L., O'Connell, K., Trautman, A., & McDonald, M. (2012). Secondary traumatic stress in school personnel. *Advances in School Mental Health Promotion, 5*(1), 38–50.

Caringi, J. C., Stanick, C., Trautman, A., & Crosby, L. (2015). Secondary traumatic stress in public school teachers: contributing and mitigating factors. *Advances in School Mental Health Promotion, 8*(4), 244–256.

Essary, J. N., Barza, L., & Thurston, R. J. (2020). Secondary traumatic stress among educators. *Kappa Delta Pi Record, 56*(3), 116–121.

Gentry, J.E., Baggerly, J., & Baranowsky, A. (2004). Training-as-treatment: Effectiveness of the certified compassion fatigue specialist training. *International Journal of Emergency Mental Health, 6*, 147–155.

Goodman, M. J. & Schorling, J. B. (2012). A mindfulness course decreases burnout and improves well-being among healthcare providers. *International Journal of Psychiatry in Medicine, 43*(2), 119–128.

Grepmair, L., Mitterlehner, F., Loew, T., Bachelor, E., Rother, W., & Nickel, M. (2007). Promoting mindfulness in psychotherapists in training influences the treatment results of their patients: A randomized, double-blind, controlled study. *Psychotherapy and Psychosomatics, 76*, 332–338.

Hydon, S., Wong, M., Langley, A. K., Stein, B. D., & Kataoka, S. H. (2015). Preventing secondary traumatic stress in educators. *Child and Adolescent Psychiatric Clinics of North America, 24*(2), 319–333.

Killian, K.D. (2008). Helping til it hurts? A multimethod study of compassion fatigue, burnout, and self-care in clinicians working with trauma survivors. *Traumatology, 14*, 32–44.

Koenig, A., Rodger, S., & Specht, J. (2017). Educator burnout and compassion fatigue: A pilot study. *Canadian Journal of School Psychology, 33*(4), 1–20.

Kulkarni, S., Bell, H., Hartman, J. L., & Herman-Smith, R. L. (2013). Exploring individual and organizational factors contributing to compassion satisfaction, secondary traumatic stress, and burnout in domestic violence service providers. *Journal of the Society for Social Work and Research, 4*(2), 114.

Ludwig, D. S., & Kabat-Zinn, J. (2008). Mindfulness in medicine. *Journal of the American Medical Association, 300*, 1350–1352.

Molnar, B. E., Sprang, G., Killian, K. D., Gottfried, R., Emery, V., & Bride, B. E. (2017). Advancing science and practice for vicarious traumatization/secondary traumatic stress: A research agenda. *Traumatology, 23*(2), 129–142.

Ortlepp, K., & Friedman, M. (2002). Prevalence and correlates of secondary traumatic stress in workplace lay trauma counselors. *Journal of Traumatic Stress, 15*, 213–222.

Prati, G., Pietrantoni, L., & Cicognani, E. (2010). Self-efficacy moderates the relationship between stress appraisal and quality of life among rescue workers. *Anxiety, Stress, and Coping: An International Journal, 23*, 463–470.

Rose, S., Bisson, J., & Wessely, S. (2003). A systematic review of single-session psychological interventions ("debriefing") following trauma. *Psychotherapy and Psychosomatics, 72*, 176–184.

Ruzek, J. I., Brymer, M., Jacobs, A. K., Layne, C. M., Vernberg, E. M., & Watson, P. J. (2007). Psychological first aid. *Journal of Mental Health Counseling, 29*, 17–49.

Samios, C., Abel, L. M., & Rodzik, A. K. (2013). The protective role of compassion satisfaction for therapists who work with sexual violence survivors: An application of the broaden-and-build theory of positive emotions. *Anxiety, Stress and Coping, 26*(6), 610–623.

Sharp-Donahoo, L. M., Siegrist, B., & Garrett-Wright, D. (2018) Addressing compassion fatigue and stress of special education teachers and professional staff using mindfulness and prayer. *The Journal of School Nursing, 34*(6), 442–448.

Sporleder, J., & Forbes, H. T. (2016). *The trauma-informed school: A step-by-step implementation guide for administrators and school personnel.* Beyond Consequences Institute.

Sprang, G., Clark, J. J., & Whitt-Woosley, A. (2007). Compassion fatigue, compassion satisfaction, and burnout: Factors impacting a professional's quality of life. *Journal of Loss and Trauma, 12*, 259–280.

Stamm, B. H. (1999). *Secondary traumatic stress: Self-care issues for clinicians, researchers, and educators.* Sidran Press.

Stamm, B. H. (2010). Comprehensive bibliography of the effect of caring for those who have experienced extremely stressful events and suffering. *The concise ProQOL manual*, 2011–2010.

Thieleman, K., & Cacciatore, J. (2014). Witness to suffering: Mindfulness and compassion fatigue among traumatic bereavement volunteers and professionals. *Social Work, 59*(1), 34–41.

Wald, H. S., Haramati, A., Bachner, Y. G., & Urkin, J. (2016). Promoting resiliency for interprofessional faculty and senior medical students: Outcomes of a workshop using mind-body medicine and interactive reflective writing. *Medical Teacher, 38*(5), 525–528.

CHAPTER 4: LEADING CHANGE IN THE OVERREPRESENTATION OF STUDENTS OF COLOR IN SPECIAL EDUCATION

Albrecht, S. F., Skiba, R. J., Losen, D. J., Chung, C.-G., & Middelberg, L. (2011). Federal policy on disproportionality in special education. *Journal of Disability Policy Studies, 23*(1), 14–25. https://doi.org/10.1177/1044207311407917

Arnold, M., & Lassmann, M. E. (2003). Overrepresentation of minority students in special education. *Education, 124*(2), 230–236.

Bryk, A. S., Gomez, L. M., Grunow, A., & LeMahieu, P. G. (2015). *Learning to improve: How America's schools can get better at getting better.* Harvard Education Press.

Capper, C. A. (2018). *Organizational theory for equity and diversity: Leading integrated, socially just education.* Routledge.

Capper, C. A., & Frattura, E (2021). *Integrated comprehensive systems for equity.* Retrieved from https://www.icsequity.org/services/professional-development/

Capper, C. A., & Frattura, E. M. (2008). *Meeting the needs of students of all abilities: How leaders go beyond inclusion.* Corwin Press.

Continu Team. (2023, October 18). *In-person vs. online training: What does the research say?* Continu. Retrieved from https://continu.com/blog/in-person-vs-online-training

Equity and Engagement/Equity and Inclusion Overview. (n.d.). Retrieved 2021, from https://www.chccs.org/equity#calendar14581/20210522/month

Escudero, B. (2019, January 6). *How to practice culturally relevant pedagogy*. Teach for America. https://www.teachforamerica.org/stories/how-to-engage-culturally-relevant-pedagogy

Ferlazzo, L. (2015, July 10). *"Culturally responsive teaching": An interview with Zaretta Hammond.* Retrieved from http://blogs.edweek.org/teachers/classroom_qa_with_larry_ferlazzo/2015/07/culturally_responsive_teaching_an_interview_with_zaretta_hammond.html

Ford, D. Y. (2012). Culturally different students in special education: Looking backward to move forward. *Exceptional Children, 78*(4), 391-405.

Frank Porter Graham Child Development Institute. (n.d.). *Topic 3: Establishing Implementation Teams*. National Implementation Research Network.

Garcia, E. (2020, February 12). *Schools are still segregated, and black children are paying a price*. Economic Policy Institute. https://www.epi.org/publication/schools-are-still-segregated-and-black-children-are-paying-a-price/

Griner, A. C., & Stewart, M. L. (2012). Addressing the achievement gap and disproportionality through the use of culturally responsive teaching practices. *Urban Education, 48*(4), 585–621. https://doi.org/10.1177/0042085912456847

Gorski, P. C. (2011). Unlearning deficit ideology and the scornful Gaze: Thoughts on authenticating the class discourse in education. *Counterpoints, 402*(1), 152–173. http://www.jstor.org/stable/42981081

Hollins, E. R. (1994, April). *The burden of acting white revisited: Planning school success rather than explaining school failure*. Paper presented at the Annual Meeting of the American Education Research Association. New Orleans.

Joyce, B. R., & Showers, B. (2002). *Designing, training and peer coaching: Our needs for learning*. Association for Supervision and Curriculum Development.

King, J. (1994). *The burden of acting white re-examined: Towards a critical genealogy of acting Black*. Paper presented at the Annual Meeting of the American Education Research Association. New Orleans.

Ladson-Billings, G. (1995). But that's just good teaching! The case for culturally relevant pedagogy. *Theory into Practice, 34*(3), 159–165. http://www.jstor.org/stable/1476635

Langley, G. J. (2014). *The improvement guide: A practical approach to enhancing organizational performance*. Jossey-Bass.

Losen, D. J., & Orfield, G. (2001, December 31). *Racial inequity in special education undefined*. Harvard Education Press. https://eric.ed.gov/?id=ED568855

Lynch, M. (2018). The hidden nature of whiteness in education: Creating active allies in white teachers. *Journal of Educational Supervision, 1*(1). https://doi.org/10.31045/jes.1.1.2

Meyer, G. & Davis, B. (2012, October 27). *Students' six: Teaching strategies that work for SoC*. Retrieved from https://sites.google.com/a/chccs.k12.nc.us/graigmeyerpresentations/students-six

Matias, C. E., & Liou, D. D. (2015). Tending to the heart of communities of color: Towards critical race teacher activism. *Urban Education, 50*(5), 601-625.

Muniz, J. (2019). *Culturally responsive teaching*. Retrieved from https://www.newamerica.org/education-policy/reports/culturally-responsive-teaching/

Park, Y., Chow, K., & Gracely, S. (2016). *Multi-tiered frameworks: Understanding RTI, PBIS, MTSS*. Student Behavior Blog. https://studentbehaviorblog.org/multi-tiered-frameworks-understanding-rti-pbis-mtss/

Schwartz, K. (2014, April 4). *Facing race issues in the classroom: How to connect with students.* KQED. https://www.kqed.org/mindshift/34806/how-can-teachers-address-race-issues-in-class-ask-students

Shapiro, E. (n.d.). *Tiered instruction and intervention in a response-to-intervention model.* Retrieved from http://www.rtinetwork.org/essential/tieredinstruction/tiered-instruction-and-intervention-rti-model#:~:text=At%20Tier%201%2C%20considered%20the,typically%20aligned%20with%20state%20standards

Siegel, K. (2007). The *impact of inclusive settings on special education student achievement* (Doctoral dissertation). Available from ProQuest Dissertations and Theses database. (UMI No. 3277341).

Steele, C., & Aronson, J. (2018). Stereotypes and the fragility of academic competence, motivation, and self-concept. In A. J. Elliot, C. S. Dweck, & D. S. Yeager (Eds.). *Handbook of competence and motivation: Theory and application* (pp. 436–453). Guilford Press.

The Equity Collaborative (2021). *Students' six: Strategies for culturally relevant teaching.* The Equity Collaborative. Retrieved from https://theequitycollaborative.com/resources/students-six/

Zamora, P. (2007, December 5). *Statement of Washington, D.C. Regional Counsel to the United States Commission on Civil Rights.* Mexican American Legal Defense and Educational Fund: Minorities in Special Education. Retrieved from www.maldef.org/education/public-policy/6.2.1Zamora minorities SpEd 1.308.pdf

CHAPTER 5: LEADING CHANGE IN ONBOARDING AND SUPPORT OF NOVICE TEACHERS

Adams, E. (2001). *A closer look at special education teachers who transfer to general education* [Unpublished master's thesis].

Anderson, D., Menlove, R., & Salzberg, C. L. (2001). Special education teacher attrition: How many are leaving? Where are they going? *The Researcher, 28*–34.

Allinder, R. M. (1995). An examination of the relationship between teacher efficacy and curriculum-based measurement and student achievement. *Remedial and Special Education, 16*(4), 247–254. https://doi.org/10.1177/074193259501600408

Bandura, A. (1977). Self-efficacy: Toward a unifying theory of behavioral change. *Psychological Review, 84*(2), 191–215. https://doi.org/10.1037/0033-295x.84.2.191

Bandura, A. (1982). Self-efficacy mechanism in human agency. *American Psychologist, 37*(2), 122–147. https://doi.org/10.1037/0003-066x.37.2.122

Bandura, A. (1984). Recycling misconceptions of perceived self-efficacy. *Cognitive Therapy and Research, 8*(3), 231–255. https://doi.org/10.1007/bf01172995

Bandura, A. (2004). *Self-efficacy: The exercise of control.* Freeman.

Berry, A. B., Petrin, R. A., Gravelle, M. L., & Farmer, T. W. (2017). Issues in special education teacher recruitment, retention, and professional development: Considerations in supporting rural teachers. *Rural Special Education Quarterly, 30*(4), 3–11. https://doi.org/10.1177/875687051103000402

Billingsley, B., & Bettini, E. (2017). Improving special education teacher quality and effectiveness. In J. M. Kauffman, D. P. Hullahan, & P. C. Pullen (Eds.), *Handbook of special education* (pp. 501–520.) Routledge.

Billingsley, B., Bettini, E., & Jones, N. D. (2019). Supporting special education induction through high leverage practices. *Remedial and Special Education, 40*(6), 365–379. https://doi.org/10.1177/0741932518816826

Billingsley, B., Carlson, E., & Klein, S. (2004). The working conditions and induction support of early career special educators. *Exceptional Children, 70*(3), 333–347. https://doi.org/10.1177/001440290407000305

Brownell, M. T., Sindelar, P. T., Bishop, A. G., Langley, L. K., & Seo, S. (2002). Special education teacher supply and teacher quality: The problems, the solutions. *Focus on Exceptional Children, 35*(2), 1–16. https://doi.org/10.17161/fec.v35i2.6794

Brownell, M. T., & Smith, S. W. (1992). Attrition/retention of special education teachers: Critique of current research and recommendations for retention efforts. *Teacher Education and Special, 15*(4), 229–248. https://doi.org/10.1177/088840649201500402

CEC. (2000, July/August). *Bright futures for exceptional learners: An action agenda to achieve quality conditions for teaching and learning.* A report by the Council of Exceptional Children.

Cheney, C. O., Krajewski, J., & Combs, M. (1992). Understanding the first year teacher: Implications for induction programs. *Teacher Education and Special Education, 15*(1), 18–24. https://doi.org/10.1177/088840649201500104

Council for Exceptional Children & CEEDAR Center. (2019). *Introducing high-leverage practices in special education: A professional development guide for school leaders.* Council for Exceptional Children & CEEDAR center. www.highleveragepractices.org.

DeAngelis, K. J., & Presley, J. B. (2011). Toward a more nuanced understanding of new teacher attrition. *Education and Urban Society, 43*, 598–626.

Embich, J. L. (2001). The relationship of secondary special education teachers' roles and factors that lead to professional burnout. *Teacher Education and Special Education: The Journal of the Teacher Education Division of the Council for Exceptional Children, 24*(1), 58–69. https://doi.org/10.1177/088840640102400109

Gersten, R., Keating, T., Yovanoff, P., & Harniss, M. K. (2001). Working in special education: Factors that enhance special educators' intent to stay. *Exceptional Children, 67*(4), 549–567. https://doi.org/10.1177/001440290106700408

Ghaith, G., & Yaghi, H. (1997). Relationships among experience, teacher efficacy, and attitudes toward the implementation of instructional innovation. *Teaching and Teacher Education, 13*(4), 451–458. https://doi.org/10.1016/s0742-051x(96)00045-5

Ghaith, G., & Shaaban, K. (1999). The relationship between perceptions of teaching concerns, teacher efficacy, and selected teacher characteristics. *Teaching and Teacher Education, 15*(5), 487–496. https://doi.org/10.1016/S0742-051X(99)00009-8

Lee, Y., Patterson, P. P., & Vega, L. A. (2011). Perils to self-efficacy perceptions and teacher-preparation quality among special education teachers. *Teacher Education Quarterly,* 61–67.

Leko, M. M., & Brownell, M. T. (2011). Special education preservice teachers' appropriation of pedagogical tools for teaching reading. *Exceptional Children, 77*(2), 229–251. https://doi.org/10.1177/001440291107700205

Leko, M. M., Brownell, M. T., Sindelar, P. T., & Kiely, M. T. (2015). Envisioning the future of special education personnel preparation in a standards-based era. *Exceptional Children, 82*, 25–43.

Means, B., & Harris, C. J. (2013). Towards an evidence framework for design-based implementation research. *Teachers College Record: The Voice of Scholarship in Education, 115*(14), 350–371. https://doi.org/10.1177/016146811311501409

Menlove, R., Garnes, L., & Salzberg, C. (2014). Why special educators leave and where they go. *Teacher Education and Special Education, 27*(4), 373–383.

McLeskey, J. (2017). *High-leverage practices in special education.* Council for Exceptional Children.

Muller, E., & Markowitz, J. (2003). *Synthesis brief: Supply and demand of special education professionals.* ED 478561. Retrieved June 30, 2020, from ERIC Database.

Perry, J. A., Zambo, D., & Crow, R. (2020). *The improvement science dissertation in practice: A guide for faculty, committee members, and their students (improvement science in education and beyond).* Myers Education Press.

Reese, W. J. (1996). Tinkering toward utopia: A century of public school reform by David Tyack, Larry Cuban. *American Journal of Education, 104*(4), 313–318. https://doi.org/10.1086/444137

Schunk, D. H. (2020). *Learning theories: An educational perspective.* Pearson.

Tichnor-Wagner, A., Wachen, J., Cannata, M., & Cohen-Vogel, L. (2017). Continuous improvement in the public school context: Understanding how educators respond to plan-do-study-act cycles. *Journal of Educational Change, 18*(4), 465–494. https://doi.org/10.1007/s10833-017-9301-4

Tyack, D. B., & Cuban, L. (1997). *Tinkering toward utopia: A century of public school reform.* Harvard University Press.

Virginia Administrative Code. (2018). Types of licenses. §§ 22.1–298.1 and 22.1–299 of the Code of Virginia. Retrieved from https://law.lis.virginia.gov/admincode/title8/agency20/chapter23/section50/

Whitaker, S. D. (2000). Mentoring beginning special education teachers and the relationship to attrition. *Exceptional Children, 66*(4), 546–566. https://doi.org/10.1177/001440290006600407

Wisniewski, L., & Gargiulo, R. M. (1997). Occupational stress and burnout among special educators: a review of the literature. *The Journal of Special Education, 31*(3), 325–346. https://doi.org/10.1177/002246699703100303

CHAPTER 6: LEADING CHANGE TO IMPROVE ACADEMIC OUTCOMES FOR TRADITIONALLY MARGINALIZED STUDENTS

Alim, H. S., & Paris, D. (2017). What is culturally sustaining pedagogy and why does it matter? In D. Paris & H. S. Alim (Eds.)., *Culturally sustaining pedagogies: Teaching and learning for justices in a changing world* (pp. 1–21). Teachers College Press.

Aronson, B., & Laughter, J. (2016, March). The theory and practice of culturally relevant education: A synthesis of research across content areas. *Review of Educational Research, 86*(1), 163–206. http://doi.org/10.3102/0034654315582066

Blazar, D. (2021, December). Teachers of color, culturally responsive teaching, and student outcomes: Experimental evidence from the random assignment of teachers to classes. (EdworkingPaper: 21–501). Retrieved from Annenberg Institute at Brown University: https://doi.org/10.26300/jym0-wz02

Craig, H. K. (2016). *African American English and the achievement gap: The role of dialectal code-switching.* Routledge.

de Brey, C., Musu, L., McFarland, J., Wilkinson-Flicker, S., Diliberti, M., Zhang, A., Branstetter, C., & Wang, X. (2019). *Status and trends in the education of racial and ethnic groups 2018* [NCES 2019-038]. US Department of Education. Washington, DC: National Center for Education Statistics. https://files.eric.ed.gov/fulltext/ED592833.pdf

Dickson, G. L., Heejung, C., & Fernandez, I. T. (2016). The development and initial validation of the student measure of culturally responsive teaching. *Assessment for Effective Intervention, 41*(3), 141-154. http://dx.doi.org/10.1177/1534508415604879

Dover, A. G. (2013). Teaching for social justice: From conceptual frameworks to classroom practices. *Multicultural Perspectives*, *15*(1), 3–11. http://doi.org/10.1080/15210960.2013.754285

Emdin, C. (2016). *For white folks who teach in the hood . . . and the rest of y'all too: Reality pedagogy and urban education*. Beacon Press.

Gay, G. (2002, March/April). Preparing for culturally responsive teaching. *Journal of Education*, *53*(2), 106–116.

Gay, G. (2013). Teaching to and through cultural diversity. *Curriculum Inquiry*, *43*(1), 48–70. https://doi.org/10.1111/curi.12002

Gay, G. (2018). *Culturally responsive teaching: Theory, research, and practice* (3rd ed.). Teachers College Press.

Hammond, Z. (2015). *Culturally responsive teaching and the brain: Promoting authentic engagement and rigor among culturally and linguistically diverse students*. Corwin.

Hinnant-Crawford, B. N. (2020). *Improvement science in education: A primer*. Myers Education Press.

Howard, T. C. (2019). *Why race and culture matter in schools: Closing the achievement gap in America's classrooms* (2nd ed.). Teachers College Press.

Karatas, K. (2020). The competencies of the culturally responsive teacher: What, why, and how? *Inquiry in Education*, *12*(2), 1–23. https://digitalcommons.nl.edu/ie/vol12/iss2/2

Karatas, K., & Oral, B. (2015). Teachers' perceptions on culturally responsiveness in education. *Journal of Ethnic and Cultural Studies*, *2*(2), 47–57. https://doi.org/10.29333/ejecs/39

Ladson-Billings, G. (1992, Autumn). Reading between the lines and beyond the pages: A culturally relevant approach to literacy teaching. *Theory into Practice*, *31*(4), 312–320. https://doi.org/10.1080/00405849209543558

Ladson-Billings, G. (1995a, Summer). But that's just good teaching! The case for culturally relevant pedagogy. *Theory into Practice*, *34*(3), 159–165. https://doi.org/10.1080/00405849509543675

Ladson-Billings, G. (1995b, Autumn). Toward a theory of culturally relevant pedagogy. *American Educational Research Journal*, *32*(3), 465–491. https://doi.org/10.3102%2F00028312032003465

Ladson-Billings, G. (2009). *The dreamkeepers: Successful teachers of African American children.* (2nd ed.). Jossey-Bass.

Ladson-Billings, G. (2014, Spring). Culturally relevant pedagogy 2.0: A.k.a. the remix. *Harvard Educational Review*, *84*(1), 74–84. https://doi.org/10.17763/haer.84.1.p2rj131485484751

Milner, R. H. IV. (2010). *Start where you are, but don't stay there: Understanding diversity, opportunity gaps, and teaching in today's classrooms*. Harvard Education Press.

Milner, R. H. IV. (2012). Beyond a test score: Explaining opportunity gaps in educational practice. *Journal of Black Studies*, *46*(6), 693–718. https://doi.org/10.1177/0021934712442539

Milner, R. H. IV. (2015). *Rac(e)ing to class: Confronting poverty and race in schools and classrooms*. Harvard Education Press.

Morris, E. W., & Perry, B. L. (2016, February). The punishment gap: School suspension and racial disparities in achievement. *Social Problems*, *63*(1), 68–86. https://doi-org.lib-proxy.radford.edu/10.1093/socpro/spv026

Paris, D. (2012, April). Culturally sustaining pedagogy: A needed change in stance, terminology, and practice. *Educational Researcher*, *41*(3), 93–97. https://doi.org/10.3102/0013189X12441244

Paris, D., & Alim, H. S. (2014, Spring). What are we seeking to sustain through culturally sustaining pedagogy? A loving critique forward. *Harvard Educational Review*, *84*(1), 85–100. https://doi.org/10.17763/haer.84.1.982l873k2ht16m77

Potter, D., & Morris, D. S. (2017). Family and schooling experiences in racial/ethnic academic achievement gaps: A cumulative perspective. *Sociological Perspectives, 60*(1), 132–167. https://doi.org/10.1177/0731121416629989

Powell, R., Cantrell, S. C., Correll, P. K., & Malo-Juvera, V. (2017). Culturally responsive instruction observation protocol (4th ed.). University of Kentucky College of Education.

Silver Creek Schools Data (2021a). ALMS teacher demographic data, 2020.

Silver Creek Schools Data. (2021b). SOL English reading pass rates for African Americans vs all students.

Silver Creek Schools Data. (2021c). SOL English reading pass rates for Black vs white students, 2018–19 and 2020–21.

Silver Creek Schools Data (2023). Student demographic data, Spring 2023.

Siwatu, K. O. (2007). Preservice teachers' culturally responsive teaching self-efficacy and outcome expectancy beliefs. *Teaching and Teacher Education, 23*, 1086–1101. https://doi.org/10.1016/j.tate.2006.07.011

Tatum, A. W. (2005). *Teaching reading to Black adolescent males: Closing the achievement gap*. Stenhouse Publishers.

US Census Bureau Silver Creek. (n.d.). *QuickFacts* table. https://www.census.gov/quickfacts/fact/table/Somewherecityvirginiacounty,Somewherecityvirginia,US/RHI125219

Virginia Department of Education. (n.d.), ALMS) *Fall Membership Build-A-Table*. https://p1pe.doe.virginia.gov/apex/f?p=180:1:::::p_session_id,p_application_name:6235606119186387108,fallmembership

Virginia Department of Education. (2021a). School quality profile: Black students in grades 6, 7, and 8 on the English Reading SOL assessments (2016–19).

Virginia Department of Education. (2021b). School quality profile: White students in grades 6, 7, and 8 on the English Reading SOL assessments (2016–19).

CASE 2: DISCIPLINE AND IN-SCHOOL SUSPENSIONS

Bloomberg, N. (2003). Effective discipline for misbehavior: In school vs. out of school suspension. *Concept: Interdisciplinary Journal of Graduate Studies* https://concept.journals.villanova.edu/index.php/concept/article/view/138/109

Cruz, R. A., and Rodl, J. E. (2018). Crime and punishment: An examination of school context and student characteristics that predict out-of-school suspension, *Children and Youth Services Review, 95*, 226–234.

Nielsen, L. (1979). Let's suspend suspensions: Consequences and alternatives. *The Personnel and Guidance Journal, 57*(9), 442–445.

CASE 3: TRANSITIONING FROM MIDDLE TO HIGH SCHOOL

Rumberger, R. W., & Rotermund, S. (2012). The relationship between engagement and high school dropout. In S. L. Christenson, A. L. Reschly, & C. Wylie (Eds.), *Handbook of research on student engagement* (pp. 491–513). Springer Science.

CASE 4: READING ACHIEVEMENT

Blevins, W. (2017). *A fresh look at phonics, grades K–2: Common causes of failure and 7 ingredients for success*. Corwin Literacy.

Morrow, L. M., & Gambrell, L. B. (2019). *Best practices in literacy instruction*. Guilford Press.

Stanovich, Keith E. (1986). Matthew effects in reading: Some consequences of individual differences in the acquisition of literacy. *Reading Research Quarterly, 22*, 360–407.

AFTERWORD

Bryk, A. S., Gomez, L. M., Grunow, A., & LeMahieu, P. G. (2015). *Learning to improve: How America's schools can get better at getting better*. Harvard Education Press.

Index

Black and Brown students:
   discipline, 9–15, 177–82
   English learners, 173–76
   enrollment, 35–62
   gifted education, 35
   opportunity gap, 131
Change ideas/interventions, 24–25, 43–45, 67–69, 88, 116–18, 143–49
Chronic absenteeism, 177–82
Culturally Relevant Pedagogy (CRP) or Culturally Responsive Teaching (CRT), 24–25, 86–87, 144
Cycles of improvement, 24–28, 45–47, 69–71, 93–97, 121–23, 149–51
Discipline and in-school suspensions. *See* Black and Brown students
Disproportionality in gifted education. *See* Black and Brown students
Driver diagram, 20–21, 43–44, 69, 92, 118, 143–45
Driver diagram template, 171
EL and immigrant students, 173–76
Fishbone diagram, 16, 41–42, 66, 85, 116, 141, 191
Fishbone diagram template, 170

Lessons learned, improvement science from, 30–33, 54–56, 77, 100–1, 128–30, 162–63, 199–202
Special education, 84, 110
Students of color. See Black and Brown students
Plan Do Study Act (PDSA). *See* Cycles of improvement.
Problem:
   cases studies, 173, 177, 183, 187, 193
   discussion questions, 170–71
   inquiry processes, 15–20, 40–43, 65–67, 84–85, 133–37
Professional development (PD) or professional learning community (PLC):
   culturally relevant pedagogy, 144–49
   implicit bias, 22–24
   secondary traumatic stress, 68–69
   high leverage practices, 116–18
Reading achievement, 193–97
Teacher
   burnout, 63–65, 193–97
   novice, 109–30
   stress and mental health, 63–77
Transition from middle to high school, 183–86

About the Contributors

Edwin Nii Bonney, PhD, is assistant professor in the Department of Educational and Organizational Leadership Development at Clemson University. His research centers on how educational leaders and educators disrupt and/or reinforce the marginalization of their minoritized, vulnerable, and racialized students' languages, cultures, and histories. He pays particular attention in his research to moments of disruption in and beyond educational spaces where students and community members are centering their languages, cultures, and histories and are reshaping what is considered "normal" or standard. He has published several articles, book chapters, and policy briefs on decolonizing educational leadership, improvement science, discourse analysis of educational policies and programs, refugee and immigrant education, school-community partnerships, and school-family engagement. He teaches courses and advises students in the Education Systems Improvement Science EdD program. He is also looking to learn and work alongside educational leaders in tackling problems of practice so that students can be equitably served.

Courtney Browning, EdD, is a passionate educational leader and advocate for school improvement and equity with 21 years of experience. Her diverse educational background includes a BA in Philosophy, BBA in Finance from James Madison University, an MS in Elementary Education, and Reading Specialist and School Leadership endorsements through Longwood University, and an EdD in Educational Leadership through Radford University. Courtney also authored the article "A School Administrator's Journey Through an EdD Program in the Midst of a Global Pandemic" in the *Journal on Transforming Professional Practice*. These experiences have equipped Courtney with a comprehensive understanding of educational systems and strategies for positive change. As the principal of an elementary school, Courtney creates inclusive and innovative learning environments, emphasizing the importance of building transformative leadership teams. Her commitment to educational change is driven by her role as a mother of three daughters, supported by her husband.

Sarah A. Capello, PhD, is assistant professor in the EdD program at Radford University. One strand of her research focuses on transformative EdD education and the preparation of PK–12 educational leaders as scholarly practitioners. She is particularly interested in rethinking research methodology courses, doctoral assessments, and dissertations in practitioner-oriented EdD programs. A second strand of research focuses on instructional supervision for pre-service and in-service teachers, particularly expanding and supporting the role of the university supervisor. Sarah has written about these topics in a variety of academic journals and scholarly books; several of those publications have been conducted in partnership with current and former doctoral students.

Megan Crew is Division Coordinator for Early Childhood and English Learner Services for Salem City Schools. She holds master's degrees in Instructional Leadership and Education. Through this work she has established an obvious platform of inclusivity, investigating the needs of her English learner students as they strive to find a home within our local public school settings. She believes all students must be nurtured by educators to see growth and academic flourish. Megan was most recently published in Virginia Association for Supervision and Curriculum Development's *VASCD Journal* in 2019 on encouraging student-led conferences and again in 2020 in a paper titled "Using Deeper Learning to Promote Social Emotional Development." Megan is a National Board Certified Teacher in Early Childhood Literacy; she is also endorsed in gifted education. Megan is a self-professed homebody; she loves the curation of "homey" spaces. Megan admits her creativity and moxie are fed by time spent with her two teenage children and husband Ben.

Jessica Cromer, EdD, is Division Superintendent of Floyd County Public Schools. She has a variety of experience in education, having served as a K–7 principal, high school assistant principal, Career and Technical Education Director, and middle school teacher. Dr. Cromer earned her BA in political science and her MA in curriculum and instruction from Virginia Tech. She then went on to earn her MS in educational leadership, and EdD in education from Radford University. Dr. Cromer is a strong advocate for public education. She believes that all students deserve access to a high-quality education, regardless of their background. In her spare time, Dr. Cromer enjoys spending time outdoors and working on the family cattle farm with her husband and son.

Wendy Durham, EdD, is an experienced educator with 26 years of service. She began her career as a fifth-grade teacher in North Carolina's Rockingham County Public Schools, where she received the Teacher of the Year award at New Vision Elementary. After six years, she became an elementary assistant principal at Stoneville Elementary, where she used data conferencing to coach teachers on how to use data to drive their instruction and raise student achievement. Dr. Durham then joined the Henry County Public School (HCPS) team and served as the principal of Drewry Mason Elementary for seven years, during which she and her faculty and staff received multiple recognitions for academic improvements, such as the Title I

Academic Improvement Award for the state of Virginia. She then assumed the role of Director of K–12 Instruction for HCPS, her current position, and one she has held for nine years. As Director, Dr. Durham oversees curriculum and instruction programming for HCPS including the implementation of instructional coaching, data conferencing, and standards-based learning initiatives. Dr. Durham holds a Doctorate in Educational Leadership from Radford University, a master of education degree from the University of Virginia, and a bachelor's degree from Radford University in Interdisciplinary Studies/ Elementary Education. She is licensed by the Virginia Department of Education in the areas of administration and supervision of PreK–12, and Elementary Education K–5.

Michelle Greene, EdD, serves as principal of McHarg Elementary School in Radford City Schools. She has a bachelor's degree in elementary education, a master's degree in reading and leadership from Radford University. She has been in education for 16 years in various roles such as classroom teacher, reading specialist, instructional coach, assistant principal, and now principal. As a literacy leader of a school, she has a strong belief that every child deserves the opportunity to read to access the world around them. She believes it is the educator's job to lay the foundation for students. She feels fortunate to work alongside exceptional educators who share this passion and have personal goals to help each child succeed.

Elisabeth Harman, EdD, is Director of Special Education and Pupil Personnel Services for a large public school division in Southwest Virginia. Previously, she served in several capacities including Associate Director of Special Education, Special Education Supervisor, Autism Specialist, Assistive Technology Consultant, General Education Teacher, and Special Education Teacher. She holds a bachelor's degree from Virginia Tech, master's degrees from both the University of Virginia and Radford University, and a doctorate from Radford University. Dr. Harman serves on various committees at both the local and state levels. She is the current President of the Virginia Council of Administrators in Special Education (VCASE). She previously served as VCASE President-Elect and on the Membership and Awards Committee. Dr. Harman served an appointment to the Governor's Children's Cabinet as a member of the Student Safety Workgroup, and she actively works with her regional colleagues in a variety of capacities. In her free time, Elisabeth enjoys savoring every minute of family time with her husband, daughter, son, golden retriever, and kitty.

Shanice Harrington, EdD, is a native of Greensboro, North Carolina. Currently, she serves as an Assistant Principal in Chapel-Hill Carrboro City Schools. She has served as an Exceptional Children's Resource Teacher and a general education classroom teacher. In addition, she has been a mentor and facilitator for African American student affinity groups within the school communities that she serves. Dr. Harrington's passion for improving the quality of education for all students through dismantling inequities has driven her educational journey. She obtained her BA in elementary education with a concentration in communication disorders and her MA in special education. Most recently, she obtained her doctoral degree in educational leadership focused on equity and social justice. Creating equitable opportunities for all students is at the center of her research. Advocacy for marginalized students is what drives her dedication to education.

Megan Hawley is an assistant principal in Montgomery County. She holds a bachelor's degree in elementary education and a master's degree in educational leadership and is pursuing a doctoral degree from Radford University. Megan has served her community as a public educator for 15 years. She has taught second, third, fourth grade, and is currently an assistant principal. She was awarded Teacher of the Year at her elementary school in 2013 and 2019 and received the Outstanding Student in the Radford University Educational Leadership program. Megan also serves on educational committees and boards. In addition to collaborating with staff and enjoying time with students, she enjoys spending time with family/friends, running, and sports.

Kelly A. Huff, EdD, is an active practitioner of improvement science implementing it continuously as a public school administrator. Her career has taken her from the secondary English classroom to high school administrator to central office administrator, all in the Virginia public school realm. Currently, she is the Regional Director at Mountain Vista Governor's School. She is the President of the Northern Virginia Council of Gifted and Talented Educators and a policy team member of the Virginia Association for Supervision and Curriculum Development. Other publications include topics on place-based education and the value of lived experiences in learning. She is an advocate for and supporter of diversity, equity, and inclusion in public education.

Amy Johnson, EdD, is a passionate public educator who has served her school community for 22 years in a variety of roles. She began her career as an elementary school teacher, transitioning to an Instructional Technology Resource Teacher, a math coach, and finally with the majority of her career as a high school administrator. She is happily married to her husband, Bryan, for 21 years. Together they have been blessed with three amazing children, Mason, Braeden, and Berkley. Amy is currently a doctoral candidate in the Ed Leadership program at Radford University eagerly awaiting the completion in December 2023. Amy is known for her devotion to students who have had fewer opportunities. She desires to support all students when finding their place, believing all students are deserving of a happy, healthy future.

Tracy Kwock, EdD, is a southwest Virginia–based educator who has worked with and supported thousands of students and teachers in every grade and subject area as a teacher, administrator, and professional development provider and coach. She is a recipient of the Golden Apple Award in Teaching and co-founder of Polaris Charter Academy, Chicago's first expeditionary learning school. She currently supports Virginia public schools and divisions to meet the needs of *all* students, especially those who have been historically marginalized, through the Radford University Training and Technical Assistance Center.

Elizabeth Motley, EdD, has served students in Henry County for 17 years. Beginning as a third grade teacher, Dr. Motley continuously sought out ways to spread change to ensure the students of Henry County have the best possible experience in building their educational foundation. In addition to being an elementary school teacher, Dr. Motley served as an elementary curriculum coordinator for five years before transitioning to be an elementary school principal for seven years at Sanville Elementary School and Drewry Mason Elementary School. Dr. Motley will continue to serve Henry County as the Dyslexia and Literacy Coordinator to implement change to benefit students in their early literacy foundation. Dr. Motley earned a BS degree from Radford University in interdisciplinary studies, elementary education, a master's degree from Averett University in education, a leadership certification from James Madison University, and most recently, a doctorate in educational leadership from Radford University.

Andrew Nester, EdD, is an assistant principal with Franklin County Public Schools. He has a BA degree in elementary education, with an algebra I endorsement, and a minor in criminal justice from the University of Virginia's College at Wise. Andrew earned his master's degree in educational leadership from Radford University. Currently, he is pursuing a doctoral degree in educational leadership from Radford University. Andrew has served as a public educator for 16 years. During his career in public education, he has held various positions in Franklin County Public Schools at the middle and high school levels, including an algebra I teacher, a football coach, dean of students, and his current position as a Building Level Assistant Principal at Franklin County High School. Andrew strives each day to form relationships and make positive connections with students and staff as he believes a great education is the foundation for success. Andrew and his wife, Brittany, have two children, Callie and Eli. They enjoy spending time outdoors together as a family.

Felicia Preston, EdD, is Director of Pupil Personnel Services for Martinsville City Public Schools. She has been a longtime employee of the school division. She holds a BS in psychology and an MS in counseling and human development from Radford University. She also holds an Endorsement in School Administration from James Madison University. Before working in the school system, Felicia worked in the community mental health sector with children and adolescents for two years. As a former school counselor, she is dedicated to building relationships with children and families as well as addressing the whole child including their social-emotional needs. She enjoys spending quality time with her husband and four children at home. They are truly her inspiration!

Kim Rygas serves as principal of Auburn Elementary School in Montgomery County. She holds a bachelor's degree in early childhood education, a master's degree in Early Childhood/Special Education, a master's degree in Educational Leadership, and is currently pursuing an EdD in Education from Radford University. In her 15 years in education, she has taught first and third grade, served as an assistant principal and adjunct instructor, and is passionate about servant leadership in K–12 schools.

She is an advocate for her students, teachers, colleagues, and learning community. She believes in the power of creating positive relationships and is honored to work alongside incredible educators who demonstrate this daily. In her free time, she enjoys spending time with her family, friends, and four dogs.

Jamie Soltis, EdD, earned his bachelor of science degree from Longwood College in 1996, his master of education degree from the University of Virginia in 2007, and his doctor of education degree from Radford University in 2023. With 25 years of experience in public education, Dr. Soltis has held various positions such as a biology and chemistry teacher, a high school assistant principal, a middle school principal, a high school principal, and a director of instruction. He currently serves as an assistant superintendent of schools and resides in southwest Virginia with his wife Dena and son Clark.

Sandy Strayer, EdD, joined Henry County Public Schools in 1992 as a teacher at Bassett High School—a position she held for nine years. She served as assistant principal at Fieldale-Collinsville High School from 2001–2004 and was assistant principal at Bassett High School during the 2004–2005 school year following consolidation. In 2005, she became principal at Collinsville Primary School and remained there until 2010, when she became Director of Secondary Instruction and Director of Career and Technical Education, a position she held for three years before moving into a role as Director of K–12 Instruction. Next, she moved into the role of Assistant Superintendent of Teaching and Learning. After three years, she changed positions to become the Assistant Superintendent for Operations. Currently, she serves as the Superintendent of Henry County Public Schools. Dr. Strayer holds a doctorate from Radford University, an education specialist degree in administration from the University of Virginia (UVA); a master's degree in professional studies from George Mason University; and a bachelor's degree from Radford University. She is licensed by the Virginia Department of Education as a division superintendent and in the areas of administration and supervision PreK–12, theater arts PreK–12, and history and social sciences. She is a member of the Virginia Association of School Superintendents, the School Superintendents Association, the Association for Supervision and Curriculum Development, the Virginia Association for Career and Technical Education, and the Virginia Department of Education Cooperative Learning Committee. She serves on the Valley Star Credit Union Supervisory Committee, UVA K12 Advisory Council, Piedmont Governor's School Board, Smart Beginnings Council, and GO TEC (Great Opportunities in Technology & Engineering Careers) Advisory Board.

Matthew Woods, EdD, has served for more than 13 years assisting students, educators, and schools in a variety of roles. His professional experience includes being a high school social studies teacher, a middle and high school assistant principal, a middle school principal, a director of student support services, an adjunct professor, and a field instructor for student teachers. Additionally, Dr. Woods hosts an education podcast, *Leading Out the Woods*, and is the author of *Digitial PDF for Educators* and the children's book series I Wanna Be . . . Dr. Woods's leadership and innovative approaches have brought him recognition from numerous organizations, including Association for Supervision and Curriculum Development (Emerging Leaders Class of 2021) and the LG Happiness League. He earned a BS in history and social ttudies from Ferrum College, an MEd in educational leadership and administration from Virginia Tech, a graduate certificate in education law and policy, and an educational specialist in middle grades education from the University of Georgia, and an EdD in educational leadership and administration from Radford University.

Maxwell M. Yurkofsky, EdD, obtained his EdD in educational policy, leadership, and instructional practice from the Harvard Graduate School of Education in 2020. He teaches in and serves as the program coordinator for the Doctor of Education Program at Radford University. He is committed to preparing school and system leaders to strategically draw on improvement science, organizational theory, leadership, and design principles to inquire into and address high-leverage problems of practice. His research centers on understanding how school systems can organize for continuous improvement toward more ambitious and equitable visions of learning. He has been published in numerous peer-reviewed journals, including *Educational Researcher*, *Educational Administration Quarterly*, *Journal of Educational Administration*, *Review of Research in Education*, *Harvard Educational Review*, *Teaching and Teacher Education*, *Computers and Education*, *Teachers College Record*, *Educational Policy*, and *Peabody Journal of Education*.

www.ingramcontent.com/pod-product-compliance
Lightning Source LLC
Chambersburg PA
CBHW060341010526
44117CB00017B/2910